Saral Jyotish

Part III

Author

V. P. GOEL

Published by

Performonks Education and Consulting Services LLP

44, Tatvam Villas, Sector 48, Sohna Road,
Gurugram, Haryana 122018
E-Mail: rashi@performonks.com

First published in 2021

Revised & Reprinted 2024

ISBN: 978 - 81- 973347- 1 – 9

Published by:

Performonks Education and Consulting Services LLP

Preface

I am encouraged to continue writing the series of Saral Jyotish after getting a big response from Astrology lovers across India and abroad.

In this part, the topic of dispositor is discussed in detail. Dispositor theory is a very basic tool to decipher the hidden results of planets. No planet acts in isolation. They act in support to each other, and the astrological meaning conveyed is the sum total of these influences on a planet. How this synthesis is done is dependent on theory of dispositor.

We have given the concept of super strong Vipreet Raj Yoga for the first time. This is derived from the parameters given in classic like Phaldeepika and Prashan Marg.

Bandhan Yoga is dealt in both Parashar and Jaimini system. This will help in solving many riddles like cure of a patient, release from prison etc.

A new approach to Shakat Yoga is discussed. With this understanding we should not be worried about presence of Shakat Yoga in a horoscope.

Upchaya House is also a hot topic. This book explains the formation of pure Upchaya House Yoga to grant continuous rise in life. Another concept of Kaal Purush Upchaya is also given which is discussed for the first time in this book.

V. P. Goel

vpgoel2019@gmail.com

My YouTube Channel: saraljyotishbyvpgoel

Books by the Author

हिंदी में	In English	In Russian
वर्ग कुंडलियों से सटीक पफलित	Comprehensive Prediction by Divisional Charts	Comprehensive Prediction by Divisional Charts
योगिनी दशा से पफलित	Snapshot Prediction using Yogini Dasha	Snapshot Prediction using Yogini Dasha
शोडाषोत्तरी दशा से पफलित	Predict Through Shodashottary Dasha	
आयु रहस्य	Unravelling Puzzle of longevity	
	Predict Through Shasti Hayani Dasha	
	Locate Disease Astrologically	Locate Disease Astrologically
जैमिनी ज्योतिष से पफलित	Predicting through Jaimini Astrology	Predicting through Jaimini Astrology
नवांश से पफलित	Predict with Navamsha	Predict with Navamsha
सप्तांश से पफलित	Predict with Saptamsha	Predict with Saptamsha
दशमांश से पफलित	Predict with Dashamsha	Predict with Dashamsha
	Predict with Trishamsha	
सरल ज्योतिष 1	Saral Jyotish 1	Saral Jyotish 1
	Saral Jyotish 2	Saral Jyotish 2
	Saral Jyotish 3	Saral Jyotish 3
	Saral Jyotish 4	Saral Jyotish 4
	Saral Jyotish 5	
	Saral Jyotish 6	
सरल षड्बल		

Contents

Chapter 1

Bandhan Yoga

Bandhan is restriction on your movements. It can be physical or mental restriction. The cause can be self-imposed or forced.

We can broadly categorize Bandhan in two categories. First is the Bandhan due to some crime committed and second is the Bandhan due to other reasons. These can be illness, kidnapping, self-imposed or religious reasons. To differentiate we should first examine the horoscope for criminal tendencies present. The presence of these condition only may not give jail, but it is only an indicator that person is inclined to use unfair means in his life.

Criminal Tendency

1. The first condition is very important. When these are present in the horoscope of persons then he is inclined to do wicked acts. If all the four conditions are present, then the person is unreliable and can commit crime or use unfair means not acceptable by society. When even one condition is present then the person is inclined to do a bad act.

   a. If the lord of Ascendant is under malefic influence only and have no association of a benefic. **This condition is a must**. If there is a benefic association with Ascendant lord, then the person tries to improve.

   b. When the Sun or the Moon are between two malefic planets.

c. Mars occupy the 7th house either from the Sun or from the Moon.

d. Mercury occupy a Prishtodaya sign. The Prishtodaya signs are Aries, Taurus, Cancer, Sagittarius and Capricorn.

2. Fourth house and fourth lord have only malefic connection. This can be a papa kartari.

3. When any of fourth lord or tenth lord is in fourth house then person is fraudulent.

4. When Saturn or Mars or Rahu is in fourth house then the mind of person is always thinking of dishonest ways.

5. Khala Yoga is present in the horoscope.

6. Third house is strong, and Mercury is afflicted in Navamsha.

7. Mercury and Moon are afflicted in Navamsha. Any benefic relation will reduce the bad effects to a greater extent. The affliction in Navamsha is important.

8. Third lord is in exchange with any other sign lord. This is Khala Yoga.

9. The lagna of Dreshkana is related to Mercury, sign of Mercury rise, or Mercury is placed in lagna, and is aspected by Moon. The person will do lowly acts.

10. Waning Moon and Mars are in a trik house in birth chart.

11. Mercury is with a malefic in ninth house in birth chart.

We take few examples to verify the above rules.

Example DOB 25 December 1960 TOB 15.53 POB Delhi

Birth Chart

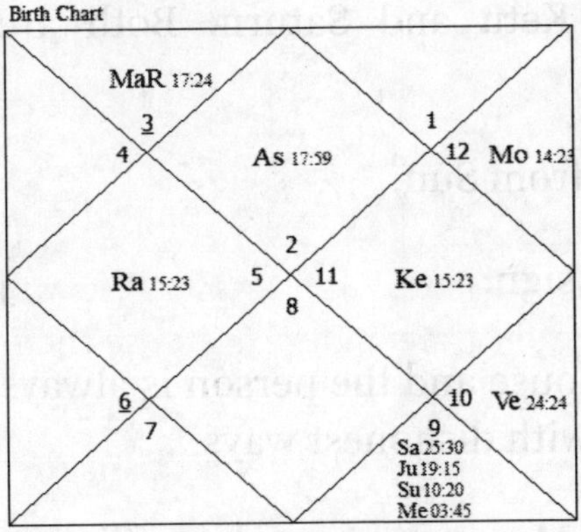

Birth Chart

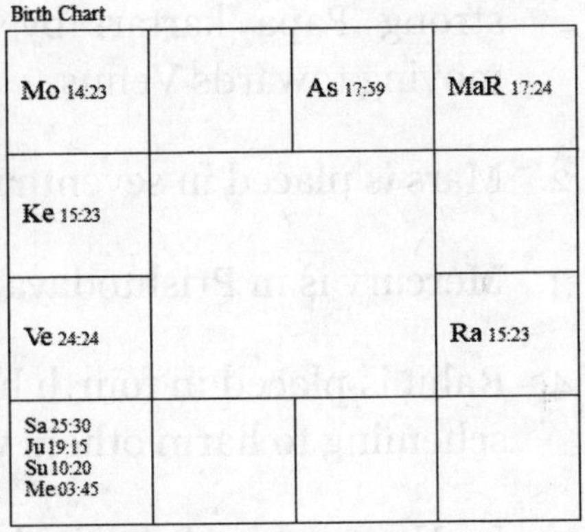

D9 Navamsha (spouse)

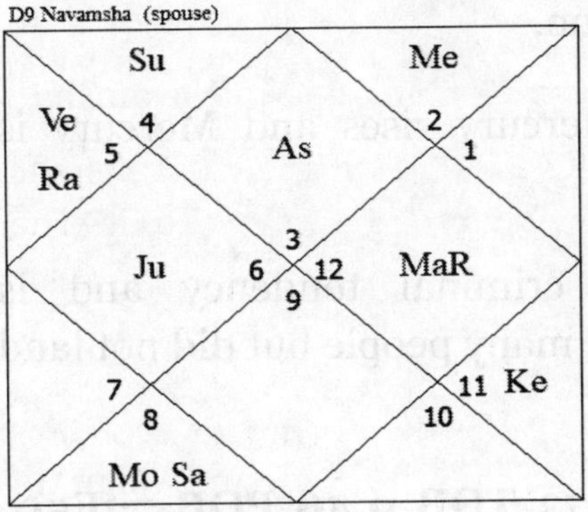

D9 Navamsha (spouse)

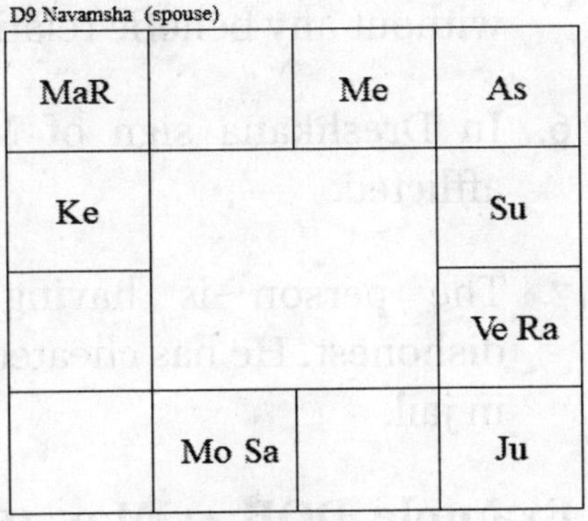

D3 Dreshkana (happiness siblings)

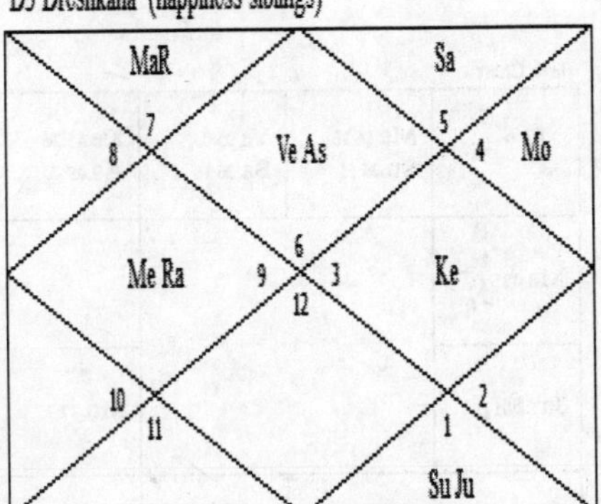

D3 Dreshkana (happiness siblings)

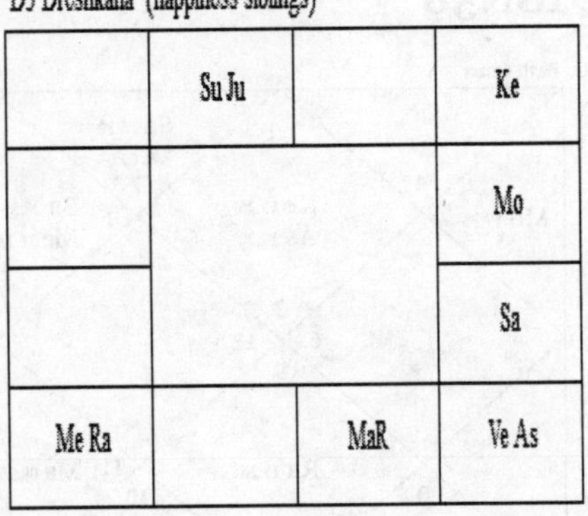

1. Lagna lord is aspected by Mars. There is no benefic relation with lagna lord. Lagna lord Venus is having strong Papa kartari by Ketu and Saturn. Both are moving towards Venus.

2. Mars is placed in seventh from Sun.

3. Mercury is in Prishtodaya sign.

4. Rahu is placed in fourth house and the person is always scheming to harm others with dishonest ways.

5. In Navamsha Moon and Mercury are under affliction without any benefic relation.

6. In Dreshkana sign of Mercury rises and Mercury is afflicted.

7. The person is having criminal tendency and is dishonest. He has cheated many people but did not land in jail.

Example DOB 11 May 1973 TOB 9.46 POB 72E50, 18N58

Birth Chart

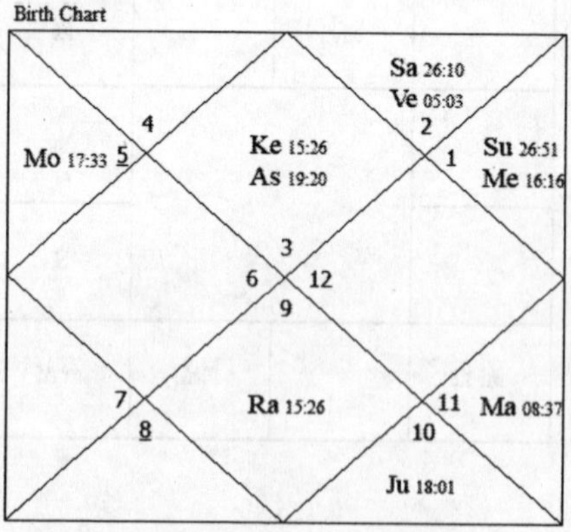

Birth Chart

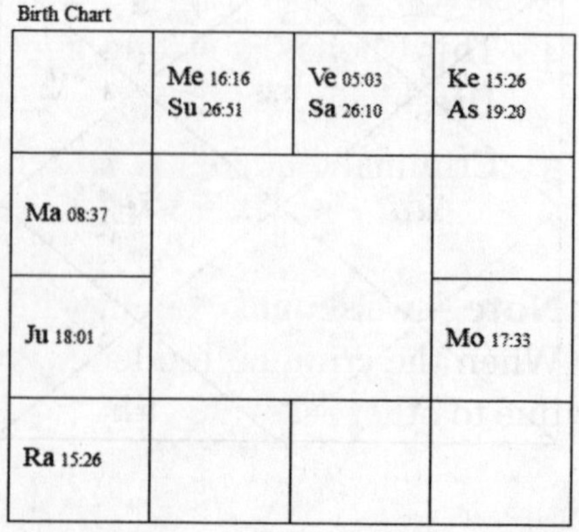

D9 Navamsha (spouse)

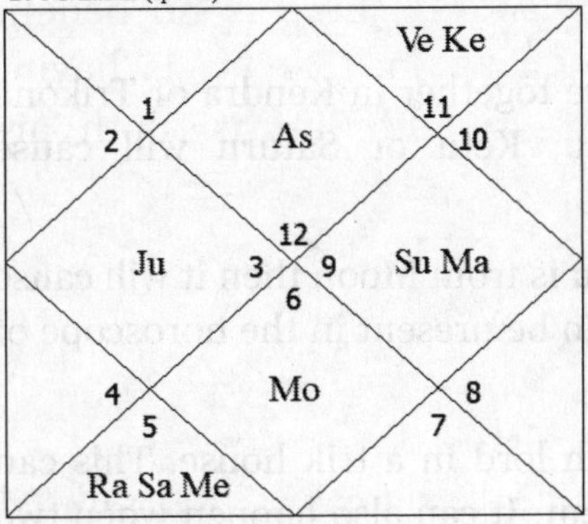

D9 Navamsha (spouse)

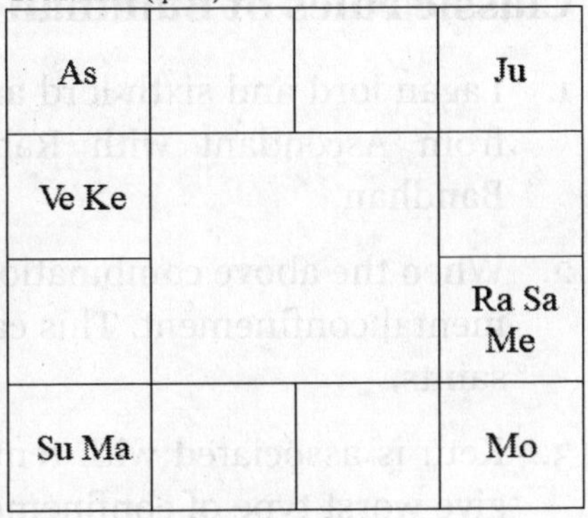

D3 Dreshkana (happiness siblings)

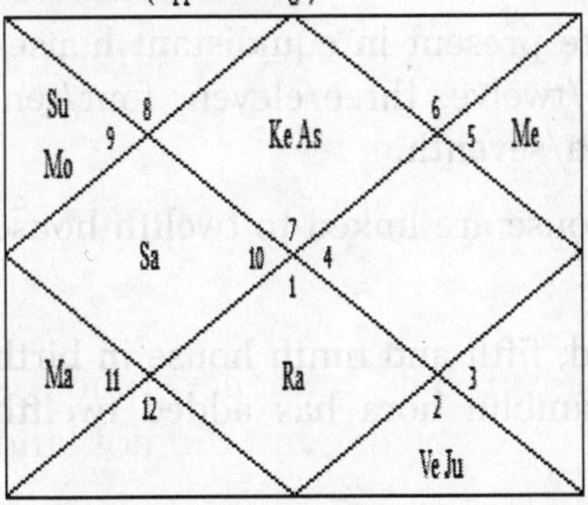

D3 Dreshkana (happiness siblings)

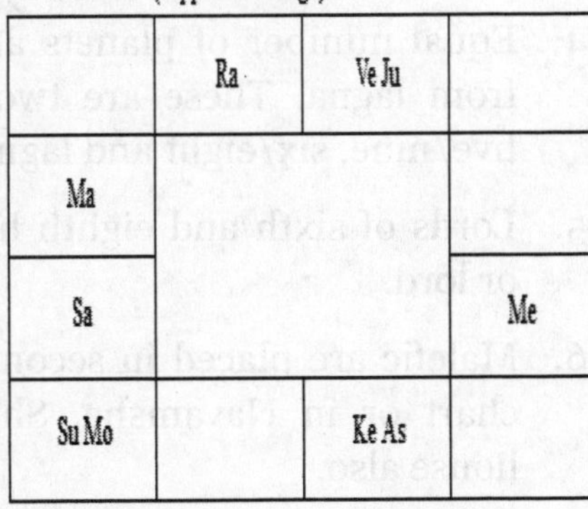

1. Lagan lord is with Sun and have no benefic relation.
2. Mars is in seventh house from Moon.
3. Mercury is in Prishtodaya sign Aries.
4. Third house is strong and Mercury is aspected by Mars in Dreshkana.
5. Criminal tendency is present in the horoscope.

Note – we should examine the horoscope for criminal tendency. When the criminal tendency is not present then the Bandhan is due to other reasons.

Classic rules of Bandhan

1. Lagan lord and sixth lord are together in Kendra or Trikona from Ascendant with Rahu, Ketu or Saturn will cause Bandhan.
2. When the above combination is from Moon then it will cause mental confinement. This can be present in the horoscope of saints.
3. Ketu is associated with tenth lord in a trik house. This can give worst type of confinement. It can also happen when two malefic are conjoined in a trik house.
4. Equal number of planets are present in equidistant houses from lagna. These are two/twelve, three/eleven, four/ten, five/nine, six/eight and lagna/seventh.
5. Lords of sixth and eighth house are linked to twelfth house or lord.
6. Malefic are placed in second, fifth and ninth house in birth chart or in Navamsha. Shambhu hora has added twelfth house also.
7. Lagna lord is combust and Sun is debilitated can cause confinement.
8. When sixth lord and eighth lord are conjoined in a Kendra or Trikona and are with Saturn or Rahu then confinement is for a long duration.
9. Combined influence of sixth lord and Saturn on lagna or lagna lord gives suffering, humiliation or hospitalization in the Antra Dasha of weaker planet.
10. Presence of Shakat Yoga can give confinement if Jupiter is related with a malefic.
11. Classics take Saturn, Mars, Rahu and Ketu as the cause of confinement. They cause confinement when they influence

certain houses of the horoscope. There are four types of confinement which are Ari, Vir, Nag and Ahi.

12. **Ari** – Ari means **enemy**. Saturn is the karaka of this Bandhan. Saturn is Karma and prarabhdha. It is the result of your past Karma. These can be the Karma of past life or of present life which you are required to pay. Usually, their imprisonment happens due to bad company they chose. People who get involved in drug trafficking, mafia, robbery, alcoholism, adultery along with their friends, tend to get caught and end up in jail. The person is friends with people who are actually his enemy.

13. **Vir** – Vir means **Brave.** Mars is the Karaka of this Bandhan. These people put up a brave face in committing crimes. This can be of three types. One is the brave acts in army while fighting an enemy in a war and is captured and taken as prisoner of war. Second type are people who get involved in civil wars, street fights, terrorism, Naxalist, mob fights against police tend to get arrested and thrown in jail. The third type are those who face arrest for crimes like murder, rape, non-payment of loans or taxes, white collar offenses, cyber-crime, cheating, real estate issues etc.

14. **Nag** - Nag is snake. This Bandhan is caused by Rahu and is a result of offending someone in public or online, promoting religious hatred or racism, mafia, drugs, bombing cities, illegal mining, possessing huge amounts of unaccounted cash etc. Usually, they start with a low life and grow to a powerful position by opposing law but end up either in jail or hiding underground. These people can never have a public life. This is also a result of black magic, witchcraft performed by them on others, and it boomeranged on them.

15. **Ahi** – Ahi is deadly serpent. This Bandhan is caused by Ketu. This is a result of unimaginable strange crimes. They are usually victims of their own greed and misdeeds. Ketu is

head-less, which indicates natives getting involved in brainless activities to get caught. Reasons can be silly but crime will be severe and so will be the punishment.

Navamsha

Navamsha is an important chart to understand the nature of the planet. The main planets to be examined in Navamsha are Moon, Mercury and the second lord of birth chart. The second lord of birth is the indicator of Samskara of the birth.

1. When all of them are afflicted in Navamsha then the person has no control on his actions.
2. Fifth lord of birth and Venus are also examined for lust and direction of intelligence of the person. They should be free from affliction to take the person on right path. Affliction of fifth lord of birth in Navamsha can make a person drug addict.
3. **Sixty fourth Navamsha** is the fourth house from Moon in Navamsha chart. Lord of this house is the lord of sixty fourth Navamsha.
4. The final verdict will be from Dreshkana. This will be discussed with Dreshkana.

Dreshkana

Dreshkana plays an important role in deciding the courage and the result of Karam undertaken. four types of Dreshkana when occupied by planet are giver of hardships like confinement among other problems. These are Sarpa, Pasha, Ayudha and Nigada Dreshkana. Beside these the twenty second Dreshkana is important.

Twenty second Dreshkana

The sign in eighth house of Dreshkana chart is the twenty second Dreshkana. The lord of this sign is called lord of twenty second Dreshkana or Khara.

Malefic Dreshkana

A table listing the other malefic Dreshkana in all signs is given. Only these four types of Dreshkana are marked.

Sign	First Dreshkana	Second Dreshkana	Third Dreshkana
Aries	Ayudha		Ayudha
Taurus		Sarpa	
Gemini		Ayudha	Ayudha
Cancer		Sarpa	Sarpa
Leo	Ayudha	Ayudha	Ayudha
Virgo			
Libra			
Scorpio	Sarpa	Sarpa/ Pasha	
Sagittarius			Ayudha
Capricorn	Nigada		
Aquarius	Ayudha	Ayudha	Ayudha
Pisces	Ayudha	Ayudha	Sarpa

Rules to analyze Dreshkana

1. Note the sign and the lord of twenty second Dreshkana. Also note the planets in these four Dreshkana. More planets in these Dreshkana more are the chances of confinement.

2. **When the lord of twenty second Dreshkana is also in a malefic Dreshkana then it is serious. This is also true for the lord of sixty fourth Navamsha.**
3. When the lord of twenty second Dreshkana or the lord of sixty fourth Navamsha is influencing lagna or lagna lord of Dreshkana then it promotes the bad effects. Sometimes this lord is influencing the lagna or lagna lord in birth horoscope.
4. The planets related to twenty second Dreshkana sign or lord are also harmful. The same applies to sixty fourth Navamsha or its lord.
5. The confinement is given by fourth, tenth, twelfth and eighth house of Dreshkana. Planets in these houses and those influenced by lords of these houses give confinement in their dasha periods.
6. Dreshkana is taken as supportive chart of Navamsha. The effects of Navamsha are highlighted in Dreshkana. If Mercury and Moon are afflicted in Navamsha and have malefic relation in Dreshkana then the bad effects of Navamsha are supported by Dreshkana. When they are afflicted in Navamsha and have benefic relation in Dreshkana then the affliction is not supported in Dreshkana and may not give bad effects.
7. Mercury is the intelligence and Moon is mind. These two gives shape to action.
8. We will be using cyclical or Parivrittitraya Dreshkana. In this Dreshkana the sequence of Dreshkana is ruled by Tatva of the sign of planet or lagna. A table for finding the cyclical Dreshkana is given.

Sr. No.	Sign	First Dreshkana	Second Dreshkana	Third Dreshkana
1.	Fiery 1, 5, 9	Aries	Taurus	Gemini
2.	Earthy 2, 6, 10	Cancer	Leo	Virgo
3.	Airy 3, 7, 11	Libra	Scorpio	Sagittarius
4.	Watery 4, 8, 12	Capricorn	Aquarius	Pisces

Shashtiamsha

The final ruling is given by D 60. We check the Shashtiamsha deity. If the planets selected in Dreshkana are in malefic Shashtiamsha then the troubles are compounded. Workout the ruling Shashtiamsha deity of the planets. It is important to check the planets pointed out in Dreshkana. When these are in malefic Shashtiamsha then the bad effects are confirmed. Some of the malefic Shashtiamsha are given.

1. Ghora – Horrible, ghastly, awful, horror, son of Angiras, female attendant of Durga and gives extreme results.
2. Rakshasa – Demon, evil spirit, servants, darkness, tailor, do sinful acts, on the wrong path.
3. Bharst – Fallen from moral standards, manufacturer of furniture, Corrupt, bad deeds.
4. Kulanghan – brings bad name to family, fallen from family traditions, actor of cinema/ stage/ TV/ radio.
5. Garal – Poison, gymnast, modern dancers.
6. Agni –Burning like fire, doing ceremonies, doer of yagna, karamkandi.
7. Gulika – Destructive, son of Saturn. Dealer of household goods.

8. Mrityu – Death, son of Mars. Engaged in transport related jobs.
9. Kaal – Destructive, son of Sun. Time.
10. Devagni – Forest fire beyond control. Related to agriculture.
11. Yama – Death like suffering.
12. Kantak – Thorn, very painful limp.
13. Vish Pradcigdha – Fully poisoned, cannot be rebuild.
14. Kulnash - Destroyer of family/ lineage.
15. Vansha Chhaya - Destroyer of family/ lineage.
16. Utpata – Destructive, revolution, fury of nature.
17. Kroor – Harsh, inauspicious.

The twelfth house lord is also checked for its placement in Shashtiamsha.

We now take few horoscopes of the person who went to jail. A step-by-step method is given on the example horoscopes.

Example James Earl Ray DOB 10 March 1928 TOB 15.00 POB Alton IL

Birth Chart

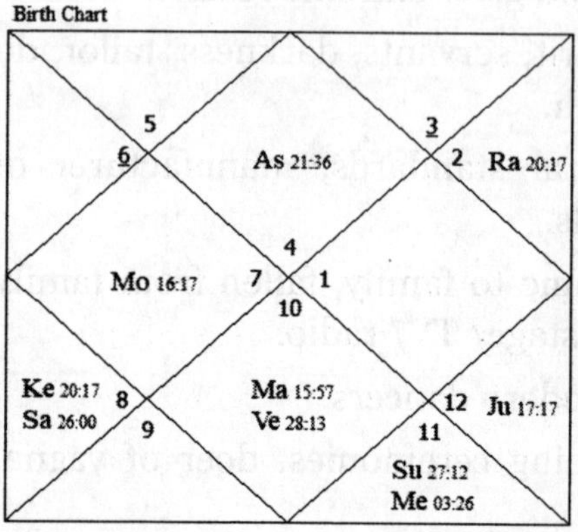

Birth Chart

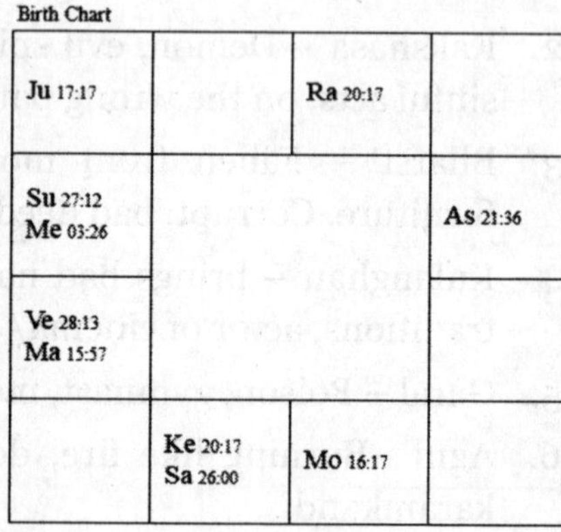

D9 Navamsha (spouse)

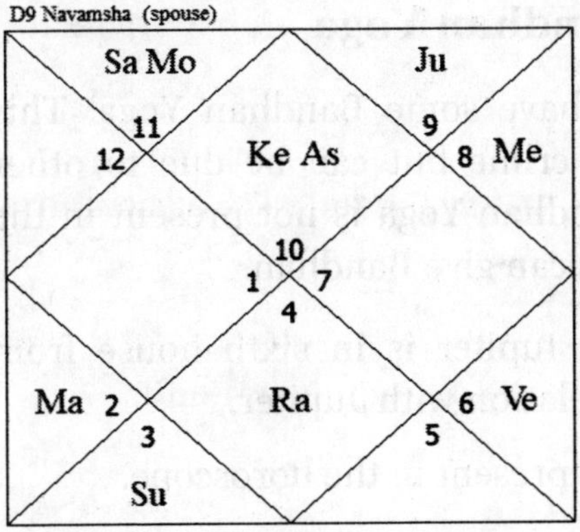

D9 Navamsha (spouse)

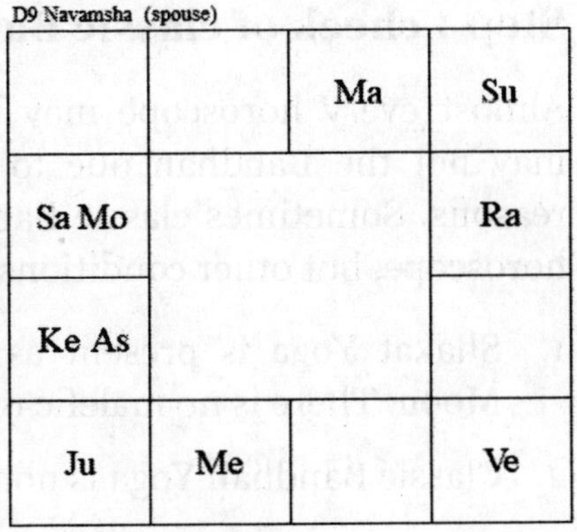

D3 Dreshkana (happiness siblings)

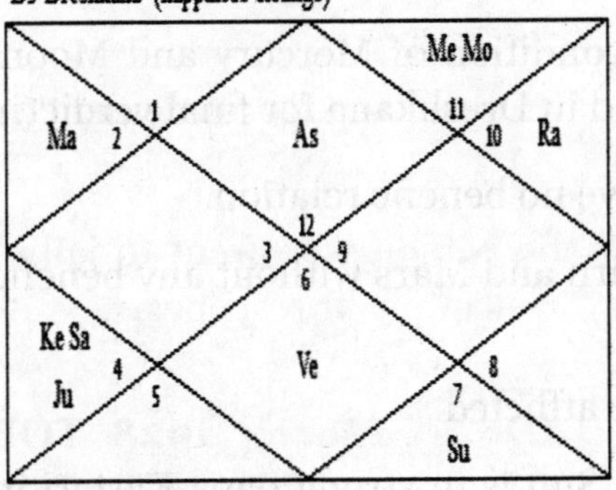

D3 Dreshkana (happiness siblings)

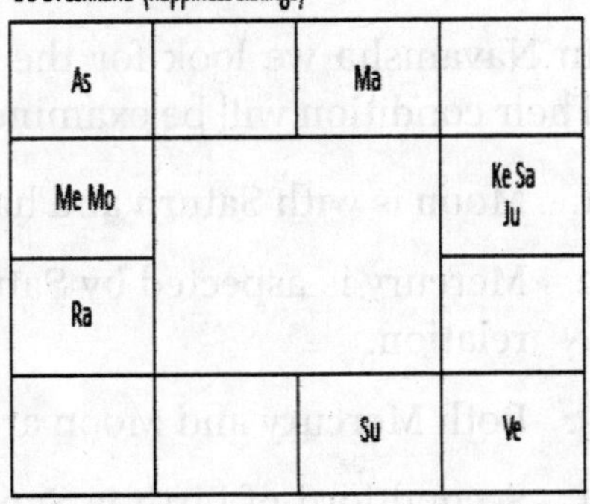

D60 Shashtiamsha (All areas)

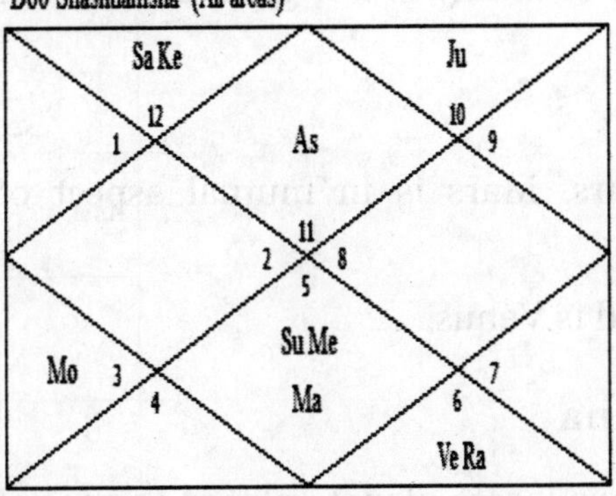

D60 Shashtiamsha (All areas)

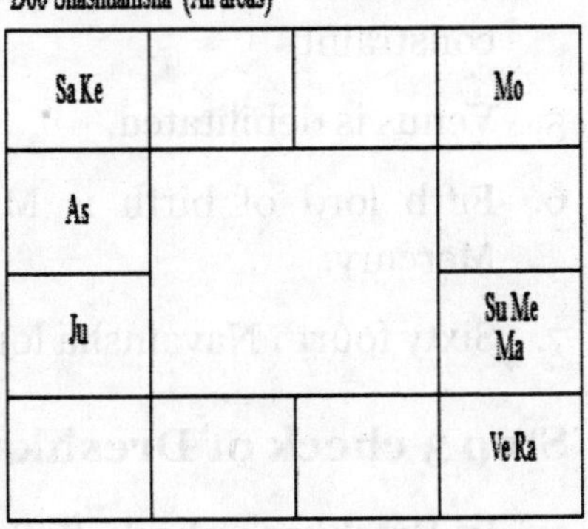

Step 1 check of classic Bandhan Yoga

Almost every horoscope may have some Bandhan Yoga. This may not the Bandhan due to crime but can be due to other reasons. Sometimes classic Bandhan Yoga is not present in the horoscope, but other conditions can give Bandhan.

1. Shakat Yoga is present as Jupiter is in sixth house from Moon. There is no malefic relation with Jupiter.
2. Classic Bandhan Yoga is not present in the horoscope.

Step 2 check of Navamsha

In Navamsha we look for the condition of Mercury and Moon. Their condition will be examined in Dreshkana for final verdict.

1. Moon is with Saturn and have no benefic relation.
2. Mercury is aspected by Saturn and Mars without any benefic relation.
3. Both Mercury and Moon are afflicted.
4. Second lord of birth is Sun. Sun is in strong papa Kartari in Navamsha. The Samskara of family is not good and he felt constraint.
5. Venus is debilitated.
6. Fifth lord of birth is Mars. Mars is in mutual aspect of Mercury.
7. Sixty fourth Navamsha lord is Venus.

Step 3 check of Dreshkana

1. In Dreshkana check, first we locate planets placed in special Dreshkana. In this horoscope, lagna is in third Dreshkana of Cancer and is in Sarp Dreshkana.
2. Next, we look for the condition of Mercury and Moon.

3. Moon is with Mercury. Moon is with Saturn in Navamsha. Moon is thus afflicted in Navamsha and in Dreshkana.
4. Mercury is in twelfth house.
5. Next, we examine eighth, fourth and twelfth house and planet in Sarp Dreshkana. This will indicate the time of confinement.
6. Mercury is in twelfth house. Venus is the lord of eighth house. Mercury is fourth lord and can give confinement.
7. No planet is placed in fourth house.
8. Jupiter is in fifth house with Saturn and Ketu. Twelfth lord is Saturn.
9. He was born in Rahu dasha. His Jupiter dasha ended when he was 21 years old.
10. **The main planets which can give Bandhan are Saturn, Mercury, Venus and Mars. Saturn is with Ketu. Saturn is aspecting Rahu and Venus. Six planets are capable of giving jail.**

Step 4 check of criminal tendency

1. Third house is strong by aspect of Jupiter. Mercury is badly afflicted in Navamsha.
2. Mercury and Moon are afflicted in Navamsha.
3. Fourth lord Venus is with Mars and is aspected by Saturn without any benefic relief.
4. Mercury and Moon are afflicted in Navamsha.
5. Lagna lord has no benefic association.

Check of Shashtiamsha

We check the placement of planets selected in Dreshkana.

Sun – Sun is in Kroor Shashtiamsha.

Moon – Moon is in Devagni Shashtiamsha.

Mercury – Mercury is in Bhrasht Shashtiamsha. Mercury is twelfth lord.

Saturn – Is in Kulanghan Shashtiamsha.

These four planets are in malefic Shashtiamsha and will give problems. Saturn, Venus and Mercury are badly afflicted in Shashtiamsha. Saturn is with Ketu; Venus is with Rahu and aspected by Saturn. Mercury is with Mars and Sun. he was in jail in Venus dasha and was not able to commit crime.

Let us see his crime record. He left school at the age of 12 years.

1. Committed a burglary in 1949 but was not jailed. The dasha was Saturn/ Saturn.
2. Arrested in armed robbery in 1952. The dasha was Saturn/ Mercury. He was jailed for 2 years.
3. Came out of jail and was again arrested for stealing money from mail orders. He was jailed for 4 years. The dasha was Saturn/ Ketu.
4. Out of jail after 4 years and caught stealing 120 Dollars from a store. Dasha was Saturn/ Sun. He was sentenced for 20 years for repeated crime. He escaped from jail in March 1968 hiding in a bakery delivery van. The Mercury Maha dasha started on 10 March 1968. Mercury was to prove worst dasha and he came out of jail.
5. He purchased a rifle on 30 March 1968. He shot an American leader on 4 April 1968 and escaped to Canada. The dasha was Mercury/ Mercury/ Moon. He was arrested on 8 June 1968 from Heathrow airport while trying to escape on a

false passport. He was now sentenced for 99 years in jail because he pleaded guilty to avoid gallows.

6. Once again escaped on 10 June 1977 but was caught on 13 June 1977. The dasha was Mercury/ Rahu/ Rahu.
7. Died in prison hospital on 23 April 1998 of disease of Kidney and liver failure. The dasha was Venus/ Mars/ Mars.

All crime were done in the dasha of Saturn and Mercury. They were the main pointer of Dreshkana chart.

Yes, he assassinated Martin Luther King.

Example Jeffery Dahmer DOB 21 May 1960 TOB 16.34 POB Milwaukee

Birth Chart

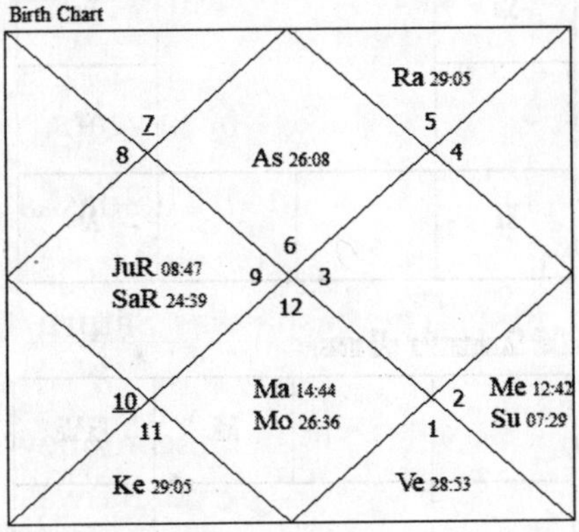

Birth Chart

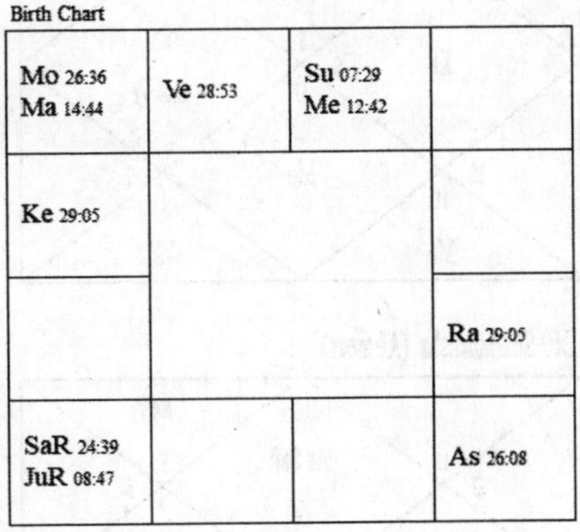

D9 Navamsha (spouse)

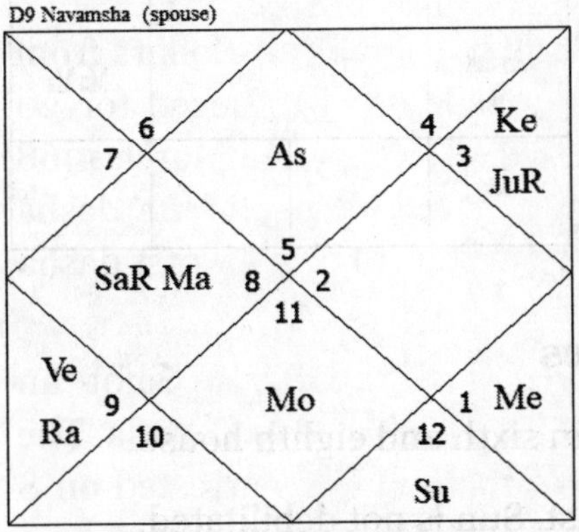

D9 Navamsha (spouse)

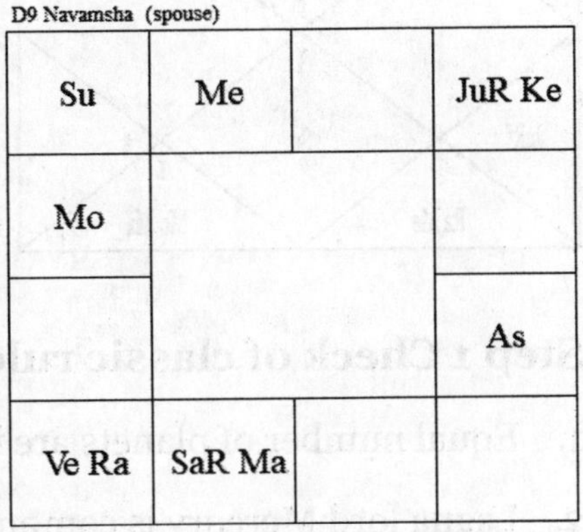

D3 Dreshkana (happiness siblings)

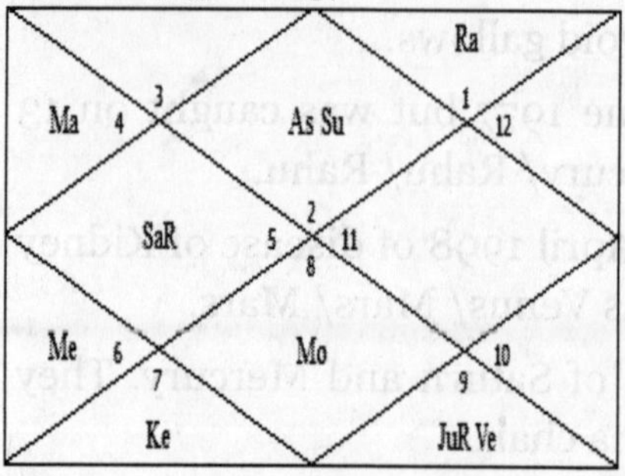

D3 Dreshkana (happiness siblings)

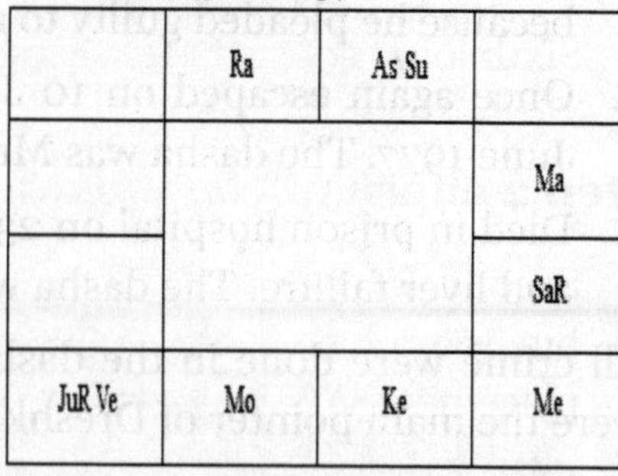

D3 Iyer Parivriti Traya Dreshkana (happiness siblings)

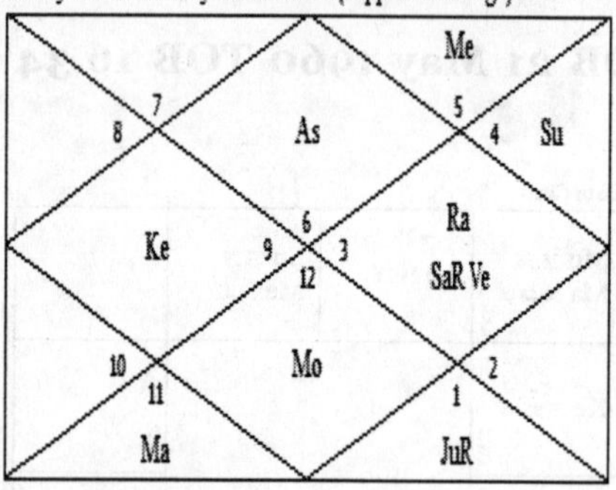

D3 Iyer Parivriti Traya Dreshkana (happiness siblings)

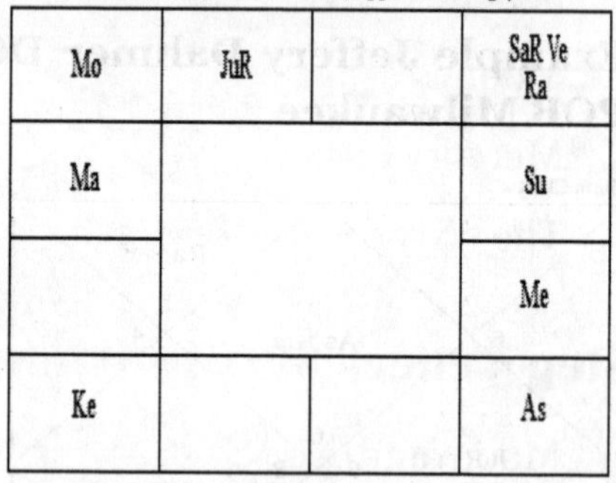

D60 Shashtiamsha (All areas)

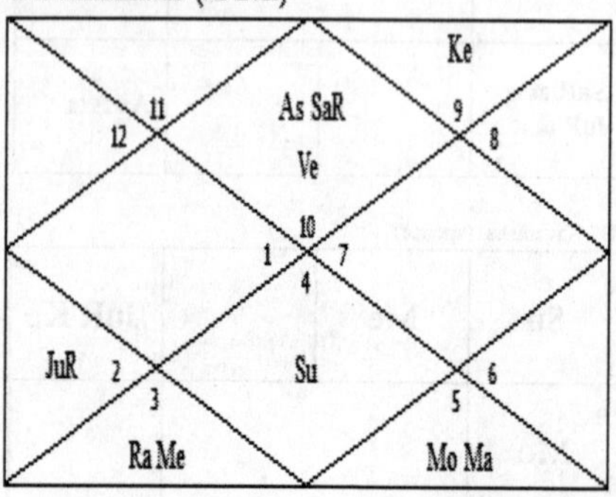

D60 Shashtiamsha (All areas)

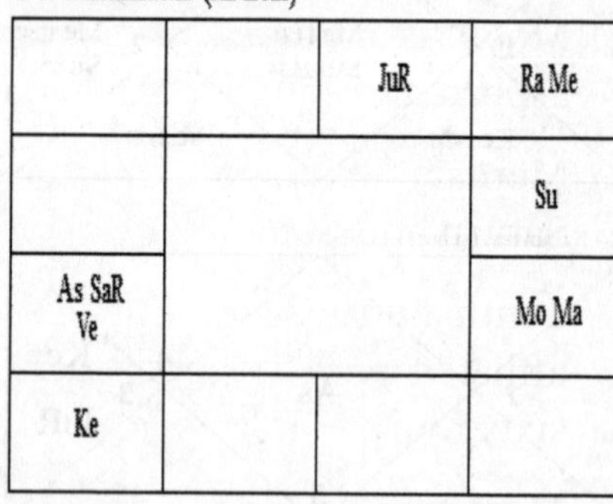

Step 1 Check of classic rules

1. Equal number of planets are in sixth and eighth house.

2. Lagna lord Mercury is combust. Sun is not debilitated.

3. Lord of sixth and eighth house are in Kendra.
4. Sixth lord is Saturn. It is aspecting lagna and gives suffering.

Step 2 check of Navamsha

1. Second lord of birth horoscope is with Rahu in Navamsha but is protected by aspect of Jupiter. The drawback is the placement of Venus and Jupiter in RKA.
2. Fifth lord of birth is with Mars in Navamsha and have no benefic relief.
3. Moon is aspected by Mars and afflicted Jupiter.
4. Mercury has no relation but is placed in ninth house.
5. The sixty fourth Navamsha is Taurus and its lord is Venus.

Step 3 check of Dreshkana

1. Moon and Mercury are in Sarp Dreshkana. Venus, Rahu, Saturn, Ketu and Mars are in Ayudha Dreshkana.
2. Moon is afflicted in Navamsha. In Dreshkana Moon is aspected by Saturn and gives more problems.
3. Mercury was neutral in Navamsha. Mercury is aspected by Saturn and Mars in Dreshkana.
4. Tenth house has Saturn, Rahu and Venus. Venus is badly afflicted and has no benefic relation. Venus is the lord of sixty fourth Navamsha also.
5. Mars is the lord of twenty second Dreshkana.
6. Eighth house has Jupiter. Jupiter is not aspected by any planet.
7. Mercury is placed in twelfth house.

8. Fourth house has Ketu. Ketu is aspected by Saturn, Venus and Jupiter.
9. Planets which can give confinement are Venus, Saturn, Rahu, Ketu, Mercury and Moon. Six planets are harmful. His confinement was in Venus period.

Step 4 check of criminal tendency

1. Lagan lord is with a malefic and has no benefic relation.
2. Mercury is in Prishtodaya sign.
3. Fourth house and fourth lord are with Saturn. Saturn is the cause to give constant and deep thinking to devise ways of crime.
4. Saturn in fourth house gives dishonest way of actions.
5. Moon is afflicted in Navamsha.
6. Mercury is alone in Navamsha.
7. Mercury is in ninth house in birth horoscope and is with a malefic.
8. These gives a strong tendency to commit crime.

Step 5 check of Shashtiamsha

1. Three planets are in malefic Shashtiamsha.
2. Moon is in Bhrasht Shashtiamsha.
3. Mercury is in Yama Shashtiamsha.
4. Venus is in Payodhi Shashtiamsha. Payodhi is ocean and is without limit.
5. All main indicators are in malefic Shashtiamsha.
6. Venus is with Saturn and is aspected by Sun who is eighth lord.

Crime record

Dahmer was a serial killer, cannibal and necrophiliac. He committed 16 murders and one homicide. He committed his first murder on 18 June 1978 and last in 1991 when he was arrested. All crimes were committed in MD of Venus. Venus is badly placed and is with eighth lord Jupiter in Dreshkana.

His trial started on 30 January 1992 and he was sentenced for 16 life terms in prison. The capital punishment is not allowed in Wisconsin. After serving two years in jail, he was beaten to death by a fellow prisoner on 28 November 1994 in MD of Sun. sun is the lord of twelfth house of birth horoscope.

Example Berry Chuck DOB 18 October 1926 TOB 6.59 POB Overland Missouri

Birth Chart

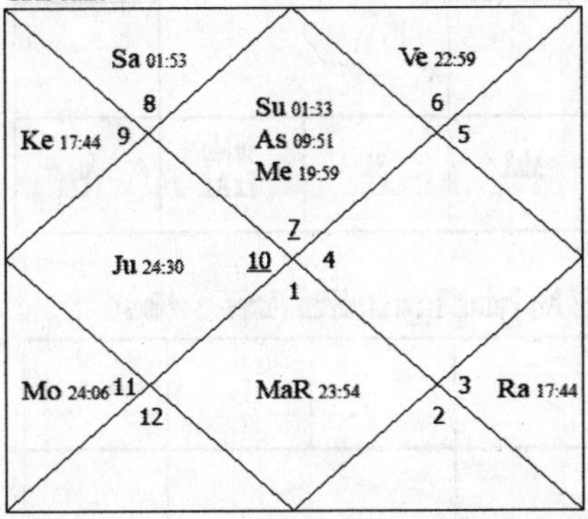

Birth Chart

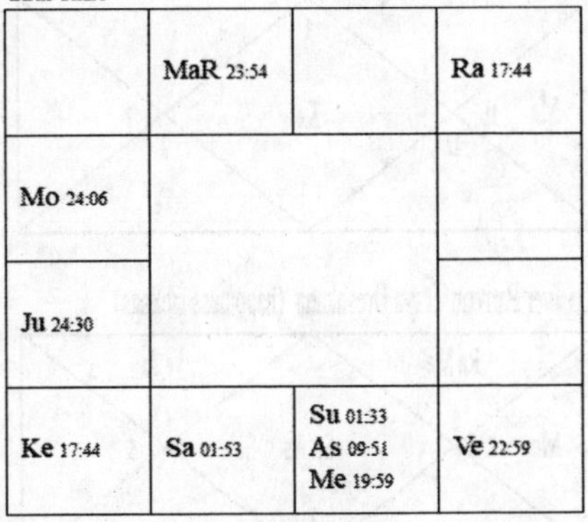

D9 Navamsha (spouse)

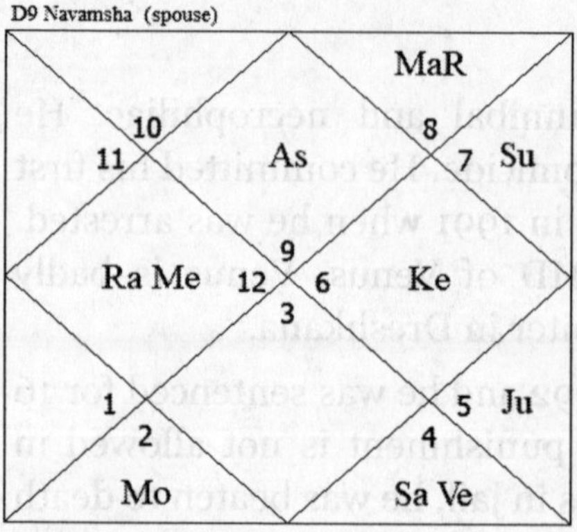

D9 Navamsha (spouse)

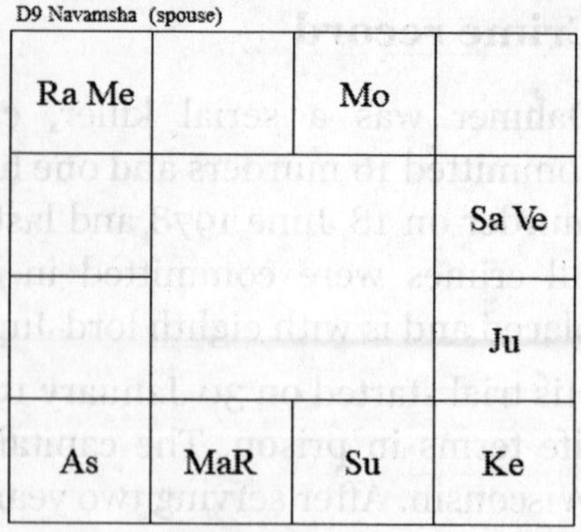

D3 Dreshkana (happiness siblings)

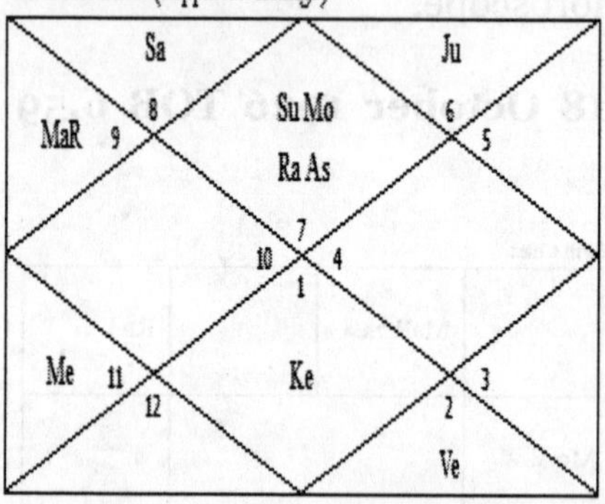

D3 Dreshkana (happiness siblings)

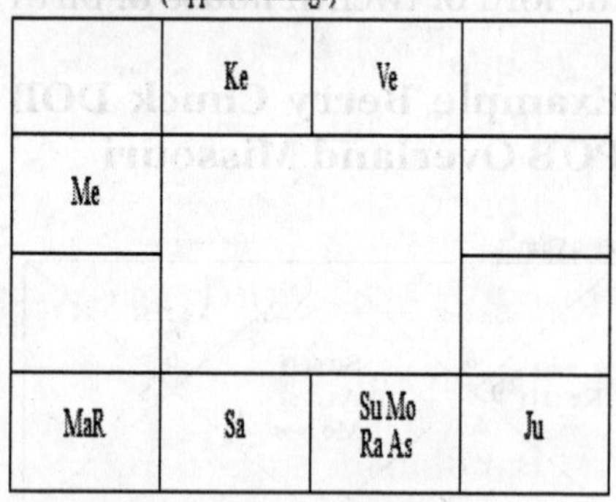

D3 Iyer Parivriti Traya Dreshkana (happiness siblings)

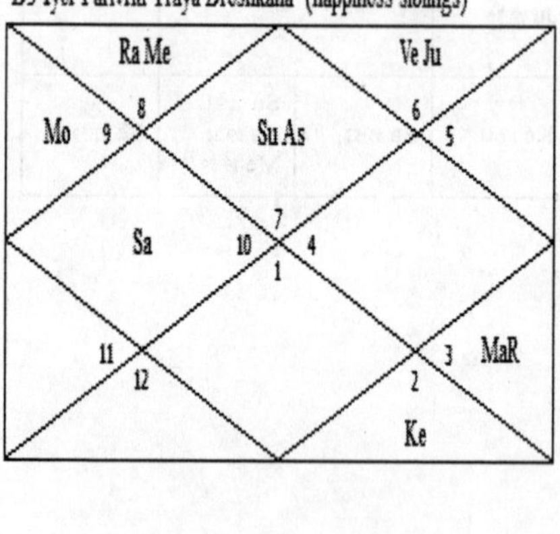

D3 Iyer Parivriti Traya Dreshkana (happiness siblings)

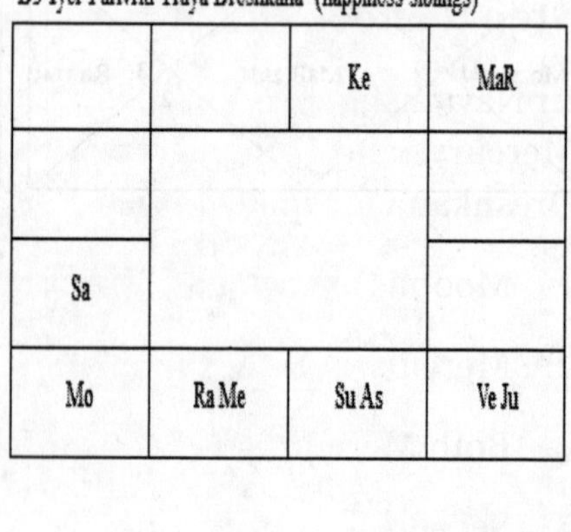

D60 Shashtiamsha (All areas)

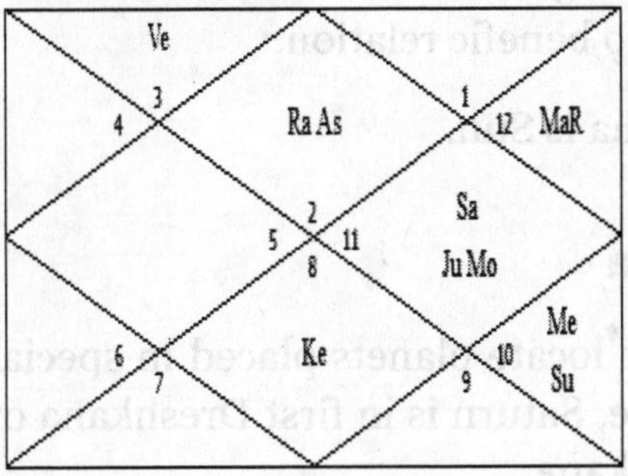

D60 Shashtiamsha (All areas)

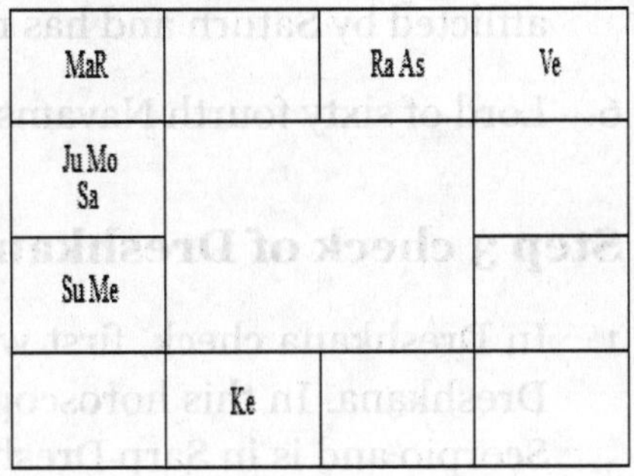

Step 1 check of classic Bandhan Yoga

1. Equal number of planets are present in second and twelfth house. Same is the condition for fifth and ninth house.
2. Lord of sixth house is aspecting twelfth house.
3. Lord of eighth house is placed in twelfth house.
4. Lagan lord is combusted and Sun is debilitated.
5. Bandhan Yogas are present in the horoscope.

Step 2 check of Navamsha

In Navamsha we look for the condition of second lord of birth, Mercury and Moon. Their condition will be examined in Dreshkana for final verdict.

1. Moon is aspected by Mars and have no benefic relation.
2. Mercury is with Rahu without any benefic relation.
3. Both Mercury and Moon are afflicted.
4. Second lord of birth is Mars. Mars is not afflicted in Navamsha. The samskara are good.

5. The fifth lord and Venus are together in Navamsha. Venus is afflicted by Saturn and has no benefic relation.

6. Lord of sixty fourth Navamsha is Sun.

Step 3 check of Dreshkana

1. In Dreshkana check, first we locate planets placed in special Dreshkana. In this horoscope, Saturn is in first Dreshkana of Scorpio and is in Sarp Dreshkana.

2. Rahu, Jupiter and Moon are in Ayudha Dreshkana.

3. The lord of twenty second Dreshkana is Venus.

4. Next, we look for the condition of Mercury and Moon. Moon is aspected by Mars and gives more problems.

5. Mercury is with Rahu and is free to do harm.

6. Next, we examine fourth, eighth, tenth, twelfth house and planet in special Dreshkana. This will indicate the time of confinement.

7. Fourth house has Saturn. Saturn is in Sarp Dreshkana and is a serious planet to give confinement.

8. No planet is placed in tenth house. Moon is tenth lord and is aspected by Mars.

9. Jupiter and Venus are placed in twelfth house. Twelfth lord Mercury is with Rahu. Mars is aspecting them. They are serious to give jail. Venus is eighth lord and gives more problems.

10. Ketu is in eighth house and acts as Venus. Mercury is aspecting Ketu.

11. The planets to give confinement are Saturn, Venus, Mercury, Rahu, Ketu and Jupiter.

Step 4 check criminal tendency

If the horoscope shows criminal tendency, then the person can land in jail. The dasha of planets selected in step 3 should operate during crucial time.

1. Lagna has no benefic relation. Lagna lord is combust but has aspect of Jupiter.
2. Mars is in seventh from Sun.
3. Third house is strong and Mercury is afflicted in Navamsha. This gives courage to commit a crime.
4. Mercury and Moon are afflicted in Navamsha.

Check of Shashtiamsha

1. Mercury is in Vish Shashtiamsha. Mercury is the lord of twelfth house of birth horoscope.
2. Saturn is in Amrita Shashtiamsha. Preacher and can influence others.
3. Rahu and Ketu are in Kantak Shashtiamsha.
4. His Sun is eleventh lord and is in Kuber Shashtiamsha.

Rahu, Ketu and Mercury are in bad Shashtiamsha. Sun made him rich. There are other combinations which make him wealthy and famous.

Berry was an American movie star. He visited jail many times for crimes committed. At an age of 18 years, he was caught for car theft and armed robbery. He was sentenced for three years in jail. This happened from 1944 to 1947 in dasha of Saturn/ Venus. In Saturn/ Mars he became a movie star.

He again served three years in 1962 in the dasha of Mercury/ Venus.

In 1978, he got 4 months sentence for not paying 108000 Dollars of Income Tax.

He has faced charges filed by at least 59 women and that has costed him 1.2 million Dollars in fine and legal charges.

Example Bari Candy DOB 6 June 1939 TOB 4.00 POB Edna Texas

Birth Chart

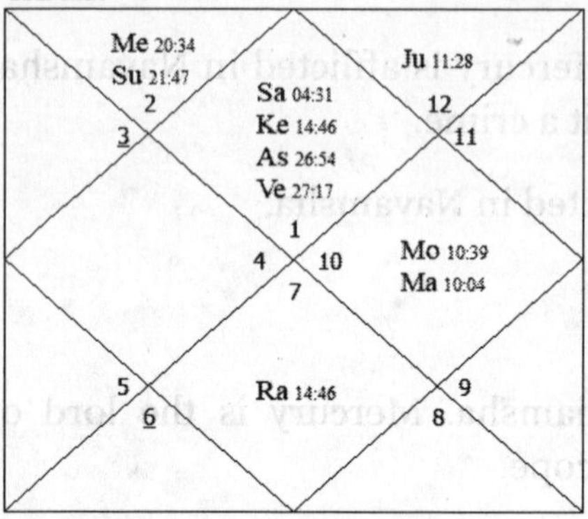

Birth Chart

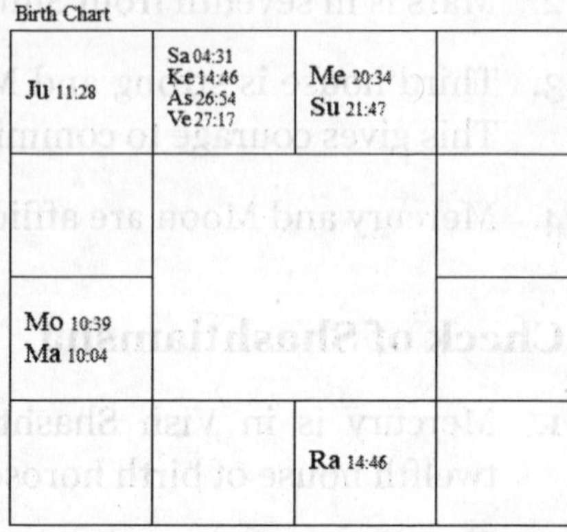

D9 Navamsha (spouse)

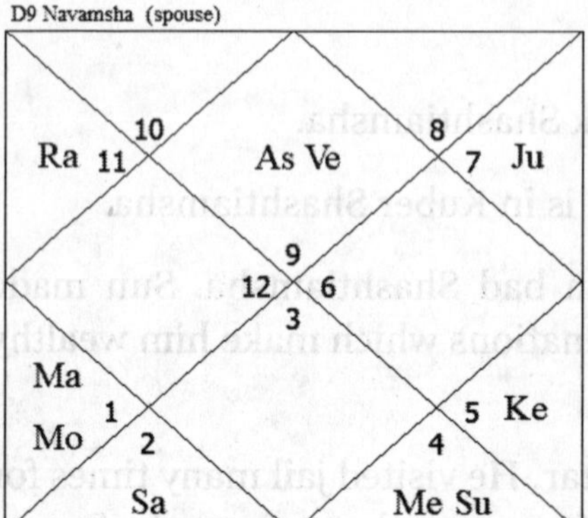

D9 Navamsha (spouse)

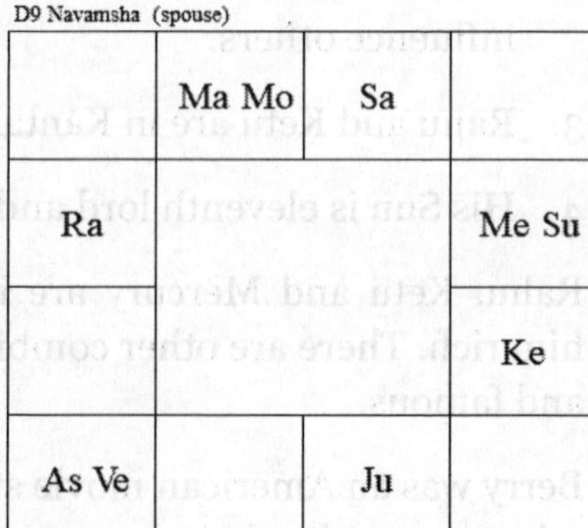

D3 Dreshkana (happiness siblings)

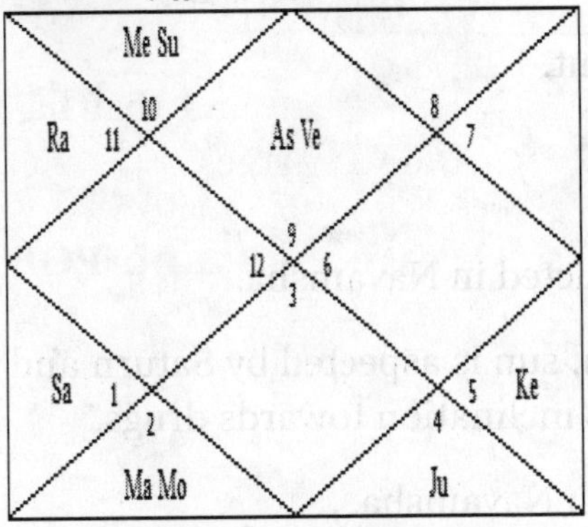

D3 Dreshkana (happiness siblings)

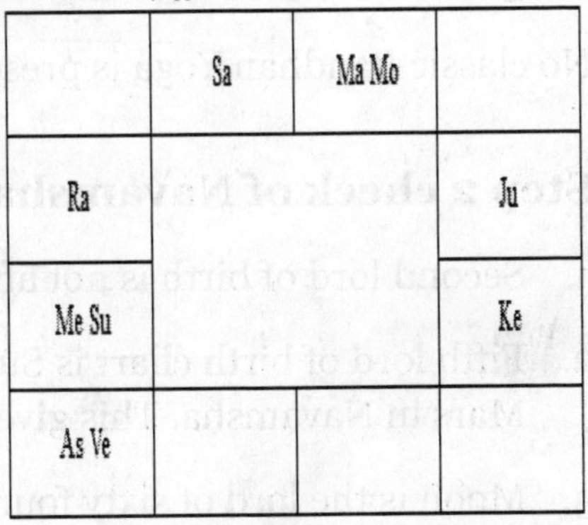

D3 Iyer Parivriti Traya Dreshkana (happiness siblings)

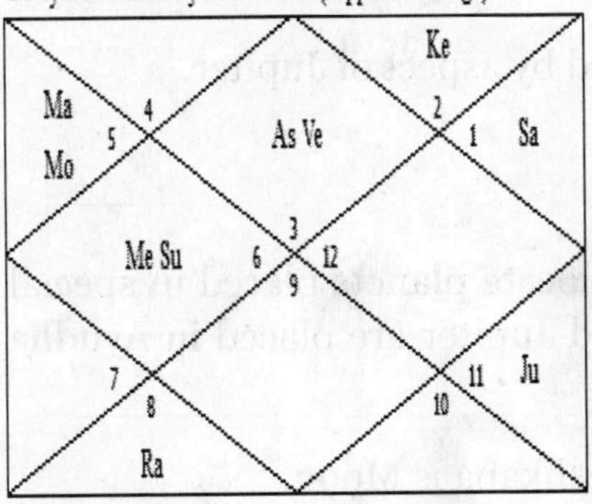

D3 Iyer Parivriti Traya Dreshkana (happiness siblings)

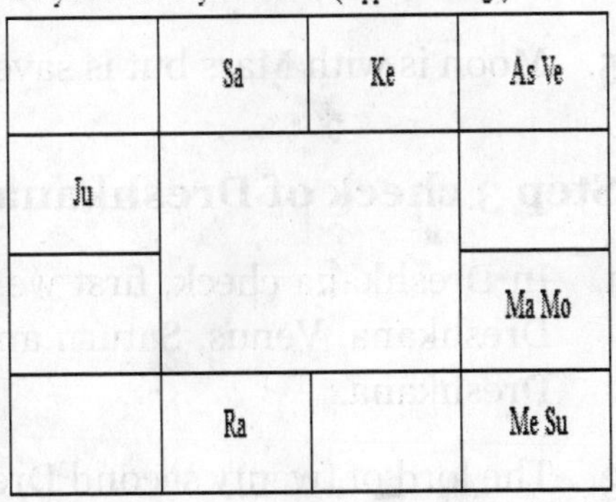

D60 Shashtiamsha (All areas)

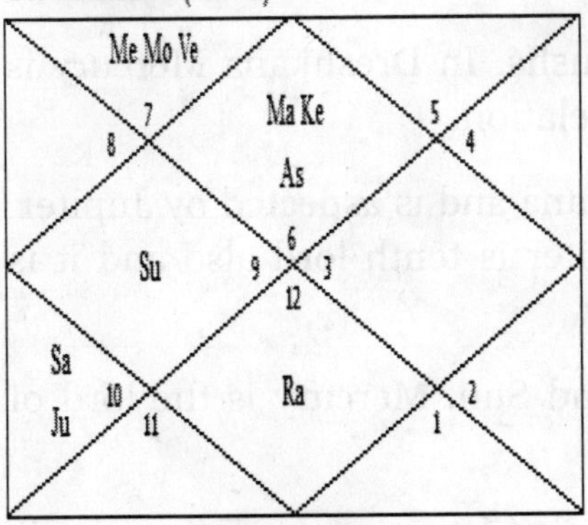

D60 Shashtiamsha (All areas)

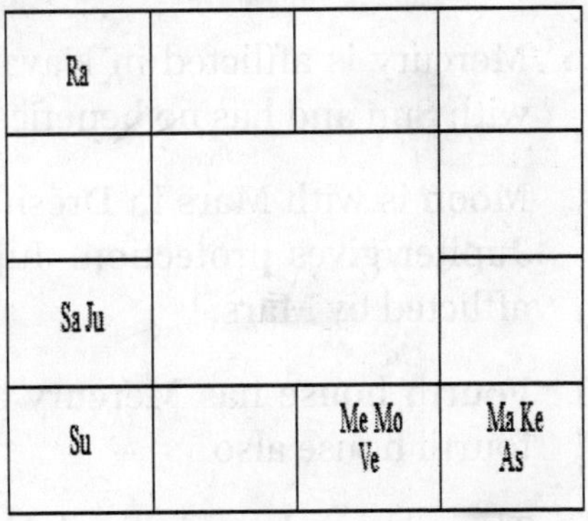

Step 1 for checking the classic Bandhan Yoga

No classic Bandhan Yoga is present.

Step 2 check of Navamsha

1. Second lord of birth is not afflicted in Navamsha.
2. Fifth lord of birth chart is Sun. sun is aspected by Saturn and Mars in Navamsha. This gives inclination towards drugs.
3. Moon is the lord of sixty fourth Navamsha.
4. Mercury is with Sun and is aspected by Mars and Saturn.
5. Moon is with Mars but is saved by aspect of Jupiter.

Step 3 check of Dreshkana

1. In Dreshkana check, first we locate planets placed in special Dreshkana. Venus, Saturn and Jupiter are placed in Ayudha Dreshkana.
2. The lord of twenty second Dreshkana is Moon.
3. Sign of Mercury is rising in Dreshkana.
4. Mercury is afflicted in Navamsha. In Dreshkana Mercury is with Sun and has no benefic relation.
5. Moon is with Mars in Dreshkana and is aspected by Jupiter. Jupiter gives protection. Jupiter is tenth lord also and it is afflicted by Mars.
6. Fourth house has Mercury and Sun. Mercury is the lord of fourth house also.
7. There is no planet in tenth house.
8. No planet is placed in eighth house.

9. Ketu is in twelfth house and have no benefic relation. We take RKA.

Step 4 check of criminal tendency

1. Mercury is in Prishtodaya sign.
2. Fourth lord has only malefic relation is with Mars and aspected by Saturn.
3. In Navamsha Mercury is with Sun and is aspected by Saturn and Mars.
4. In Navamsha Moon is with Mars but gets relief from Jupiter.

Shashtiamsha

1. Rahu and Ketu are in Gulika Shashtiamsha. They are not the planets selected in Dreshkana.
2. Venus is in Kroor Shashtiamsha but it is not involved in Dreshkana.
3. Mars is in Vish Shashtiamsha and is also the planet selected in Dreshkana. Mars is with Moon.
4. Moon is in Poorna Chandra Shashtiamsha. Moon is selected in Dreshkana but its placement in good Shashtiamsha will tone down the evil effects.
5. Rahu is afflicted by Mars and Saturn.

Candy was a highly paid dancer and a stripper. She married four times and has a daughter. She was arrested in 1957 for possession of drugs. She was sentenced for 15 years of jail but served only three years in jail. The dasha at the time of sentence was Rahu/ Jupiter. Jupiter is the lord of twelfth house. The jail sentence ended with Rahu/ Saturn. She was granted parole in

1963 and served about three years of jail. She was finally pardoned by Governor of Texas in 1968.

After release in 1963 she became a big star and a poet. She had a gentle mind but confused. Thanks to the placement of Moon in good Shashtiamsha.

Example Mahatma Gandhi DOB 2 October 1869 TOB 7.52.06 POB Porbandar

Birth Chart

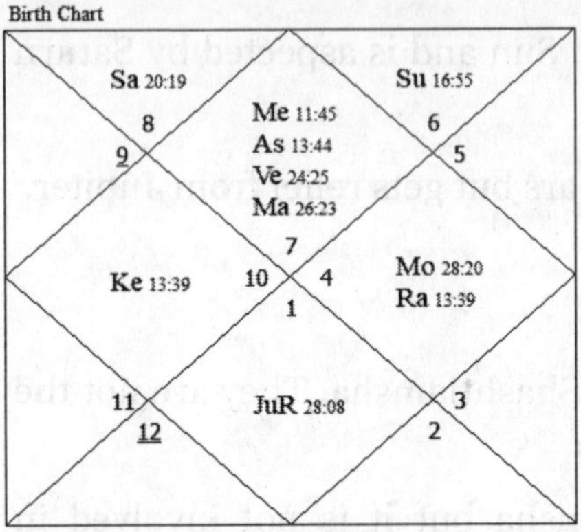

Birth Chart

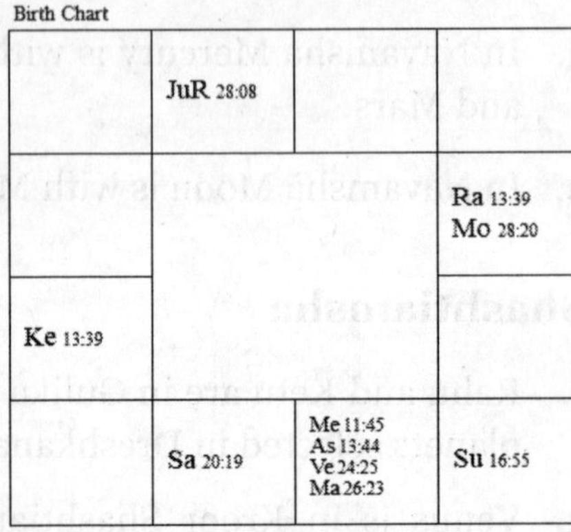

D9 Navamsha (spouse)

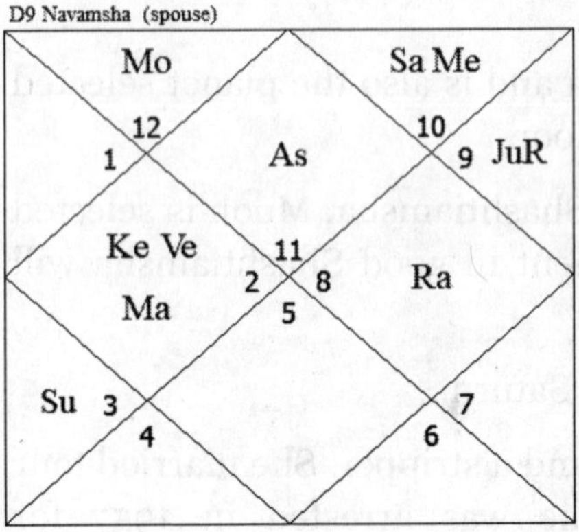

D9 Navamsha (spouse)

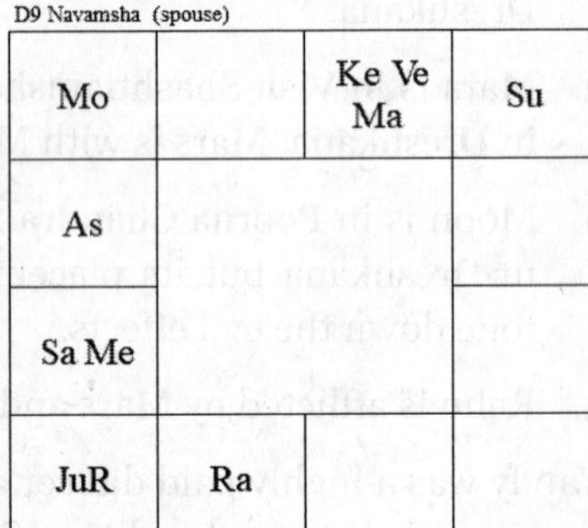

D3 Dreshkana (happiness siblings)

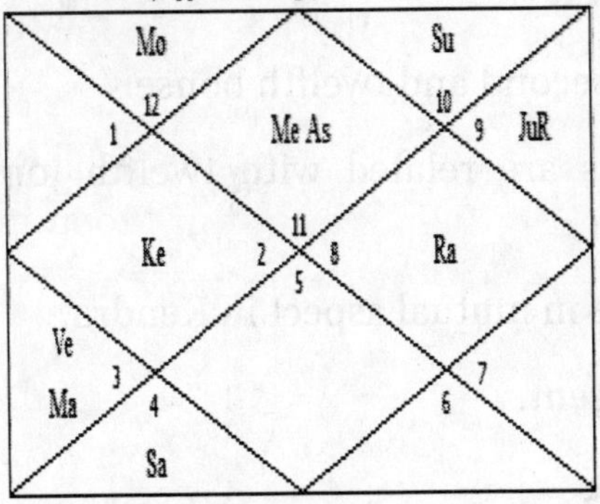

D3 Dreshkana (happiness siblings)

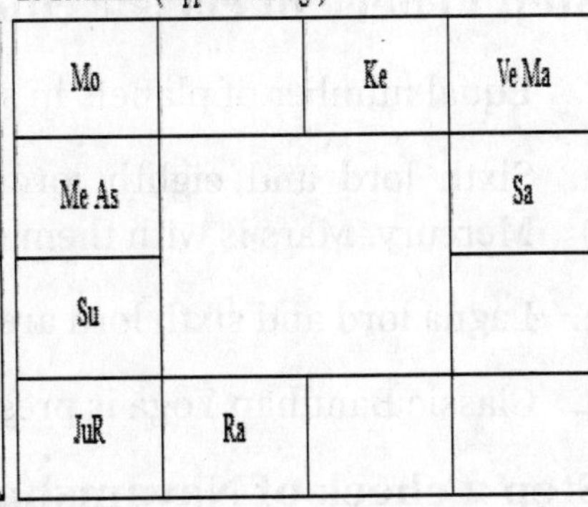

D3 Iyer Parivriti Traya Dreshkana (happiness siblings)

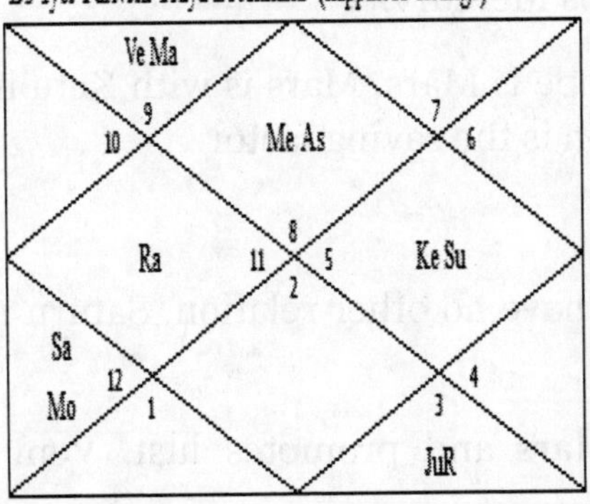

D3 Iyer Parivriti Traya Dreshkana (happiness siblings)

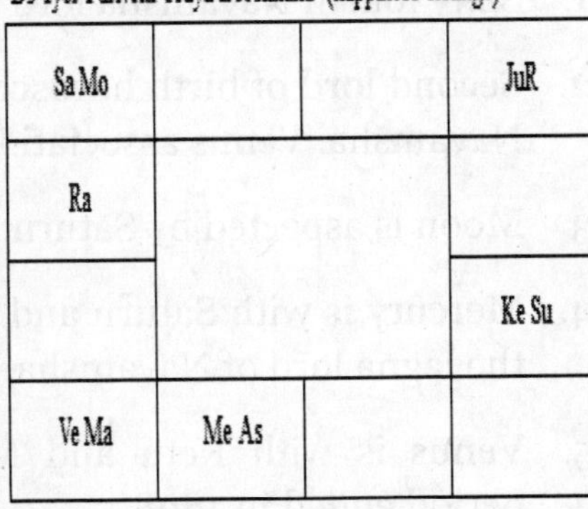

D60

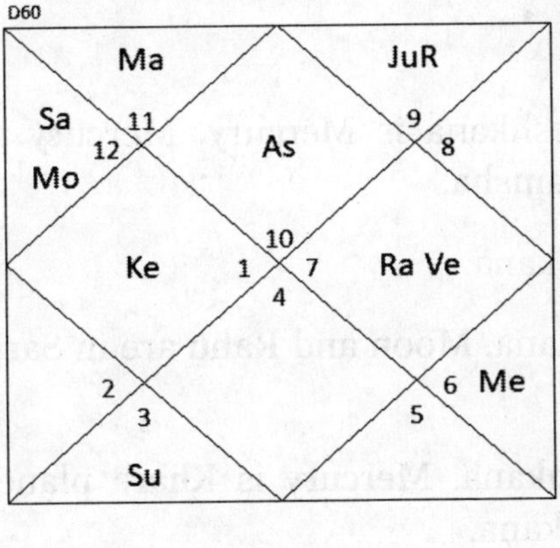

D60

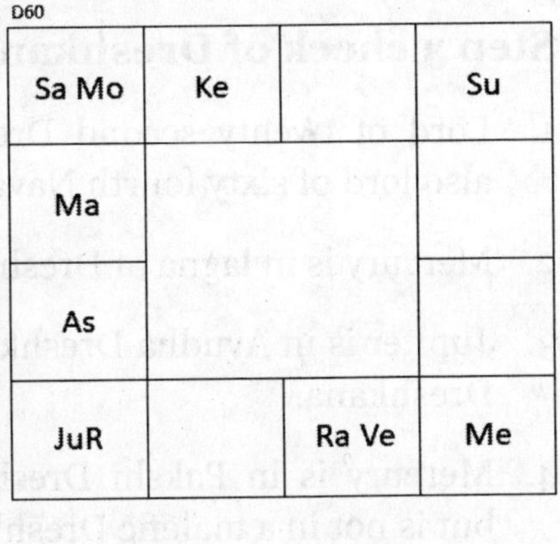

Step 1 check of classic rules

1. Equal number of planets in second and twelfth house.
2. Sixth lord and eighth lords are related with twelfth lord Mercury. Mars is with them.
3. Lagna lord and sixth lord are in mutual aspect in Kendra.
4. Classic Bandhan Yoga is present.

Step 2 check of Navamsha

1. Sixty fourth Navamsha lord is Mercury.
2. Second lord of birth horoscope is Mars. Mars is with Ketu in Navamsha. Venus association is the saving factor.
3. Moon is aspected by Saturn.
4. Mercury is with Saturn and have no other relation. Saturn is the lagna lord of Navamsha.
5. Venus is with Ketu and Mars and promotes lust. Venus period ended in 1898.

Step 3 check of Dreshkana

1. Lord of twenty second Dreshkana is Mercury. Mercury is also lord of sixty fourth Navamsha.
2. Mercury is in lagna of Dreshkana.
3. Jupiter is in Ayudha Dreshkana. Moon and Rahu are in Sarp Dreshkana.
4. Mercury is in Pakshi Dreshkana. Mercury is Khara planet but is not in a malefic Dreshkana.
5. Ketu is in tenth house with tenth lord Sun.

6. Jupiter is in eighth house. Eighth lord Mercury is not aspecting any planet.
7. No planet is in twelfth house.
8. Rahu is placed in fourth house and is aspected by Jupiter and Sun. Both Rahu and Jupiter are in special Dreshkana.
9. The planets which can give Bandhan are Sun, Rahu, Ketu, Mercury, and Jupiter.
10. Moon dasha was spent in South Africa and gave problems. Moon is in Sarp Dreshkana.
11. He was in jail in Rahu and Jupiter dasha.

Step 4 check of criminal tendency

1. Lagna lord is with Mercury and aspected by Jupiter. This is a major factor, and the person is not a criminal.
2. Fourth house has Ketu aspected by Moon. Fourth lord is Saturn. Saturn is aspecting fourth house. Saturn is not afflicted.
3. Third house is strong, and Mercury is afflicted in Dreshkana.
4. In Navamsha Mercury and Moon are afflicted by Saturn but Saturn is lagna lord of Navamsha.
5. Sixth lord is retrograde and gives a guilty feeling.
6. Criminal tendencies are not present. The cause of Bandhan is not crime.

Step 5 check of Shashtiamsha

1. Sun and Rahu are in malefic Shashtiamsha.
2. Mercury is in Maheshwar Shashtiamsha. Mercury is the lord of twelfth house of birth horoscope.

3. Mercury is the most afflicted planet. Mercury is aspected by Saturn and Mars. Mercury dasha lasted till 3 years of age and he was under strict family discipline.

He was arrested and put in jail on several occasion. His first arrest was on 10 March 1922 in the dasha of Rahu/ Rahu.

Example J L Nehru DOB 14 November 1889 TOB 23.05 POB Allahabad

Birth Chart

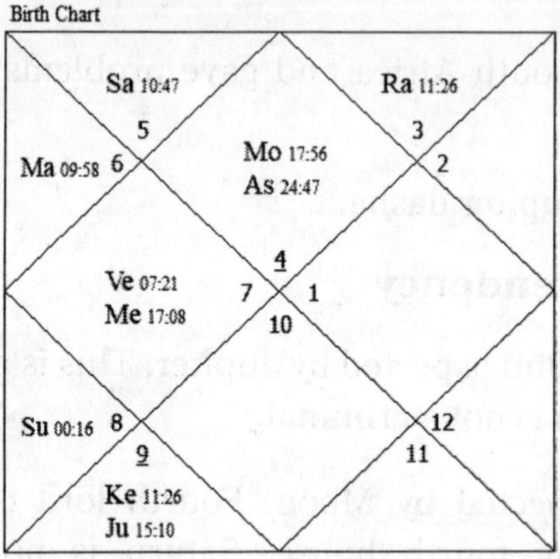

Birth Chart

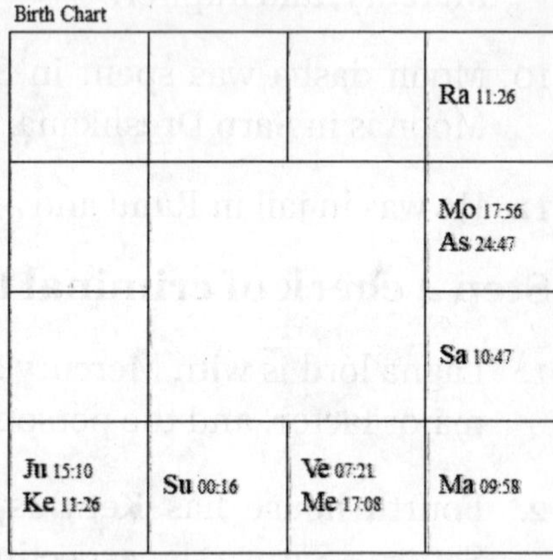

D9 Navamsha (spouse)

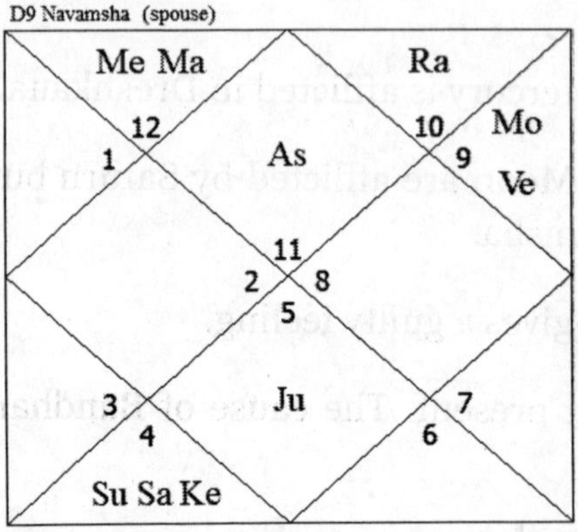

D9 Navamsha (spouse)

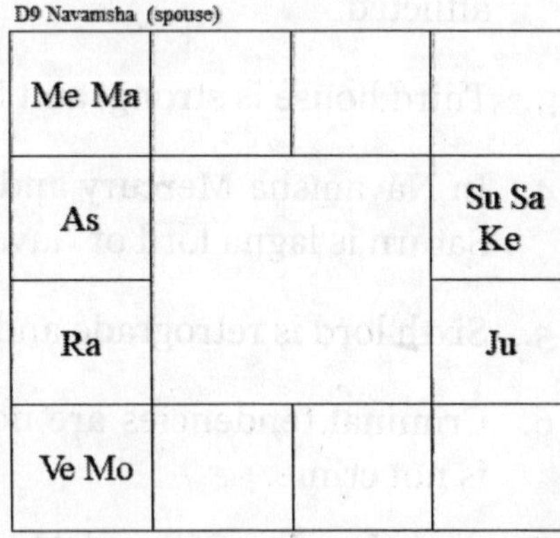

D3 Dreshkana (happiness siblings)

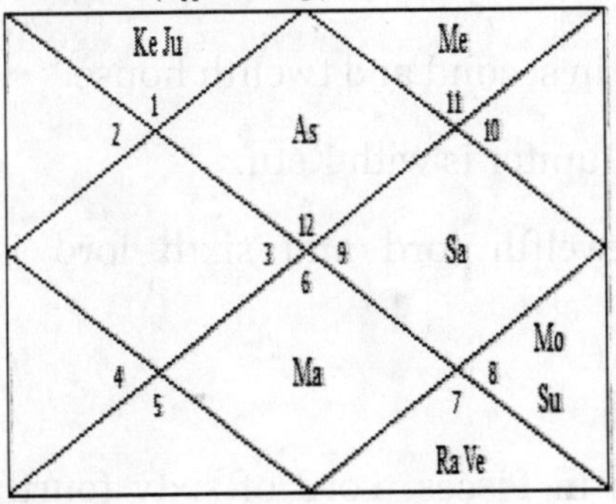

D3 Dreshkana (happiness siblings)

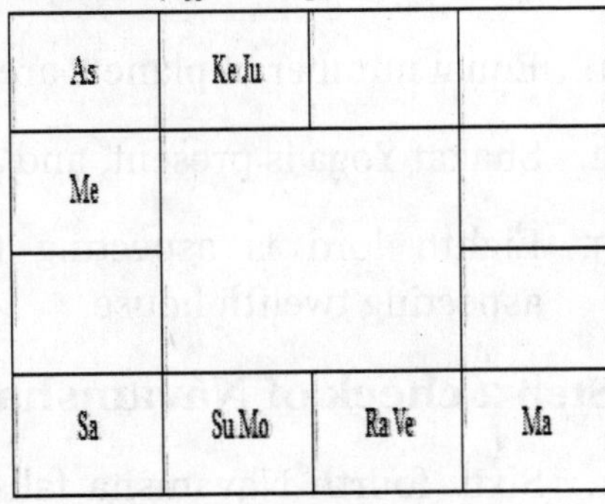

D3 Iyer Parivriti Traya Dreshkana (happiness siblings)

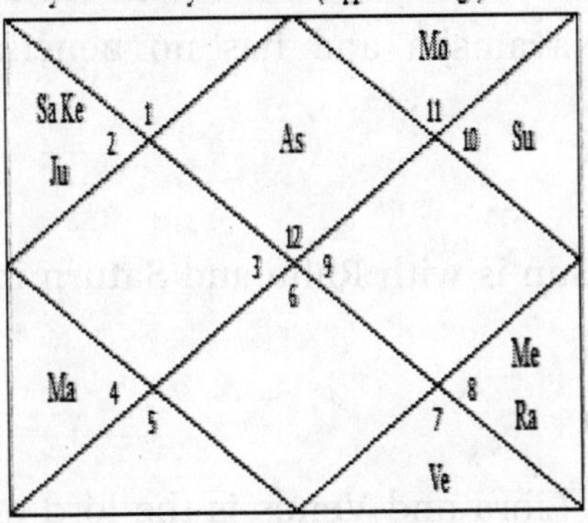

D3 Iyer Parivriti Traya Dreshkana (happiness siblings)

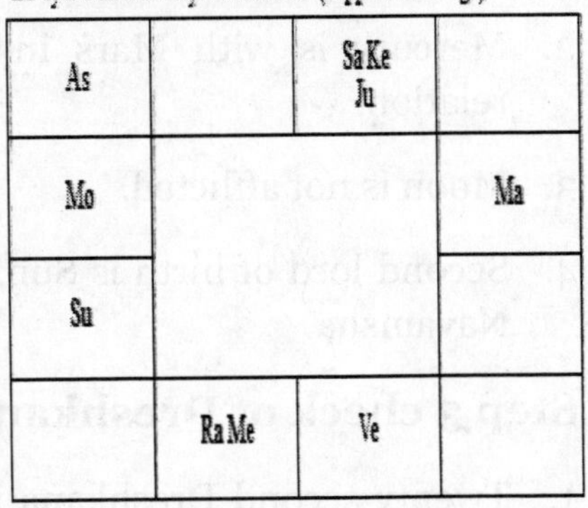

D60

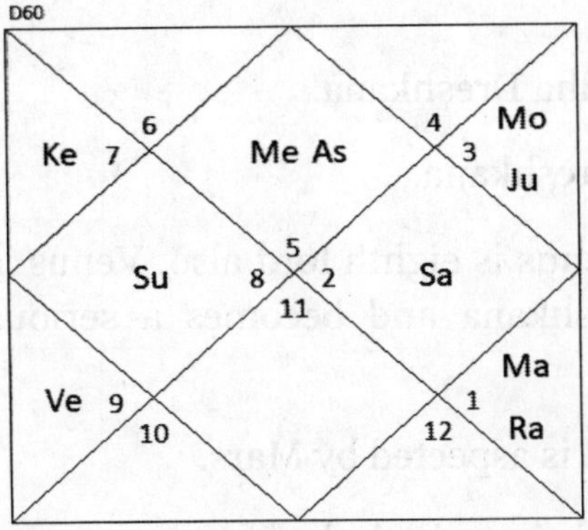

D60

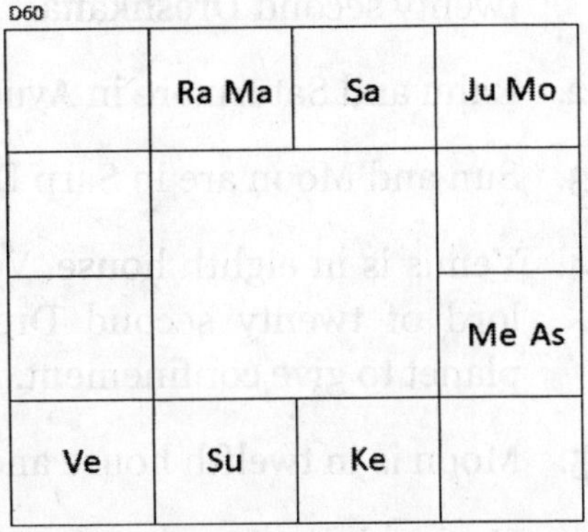

Step 1 check of classic rules

1. Equal number of planets are in second and twelfth house.
2. Shakat Yoga is present, and Jupiter is with Ketu.
3. Eighth lord is aspecting twelfth lord and sixth lord is aspecting twelfth house.

Step 2 check of Navamsha

1. Sixty fourth Navamsha falls in Pisces. Lord of sixty fourth Navamsha is Jupiter.
2. Mercury is with Mars in Navamsha and has no benefic relation.
3. Moon is not afflicted.
4. Second lord of birth is Sun. Sun is with Rahu and Saturn in Navamsha.

Step 3 check of Dreshkana

1. Twenty second Dreshkana is Libra and Venus is the lord of twenty second Dreshkana.
2. Rahu and Saturn are in Ayudha Dreshkana.
3. Sun and Moon are in Sarp Dreshkana.
4. Venus is in eighth house. Venus is eighth lord also. Venus is lord of twenty second Dreshkana and becomes a serious planet to give confinement.
5. Moon is in twelfth house and is aspected by Mars.
6. He faced first imprisonment in 1921 in dasha of Venus.
7. The jail yatra continued in Sun and Moon dasha. The longest imprisonment was from 1942 to 1945. It was in Moon MD.

Step 4 check of criminal tendency

1. Lord of Ascendant is Moon. Moon is in Papa Kartari and has no benefic association.
2. Moon is between two malefic planets.
3. Third house is strong, and Mercury is afflicted in Dreshkana.
4. Fourth house and lord are aspected by Saturn.

Step 5 Check of Shashtiamsha

1. Sun is aspected by Saturn and Mars.
2. Moon is not afflicted. It is with Jupiter and aspected by Venus. The confinement cannot be harsh.

Example Mandela DOB 18 July 1918 TOB 14.54 POB Mvezo South Africa

Birth Chart

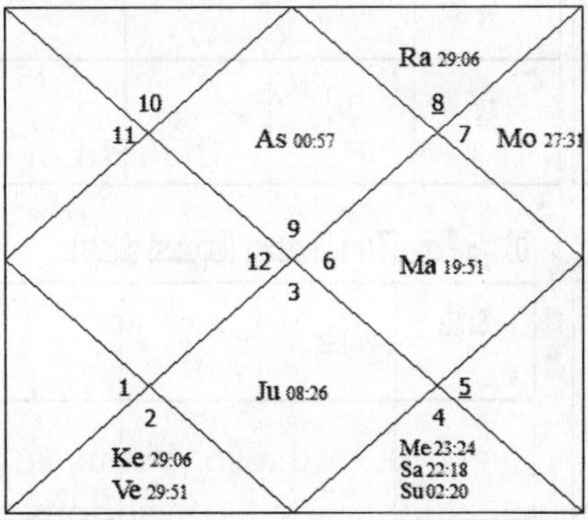

Birth Chart

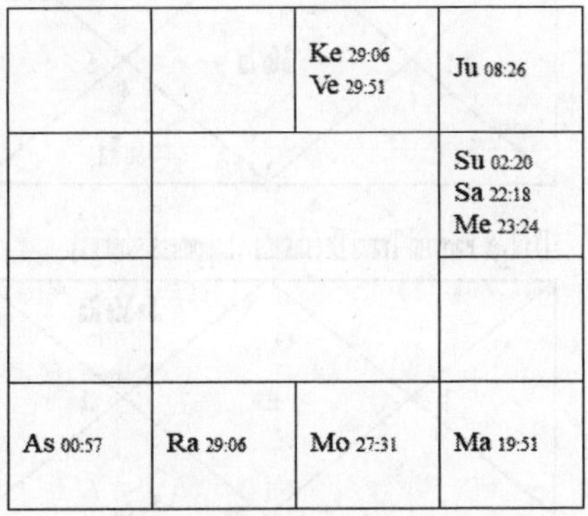

D9 Navamsha (spouse)

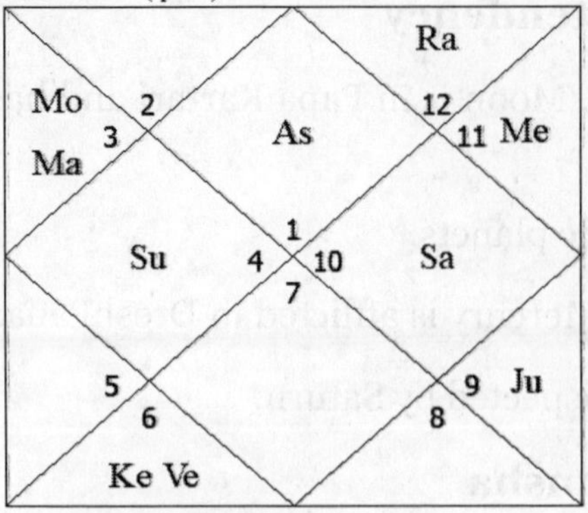

D9 Navamsha (spouse)

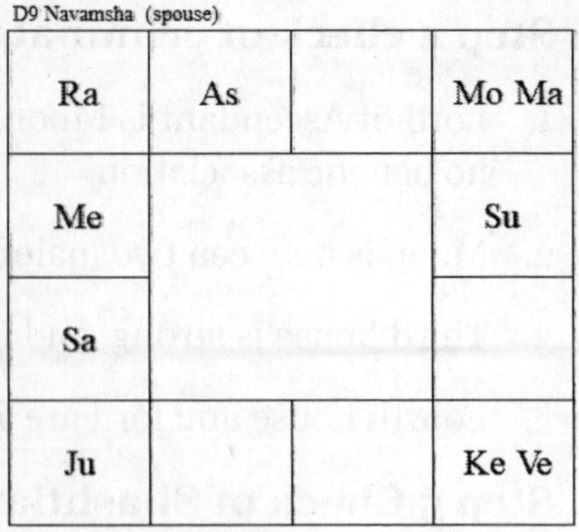

D3 Dreshkana (happiness siblings)

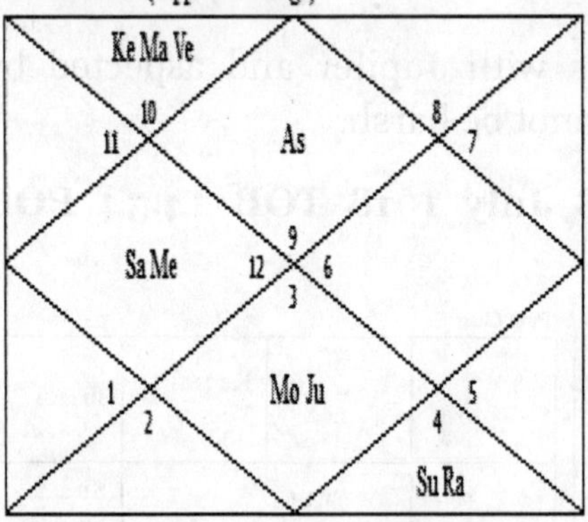

D3 Dreshkana (happiness siblings)

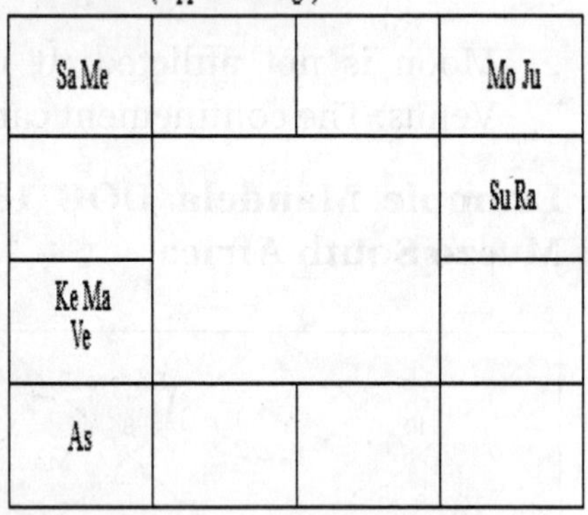

D3 Iyer Parivriti Traya Dreshkana (happiness siblings)

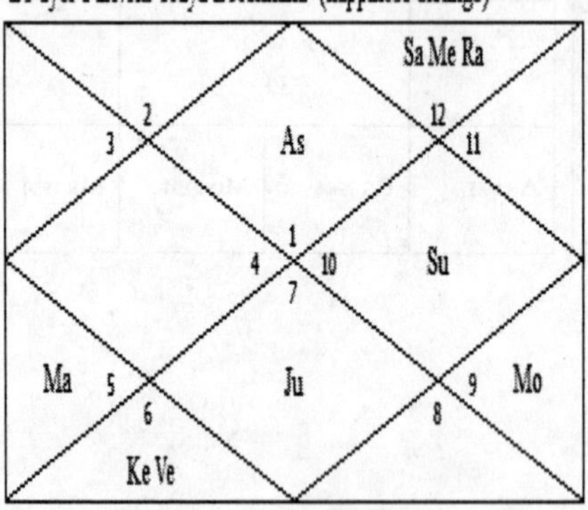

D3 Iyer Parivriti Traya Dreshkana (happiness siblings)

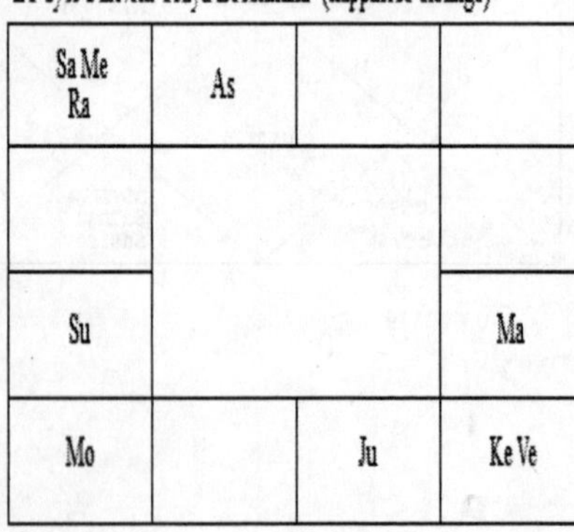

D60 Shashtiamsha (All areas)

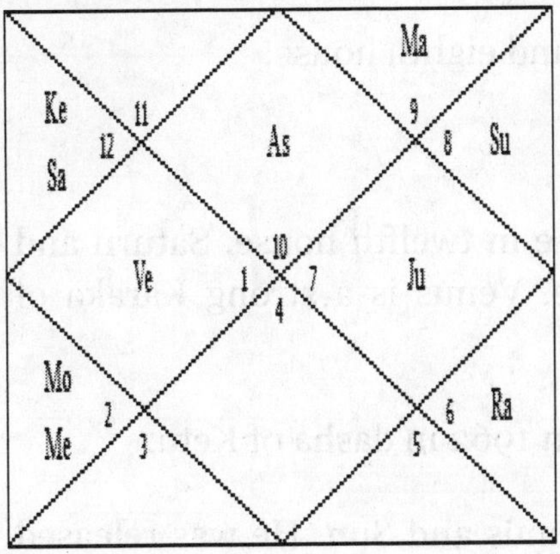

D60 Shashtiamsha (All areas)

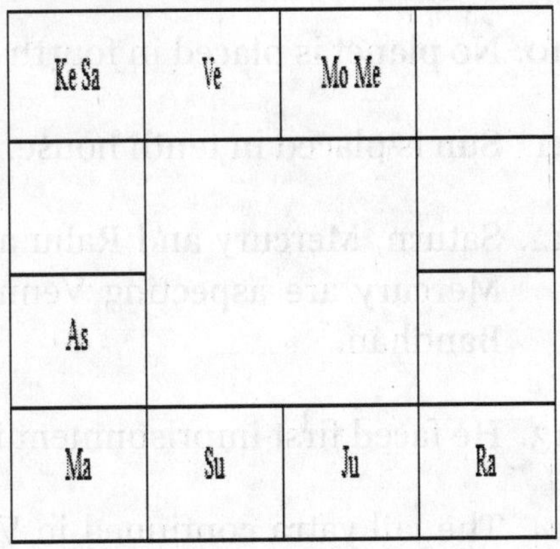

Step 1 check of classic rules

No classic Bandhan Yoga is present.

Step 2 check of Navamsha

1. Sixty fourth Navamsha falls in Virgo. Lord of sixty fourth Navamsha is Mercury.
2. Mercury is in Papa Kartari has no benefic relation.
3. Moon is with Mars but is aspected by Jupiter.
4. Second lord of birth is Saturn. Saturn is aspected by Sun and Mars and is afflicted.
5. Venus is with Ketu and is aspected by Mars. Mars is fifth lord of birth. Lust is present.

Step 3 check of Dreshkana

8. Twenty second Dreshkana is Cancer and Moon is the lord of twenty second Dreshkana.

9. Mercury and Saturn are in Sarp Dreshkana.

10. No planet is placed in fourth and eighth house.

11. Sun is placed in tenth house.

12. Saturn, Mercury and Rahu are in twelfth house. Saturn and Mercury are aspecting Venus. Venus is a strong Karaka of Bandhan.

13. He faced first imprisonment in 1962 in dasha of Ketu.

14. The jail yatra continued in Venus and Sun. He was released in 1990 in Sun dasha.

Step 4 check of criminal tendency

1. Lord of Ascendant is not afflicted. This is an important factor.

2. Moon is between two malefic planets.

3. Mercury is in Prishtodaya sign Cancer. Mercury is with Saturn and Sun.

4. Mercury is lord of sixty fourth Navamsha.

Step 5 Check of Shashtiamsha

1. Venus is in Ghora Shashtiamsha. It is awful Shashtiamsha.

2. Venus was the selected planet for Bandhan Yoga.

Bandhan Yoga Jaimini

Bandhan means confinement. It can be forced or self-imposed isolation. Jaimini system is very useful to see this combination and gives important clues to see the promise and timing of the isolation.

Dreshkana plays an important role in assessment of Bandhan Yoga. Dreshkana are one third division of a sign. The Dreshkana belonging to Sarpa, Pasha, Ayudha and Nigada category are capable of putting a person in confinement or isolation. These have been listed earlier. For easy reference we are reproducing the table of these special Dreshkana again.

Sign	First Dreshkana	Second Dreshkana	Third Dreshkana
Aries	Ayudha		Ayudha
Taurus		Sarpa	
Gemini		Ayudha	Ayudha
Cancer		Sarpa	Sarpa
Leo	Ayudha	Ayudha	Ayudha
Virgo			
Libra			
Scorpio	Sarpa	Sarpa/ Pasha	
Sagittarius			Ayudha
Capricorn	Nigada		
Aquarius	Ayudha	Ayudha	Ayudha
Pisces	Ayudha	Ayudha	Sarpa

Rules for promise

1. Mark the Karkamsha (KL) lagan in the birth horoscope.
2. Mark the planets placed in Sarpa, Nigada or Ayudha D3.
3. The KL or twelfth from KL will be connected to planets in special Dreshkana by aspect or conjunction to cause confinement.
4. KL or twelfth from KL is in kartari caused by one of these planets.
5. This connection makes a person to go in confinement or isolation. Type of confinement will depend on the signification of planets. Malefic especially Rahu and Ketu gives imprisonment in jail. Jupiter gives isolation for spiritual pursuits. Moon is the cause of isolation by self-desire and efforts. The lordship of planet indicates the reason of confinement.

Timing

1. The isolation will happen in the dasha of Rashi connected to these planets. This can also happen in the dasha of KL sign.

We will now examine a few examples.

Example 1 K. N. Rao. DOB 13 October 1931, TOB 07.53, POB Machilipatnam

Birth Chart

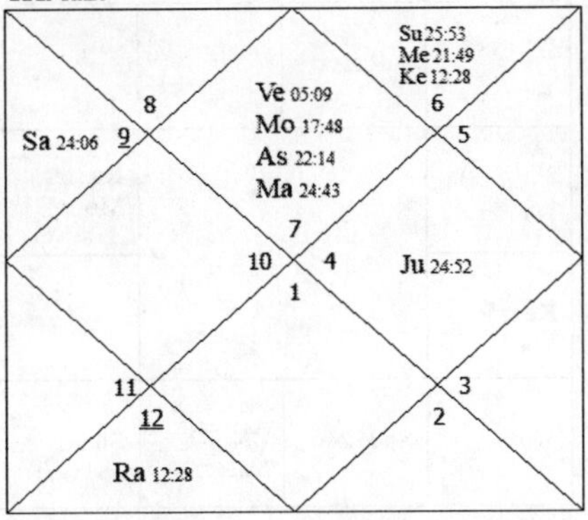

Birth Chart

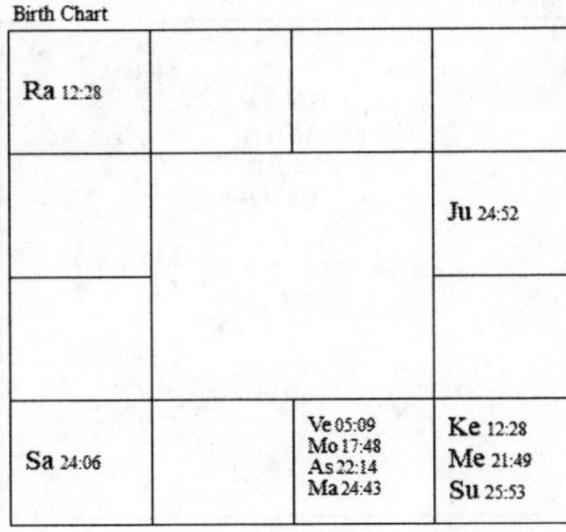

AK	AmK	BK	MK	PK	GK	DK
Sun	Jupiter	Mars	Saturn	Mercury	Moon	Venus

Jupiter is in third Dreshkana of Cancer and is in Sarpa Dreshkana. Saturn and Rahu are in Ayudha Dreshkana. The KL is Leo. Twelfth house from Leo is Cancer. Jupiter is placed there. Bandhan Yoga is present.

Bandhan Yoga can manifest in the dasha of fixed signs and that of Cancer. Dasha of Scorpio was from 1943 to 1954. Jupiter is lord of sixth house. This was due to illness and for gain of wisdom. Dasha of Aquarius was from 1962 to 1964. This was period great learning as Aquarius is fifth house. Dasha of Cancer operated from 1986 to 1995 and related to confinement to karma and illness. Dasha of Leo started in 1995. In Leo/ Aquarius he had to remain in bed due to problems in legs.

Example Mahatma Gandhi DOB 2 October 1869 TOB 7.52.06 POB Porbandar

Birth Chart

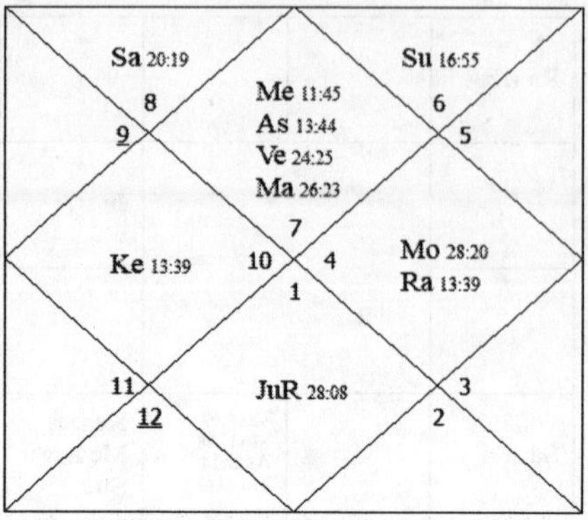

Birth Chart

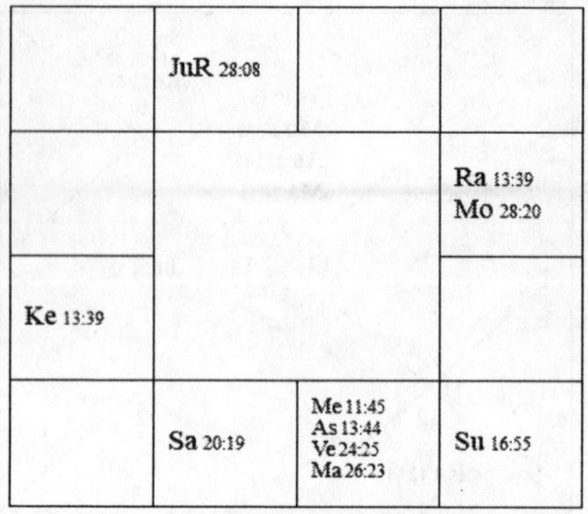

AK	AmK	BK	MK	PK	GK	DK
Moon	Jupiter	Mars	Venus	Saturn	Sun	Mercury

Rahu is in second D3 of Cancer and Moon is in third D3 of Cancer. Jupiter is in Ayudha Dreshkana. Saturn is placed in Sarpa/ Pasha Dreshkana.

Karkamsha lagna is Pisces and twelfth house is Aquarius which is aspected by Moon, Jupiter and Rahu. Bandana is present.

Dasha of Taurus was from 1922 to 1927. Cancer operated from 1931 to 1943 and he was in jail during these periods.

Example J L Nehru DOB 14 November 1889 TOB 23.05 POB Allahabad

Birth Chart

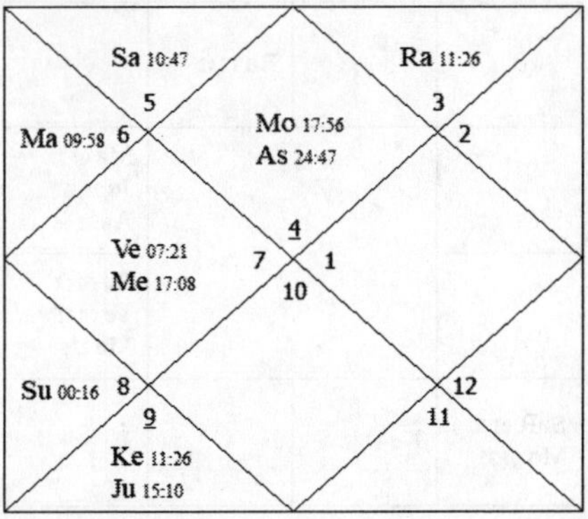

Birth Chart

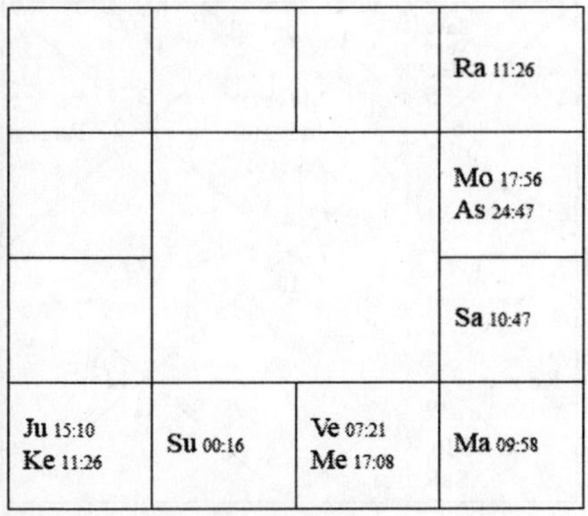

AK	AmK	BK	MK	PK	GK	DK
Moon	Mercury	Jupiter	Saturn	Mars	Venus	Sun

Moon is in second Dreshkana in Cancer. Sun is in first Dreshkana in Scorpio. Rahu and Saturn are in Ayudha Dreshkana. Karkamsha lagna is Sagittarius. The twelfth house Scorpio is having Sun and is aspected by Moon.

The dasha of Aquarius, Capricorn, Sagittarius and Scorpio operated from 1918 to 1944. This was the period of imprisonment. Sun indicates Government.

Example 4 Aurobindo Ghosh, DOB 15 August 1872, TOB 05.08 POB Calcutta

Birth Chart

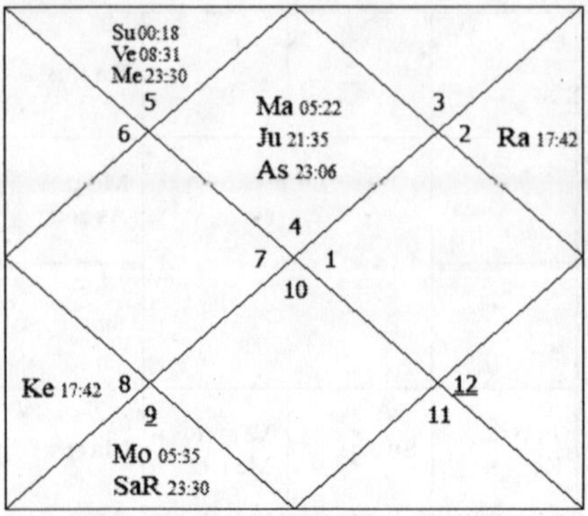

Birth Chart

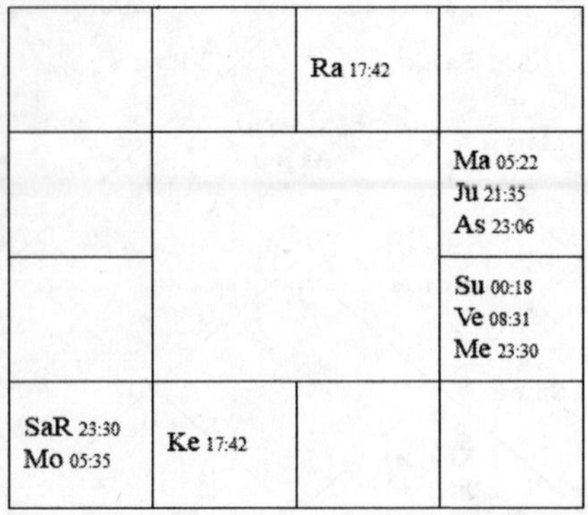

AK	AmK	BK	MK	PK	GK	DK
Mercury	Saturn	Jupiter	Venus	Moon	Mars	Sun

Jupiter is in third Dreshkana of Cancer. Rahu is in second Dreshkana of Taurus and Ketu is in second D3 of Scorpio. Sun, Venus and Mercury are in Ayudha Dreshkana. Five planets are in special Dreshkana. This gives imprisonment and confinement.

Scorpio is the KL. Twelfth from Scorpio is Libra. Libra is aspected by four planets in special Dreshkana.

He was in jail for one year in 1918 and 1919 and had divine vision. The dasha was Libra. His life of a great yogi mostly was spent in isolation.

Example 5 Saddam Husain DOB 28 April 1937, TOB 08.16, POB Tikrit.

Birth Chart

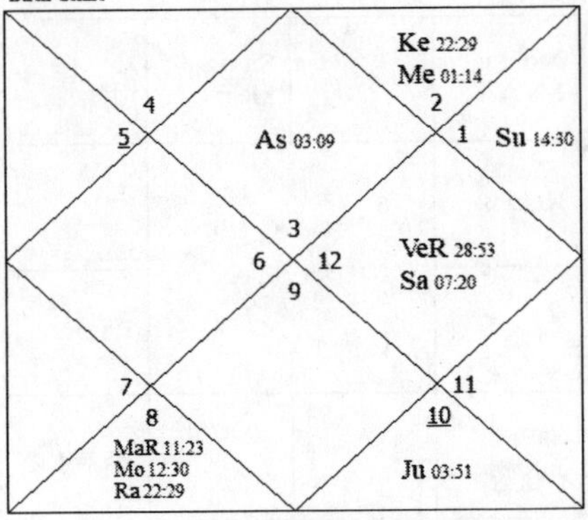

Birth Chart

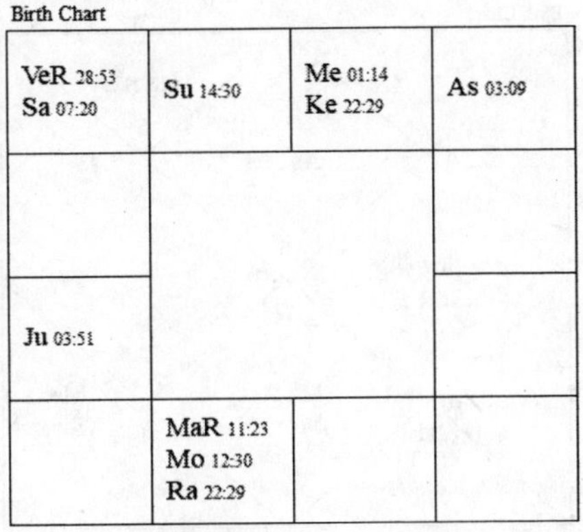

AK	AmK	BK	MK	PK	GK	DK
Venus	Sun	Moon	Mars	Saturn	Jupiter	Mercury

Moon and Mars are in second Dreshkana of Scorpio. Jupiter is in first Dreshkana of Capricorn. Venus and Saturn are in Ayudha Dreshkana.

The Karkamsha lagna is Pisces and twelfth from it is Aquarius. Aquarius is in kartari caused by Jupiter and Saturn.

Dasha of Aquarius was from 1967 to 1970 and he was imprisoned for terror activity. Cancer is aspected by Moon and Mars. The dasha of Cancer started in 2000 and he had to go into hiding and was executed in 2006. Almost all signs have relation with planets in special Dreshkana. He remained in isolation throughout his life.

Example 6 Dahmer Jeffrey DOB 21 May 1960, TOB 16.34, POB Milwaukee.

Birth Chart

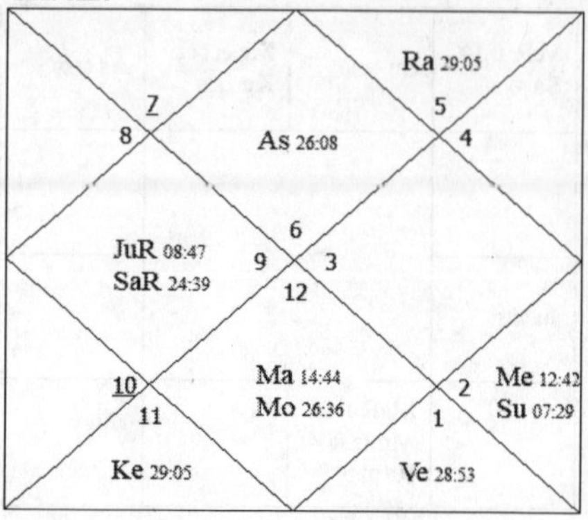

Birth Chart

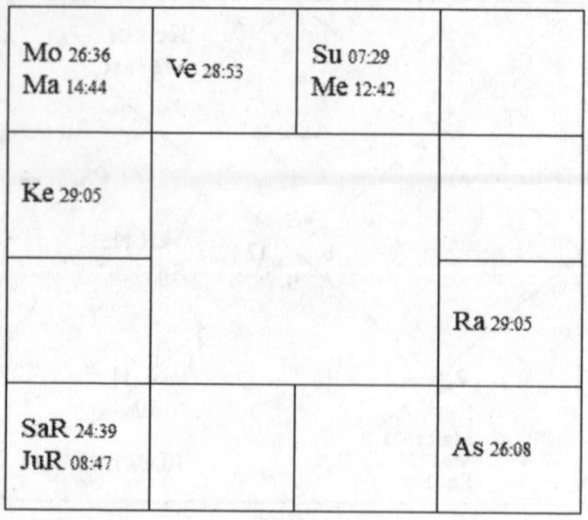

AK	AmK	BK	MK	PK	GK	DK
Venus	Moon	Saturn	Mars	Mercury	Jupiter	Sun

Mercury is in second Dreshkana in Taurus. Moon is in third Dreshkana in Pisces. Venus, Rahu, Saturn, Ketu and Mars are in Ayudha Dreshkana. Seven planets are in special Dreshkana. Karkamsha lagna is Sagittarius. It is aspected by Mercury and Saturn. Moon is placed in Sagittarius. Mars also joins it. All dual signs are afflicted. He was arrested in Pisces dasha. Aries started in 1992 and he was sentenced to 16 life terms. Venus (AK) is placed in Aries. He was killed by fellow inmate in prison on 28 November 1994.

Example 7 DOB 18 November 1933, TOB 16.02, POB Hapur

This chart belongs to a lady who was bed ridden since 2012 after Aries dasha started.

Birth Chart

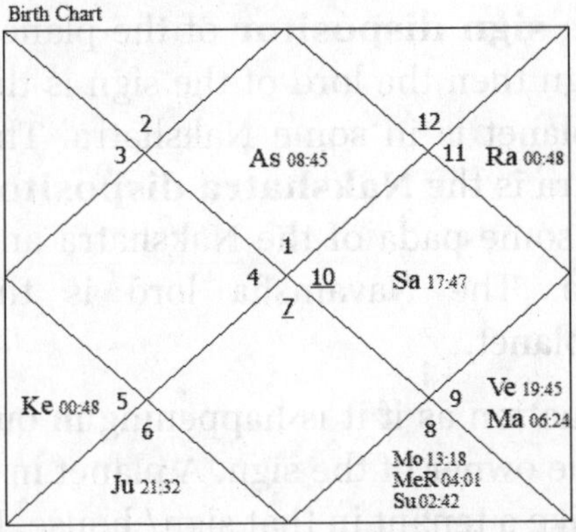

Birth Chart

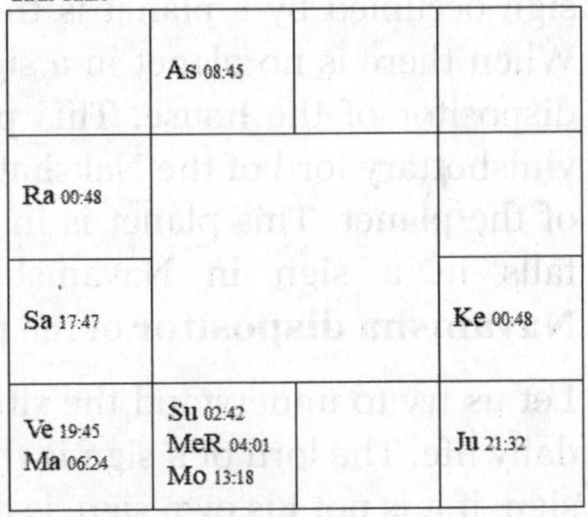

AK	AmK	BK	MK	PK	GK	DK
Jupiter	Venus	Saturn	Moon	Mars	Mercury	Sun

Three planets Sun, Mercury and Moon are in first and second Dreshkana of Scorpio. Three planets Saturn, Rahu and Ketu are in Ayudha Dreshkana.

Karkamsha lagan is Cancer which is aspected by all three planets in Sarp Dreshkana. Aries also receive the aspect of four planets in special Dreshkana.

Aries dasha started in November 2011 and she developed problem in lower portion of body and is in bed since then. She expired on 5 August 2019 and remained in bed in entire Aries Dasha.

Chapter 2
Dispositors

Every planet is placed in a sign at some longitude. The lord of the sign occupied by a planet is the **sign dispositor** of the planet. When there is no planet in a sign then the lord of the sign is the dispositor of the house. This planet is in some Nakshatra. The vimshottary lord of the Nakshatra is the **Nakshatra dispositor** of the planet. This planet is in some pada of the Nakshatra and falls in a sign in Navamsha. The Navamsha lord is the **Navamsha dispositor** of the planet.

Let us try to understand the situation as if it is happening in our daily life. The lord of a sign is the owner of the sign. A planet in a sign, if it is not his own sign, is like a tenant in that sign/ house. It is on the lord of the sign to decide the comfort or liberty to be given to his tenant. A strong landlord will impose his wishes on the tenant and the tenant may also feel that he is in a good house. A weak land lord cannot impose himself on the tenant and the tenant will take liberties. Their mutual relation will also decide the comfort of stay of the tenant. If they are friends, both will be happy.

Now we examine the tenant. In case the tenant is a bad character then the house owner will suffer. The tenant will not keep the house in good shape and harm the house. The owner will not be in happy frame of mind and cannot discharge his duties because he is now focused on saving his house.

Importance of dispositor

Many strong Yogas are formed taking the dispositor of the planet as the base. We will discuss these Yogas to highlight the importance of dispositor in Astrology. These Yoga gives a clue to assess the importance of dispositor in a horoscope. The highlight is the status and relation of dispositor of Kendra and Trikona.

Normally we take the mutual relation of Kendra and trikona as raj Yoga. These Yoga gives same importance to the dispositor of these house lords.

Parijata Yoga

Note the following.

a. Dispositor of lagna lord.

b. Dispositor of the dispositor of lagna lord.

c. Navamsha lord of the dispositor of dispositor of lagna lord.

When the planet b or c is in Kendra or Trikona from lagna or is exalted, the result is Parijata Yoga. A person born in Parijata Yoga will be a king destined to be happy in middle and later part of his life. He will be respected by other kings, fond of war, possessing elephants and horses, attentive to his duty and engagements and have compassionate disposition.

Bharati Yoga

When the Navamsha lord of second or fifth or eleventh lord is exalted and is conjoined with ninth lord, Bharati Yoga is caused.

The condition that lords of these three houses be in exaltation will be very rare, we can take the formation of Bharati Yoga with individual lord and thus Bharati Yoga can be caused in three ways.

1. With Navamsha lord of second lord is in exaltation and is with ninth lord.

2. With Navamsha lord of fifth lord is in exaltation and is with ninth lord.

3. With Navamsha lord of eleventh lord is in exaltation and is with ninth lord.

Person with Bharati Yoga will be world famous, reputed scholar, fond of music, romantic, handsome and religiously inclined.

Pushkala Yoga

When the dispositor of Moon and Lagna lord are conjoined in Kendra in a friendly sign and the lagna is aspected by a strong planet then Pushkala Yoga is caused.

The following conditions are necessary to create a Pushkala Yoga.

1. Dispositor of Moon and dispositor of lagna lord are conjoined in a Kendra.
2. The sign in which they are conjoined should be a friendly sign for both.
3. Lagna is aspected by a strong planet.

Another version of Pushkala Yoga given by B. V. Raman is as under.

1. Moon is associated with lord of lagna.
2. The lord of the sign occupied by Moon (dispositor of Moon) should be in Kendra or in the sign of an intimate friend.
3. The dispositor of Moon is aspecting lagna.
4. Lagna is occupied by a powerful planet.

The person born with Pushkala Yoga is wealthy, have a sweet speech, famous, honoured by king and is a lord.

Gauri Yoga

There are two versions of Gauri Yoga.

1. The Navamsha dispositor of tenth lord is exalted in tenth house and is with lagna lord.

2. The lord of ninth house and Moon are in their own or exaltation signs and are placed in Kendra or trikona.

B. V. Raman is in favour of the first version of Gauri Yoga. The person with Gauri Yoga will be spiritual, hardworking, is affectionate, beautiful, have great communication skill, talented children and his married life will be good.

Neechbangha Raj Yoga

Neechbangha raj Yoga is caused by the dispositor of the debilitated planet. The dispositor of exaltation sign also cause this Yoga. It is a well-known Yoga and need no elaboration.

Srinath Yoga

A Srinath Yoga is caused when the following conditions are met.

1. Seventh lord is exalted.
2. Seventh lord is placed in tenth house.
3. Dispositor of seventh lord joins ninth lord in tenth house.
4. The person born with Srinath Yoga has some special quality. He has unlimited grace of Lord Vishnu. He is a good speaker and is loved by all. He will love his family.
5. Srinath Yoga is possible only for Sagittarius Ascendant horoscope.

Example Lal Bahadur Shastri DOB 9 October 1904 TOB 11.17 POB Varanasi

Birth Chart

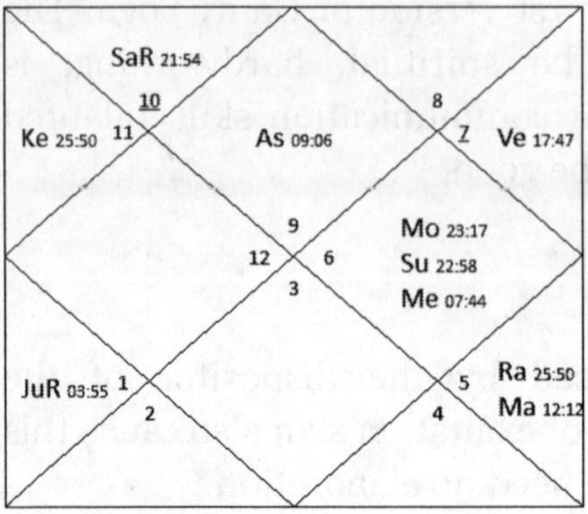

Birth Chart

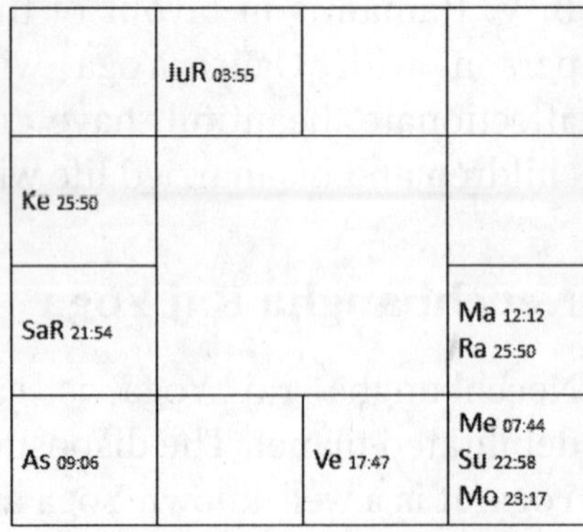

D9 Navamsha (spouse)

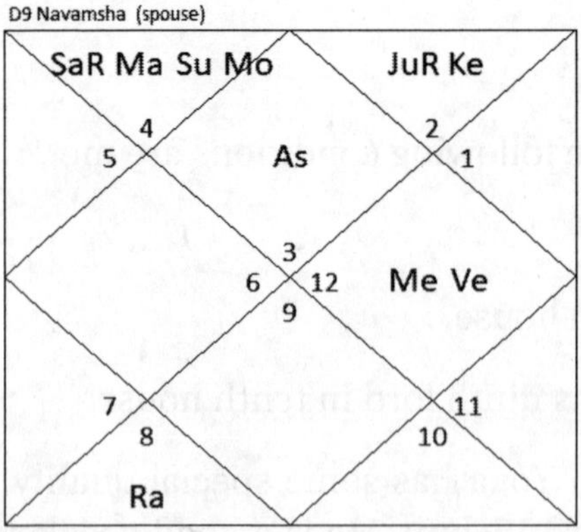

D9 Navamsha (spouse)

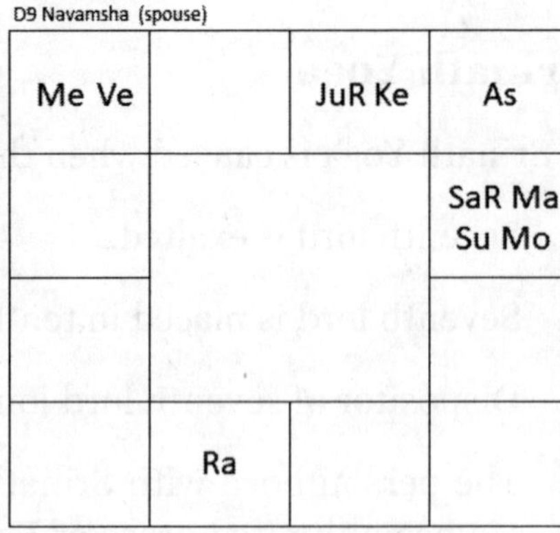

Srinath Yoga

1. Seventh lord is Mercury and is exalted in tenth house.
2. The dispositor of seventh lord is Mercury.
3. Ninth lord Sun is with Mercury in tenth house.
4. All conditions of Srinath Yoga are met.

Example Aurobindo DOB 15 August 1872 TOB 5.00 POB Calcutta

Birth Chart

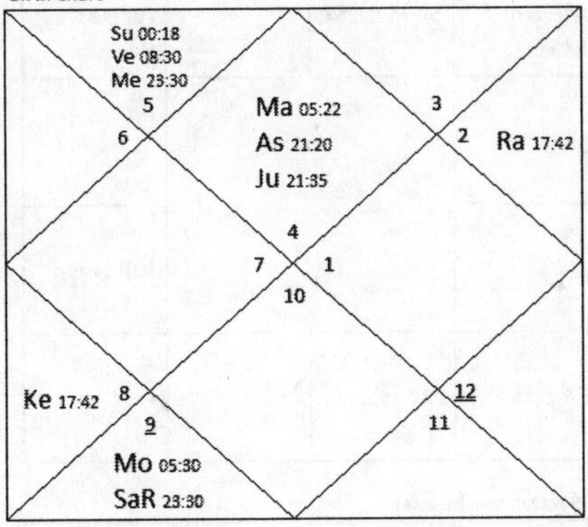

Birth Chart

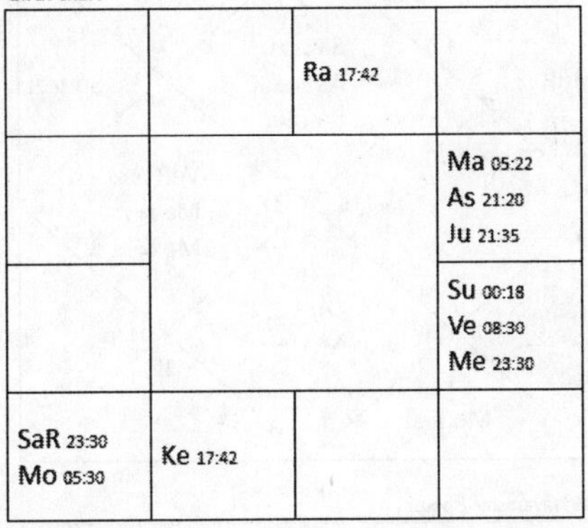

D9 Navamsha (spouse)

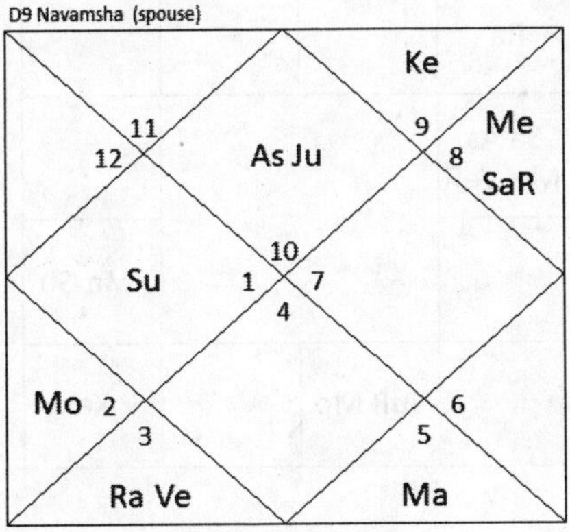

D9 Navamsha (spouse)

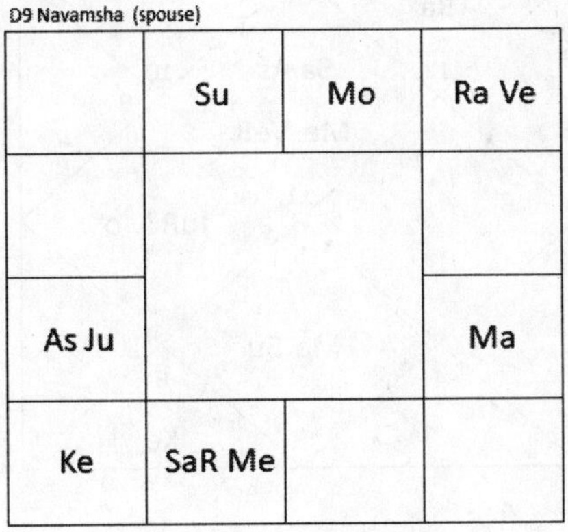

Pushkala Yoga

1. Lagna lord is Moon.
2. The dispositor of Moon is Jupiter.
3. Jupiter is in Kendra in lagna and is exalted.
4. All conditions of Pushkala Yoga are met.

Example DOB 30 April 1945 TOB 9.27 POB Delhi

Birth Chart

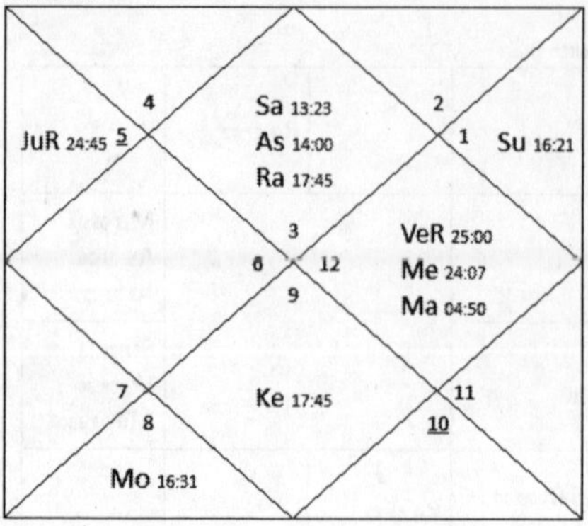

Birth Chart

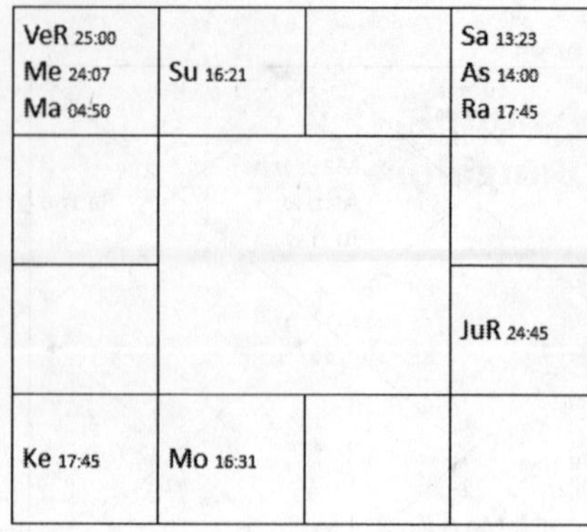

D9 Navamsha (spouse)

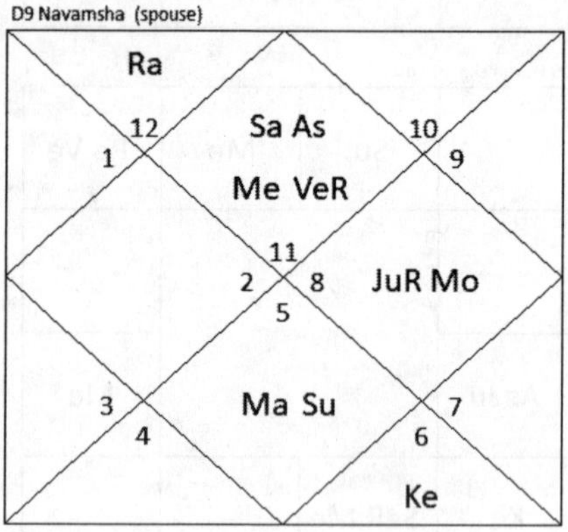

D9 Navamsha (spouse)

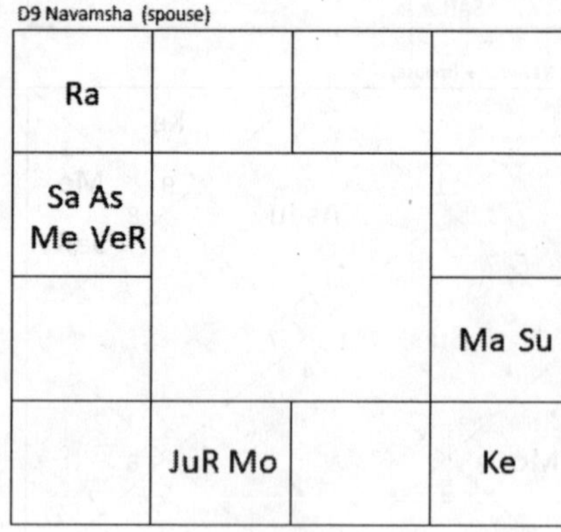

Parijata Yoga

1. Lagna lord is Mercury and the dispositor of Mercury is Jupiter.
2. The dispositor of Jupiter is Sun.
3. Sun is exalted.
4. The Navamsha dispositor of Jupiter is Mars.
5. Mars is placed in a Kendra.

Bharati Yoga

1. Navamsha lord of eleventh lord is Sun.

2. Sun is exalted but it is not with ninth lord.
3. All conditions of Bharati Yoga are not met.

Example B V Raman DOB 8 August 1912 TOB 19.15 POB Bangalore

Birth Chart

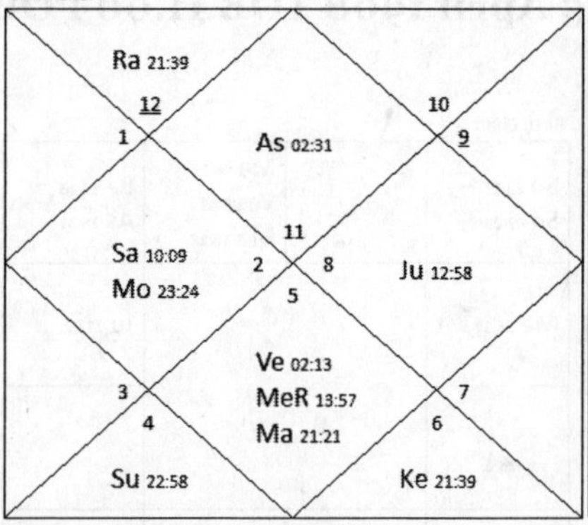

Birth Chart

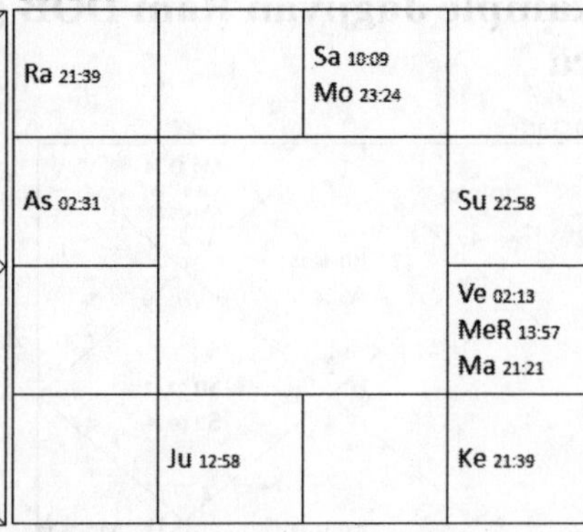

D9 Navamsha (spouse)

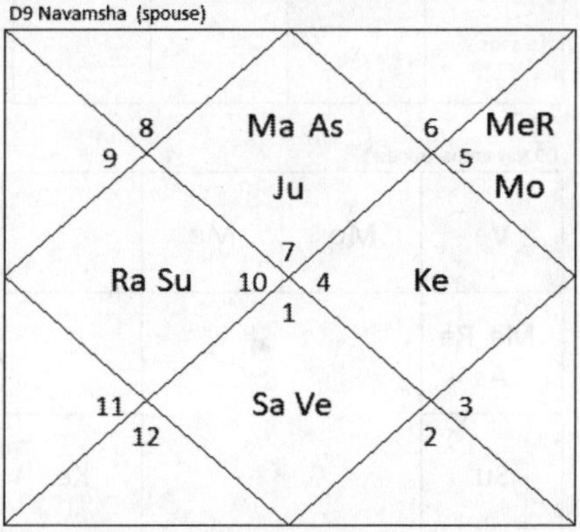

D9 Navamsha (spouse)

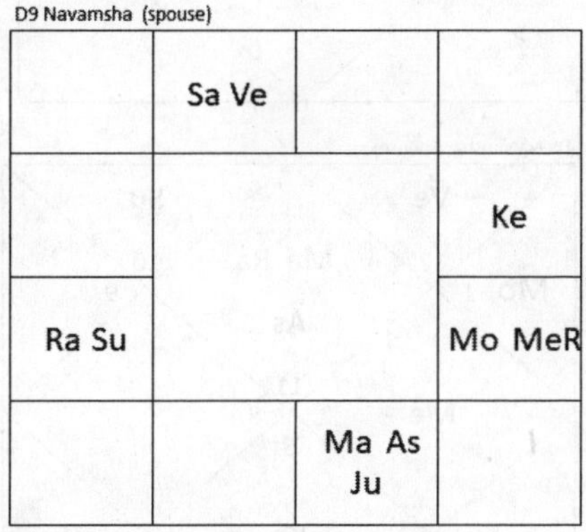

Pushkala Yoga 1

1. Dispositor of Moon and lagna lord is Venus.
2. Venus is in Kendra.
3. Venus is in a neutral sign and not in friendly sign.
4. Lagna is strong as it is aspected by its lord Saturn and three other planets.

Pushkala Yoga 2

1. Moon is with lagna lord Saturn.
2. Dispositor of Moon is in Kendra.
3. Dispositor of Moon is aspecting lagna. Lagna has no planet.

Example Jagjivan Ram DOB 5 April 1908 TOB 11.00 POB Ara

Birth Chart

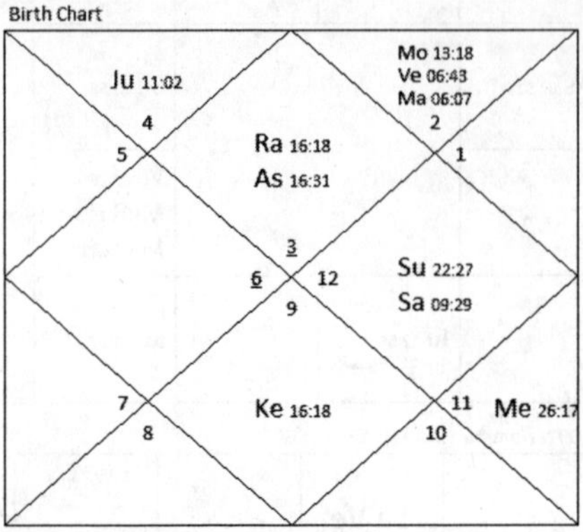

Birth Chart

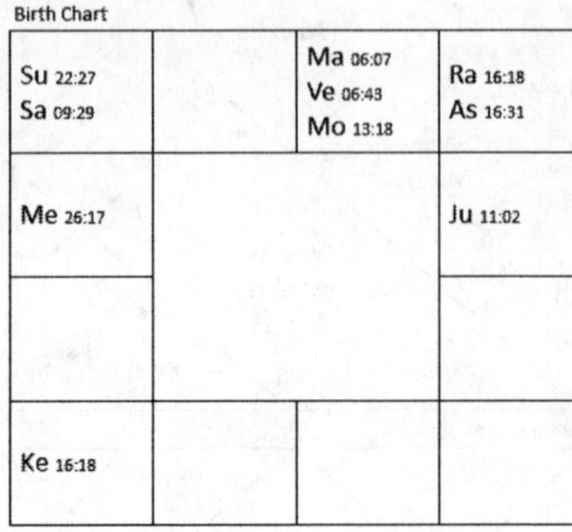

D9 Navamsha (spouse)

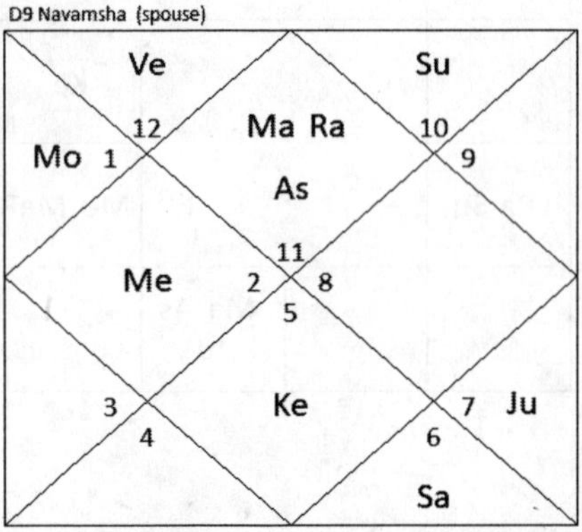

D9 Navamsha (spouse)

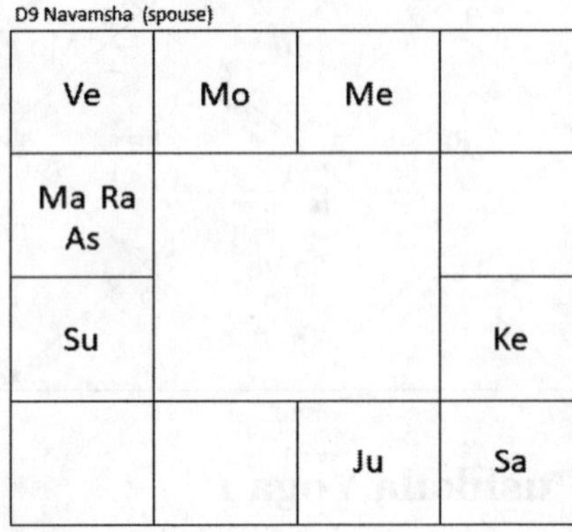

1. Lagna lord is Mercury. The dispositor of Mercury is Saturn.
2. Dispositor of Saturn is Jupiter.
3. Jupiter is exalted.

Bharati Yoga

1. Fifth lord is Venus. Venus is in Pisces in Navamsha.
2. The Navamsha dispositor of Venus is Jupiter.
3. Jupiter is exalted in birth chart.
4. Venus is exalted in Navamsha.
5. Jupiter is not with ninth lord in birth horoscope.

Example Einstein DOB 14 March 1879 TOB 11.28 POB Ulm

Birth Chart

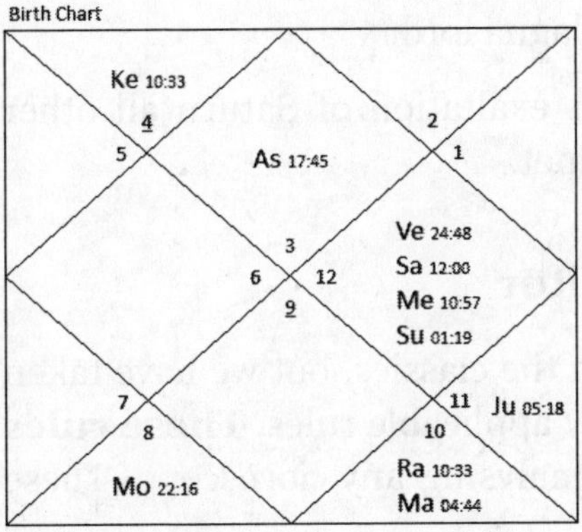

Birth Chart

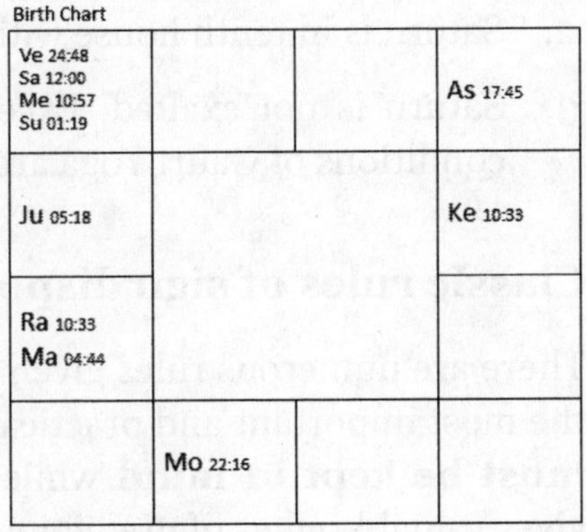

D9 Navamsha (spouse)

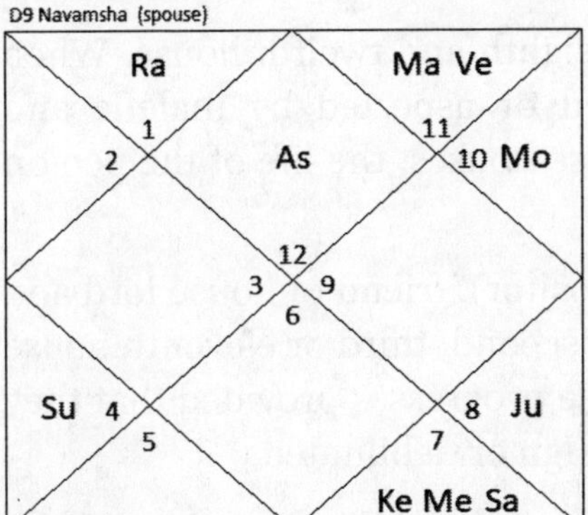

D9 Navamsha (spouse)

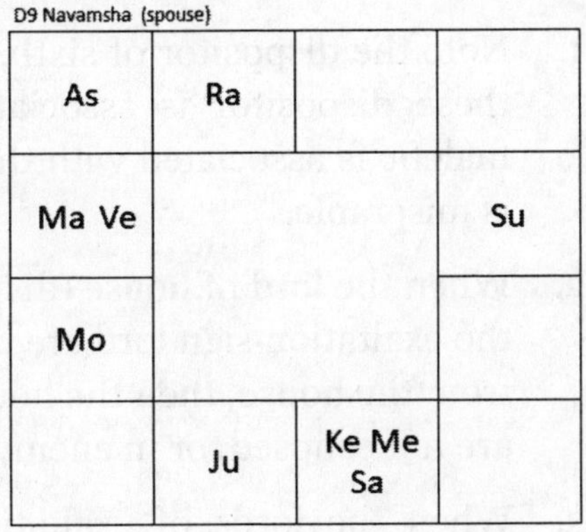

Parijata Yoga

1. Lagna lord is Mercury. Dispositor of Mercury is Jupiter.
2. Dispositor of Jupiter is Saturn.
3. Navamsha dispositor of Jupiter is Mars.
4. Mars is exalted and causes Parijata Yoga.

Gauri Yoga

1. Dispositor of tenth lord is Saturn.
2. Saturn is in tenth house with lagna lord.
3. Saturn is not exalted. Except exaltation of Saturn all other conditions of Gauri Yoga are met.

Classic rules of sign dispositor

There are numerous rules given in the classics, but we have taken the most important and practically applicable rules. **These rules must be kept in mind** while analysing any horoscope. These gives valuable clues of prediction.

1. Note the dispositor of sixth, eighth and twelfth house. When these dispositor is associated or aspected by malefic and malefic is associated with these houses, the life of the person is miserable.
2. When the lord of house (dispositor), friend of house lord and the exaltation sign lord are in second, third or eleventh house from the house, then the house progresses provided that they are not eclipsed, or in enemy sign or debilitated.
3. When the lords of exaltation and debilitation sign of the dispositor are in Kendra from the planet then a king is born.
4. Check if there is a debilitated planet in Kendra? Note the exaltation sign lord of its dispositor. If this lord is also in Kendra, then the person is king. For example, Sun is

debilitated in Kendra. Venus is the dispositor. The exaltation sign of Venus is Pisces. Therefore, Jupiter should also be in Kendra.

We give a ready table for application of this important rule.

Sr. No.	Planet	Debilitation Dispositor	Sign of exaltation of Dispositor	Planet to be in Kendra
1	Sun	Venus	Pisces	Jupiter
2	Moon	Mars	Capricorn	Saturn
3	Mars	Moon	Taurus	Venus
4	Mercury	Jupiter	Cancer	Moon
5	Jupiter	Saturn	Libra	Venus
6	Venus	Mercury	Virgo	Mercury
7	Saturn	Mars	Capricorn	Saturn

We observe from the table that Saturn is the only planet who does not need support from any other planet when it is debilitated in Kendra.

General rules

1. The friendship between planet and its dispositor is an important factor. We should check the natural and tatkalika friendship between them. The check is to see as to how the planet treats the dispositor. For example, Sun is placed in the sign of Mercury. Sun considers Mercury as neutral. So, we will say that Sun is in a sign of neutral planet. Mercury takes Sun as a friend. Good results are experienced when they are fast friends. We cannot expect good and favourable results if they are bitter enemy. For other relations the results are modified accordingly. Worst results are expected when they are placed in 6/ 8 from each other and are enemy or bitter enemy.

We give a ready table of natural friendship of planets.

Planet	Friend	Enemy	Neutral
Sun	Moon, Mars, Jupiter	Venus, Saturn	Mercury
Moon	Sun, Mercury	Nil	Mars, Jupiter, Saturn, Venus
Mars	Sun, Moon, Jupiter	Mercury	Venus, Saturn
Mercury	Sun, Venus	Moon	Mars, Jupiter, Saturn
Jupiter	Sun, Moon, Mars	Venus, Mercury	Saturn
Venus	Mercury, Saturn	Sun, Moon	Mars, Jupiter
Saturn	Mercury, Venus	Sun, Moon, Mars	Jupiter

2. The placement of dispositor from the planet is also important. The dispositor should be in Kendra or trikona or in eleventh house from planet for good results. Placement of dispositor in trik houses from the planet will not give good results.

3. The condition of dispositor is also checked. A strong and associated with benefics dispositor will promote the effects of the house lord. A weak and associated with malefic dispositor will not promote the effects of the house lord.

4. A favourable dispositor will help the planet to deliver its results whether they are good or bad. It is therefore desired that the dispositor of good planets are in favourable position. The reverse is also true. When the dispositor of a bad planet is in favourable position from planet then it will help the planet to deliver its bad effects.

5. A planet can be the lord of two houses. By judgement of dispositor of a planet we cannot decide the results of both

houses. For this judgement, we have to check it from both houses individually since the results of a planet can be different for each house.

6. **When the dispositor of house or planet is aspecting the house or planet then the strength of house or planet increases.**

Dispositor of Nodes

It is well known that the nodes act as the lord of the signs in which they are placed. They act as their own dispositors. They will give good results under the following conditions.

1. Their dispositor is not a lord of trik, third or eleventh house. This can be the case when nodes are placed in these houses.
2. Their dispositor is a functional benefic.
3. The placement of their dispositors from the node is important. Placement in Kendra, Trikona or in eleventh is good. The placement in trik house is not considered good.

This is the basic condition to assess the results of Rahu and Ketu. Their results depend on the condition of their dispositor.

Rahu and Ketu are always in one seven axes. Their dispositors are fixed as a set of planets. These are Aries/ Libra, Taurus/ Scorpio, Gemini/ Sagittarius, Cancer/ Capricorn, Leo/ Aquarius, Virgo/ Pisces. Thus, their dispositor are the set of Mars/ Venus, Mercury/ Jupiter, Moon/ Saturn and Sun/ Saturn.

Classic rules for Navamsha dispositor

Classics have dealt with Navamsha dispositor of lords of every house for delineation of results of a house. Jataka Tatva is a good example. We are not giving the numerous rules given in classics and request the readers to refer to them. We are only giving few rules to convey the importance of Navamsha dispositor.

1. The Navamsha dispositor of a debilitated planet is in Kendra or Trikona in a movable sign and the Ascendant is also a movable sign. This confers a raj Yoga.
2. The Navamsha dispositor of an exalted planet is placed in Kendra or Trikona in a friendly or exaltation sign and the lagna lord is strong. This causes **Mridang** Yoga. The person will be respected by rulers, famous, attractive and commands much influence.
3. When the Navamsha dispositor of sixth lord and the Navamsha dispositor of ninth lord are together with Sun and a fixed lagna is aspected by sixth lord then **Chandika** Yoga is caused. The person is aggressive, charitable, wealthy, minister and have a long happy life of fame.
4. When the Navamsha dispositor of waxing Moon is exalted and birth is in daytime then **Garuda** Yoga is caused. The person is respected by pious, feared by enemies and faces danger from poison in thirty fourth year.
5. When the Navamsha dispositor of fourth lord is placed in twelfth house then the person will lose all his property.
6. When the Navamsha dispositor of fourth lord is strong and occupy a Kendra/ trikona then his mother will be long lived.
7. When the Navamsha dispositor of fifth lord is aspected by benefics then the person is very intelligent.
8. The Navamsha dispositor of every house is checked for its placement in birth chart. The placement in trik houses is considered bad. When a planet is lord of two houses, the results for both houses may not be same. In such case it is good to check the placement of dispositor from the house for giving final ruling.
9. The natural benefics promote Jeeva when they are dispositors of a planet.

A close observation of the rules given for Navamsha dispositor will reveal the following.

1. Navamsha dispositor of the lord of a house should be,
    a. Well placed in Kendra or Trikona.
    b. The mutual position of planet and its Navamsha dispositor.
    c. The mutual position of sign dispositor and the Navamsha dispositor of the planet.
    d. Have relation with benefics.
    e. Is exalted.
    f. It should not be in trik houses
    g. It should not have malefic relation.

When these conditions are met then the good results of the house are experienced. Opposite to it will harm the significations of the house.

Dispositor of Karaka

1. Generally, there are two types of Karaka. One is the planetary fixed Karaka and other is the fixed Karaka of house. We can make use of both Karaka to assess the beauty of the Karaka is present or not.
2. The dispositor of planetary Karaka in birth chart is checked for its placement from the karaka. It should not be placed in trik houses from the karaka planet. For example, if dispositor of Venus is in sixth or eighth house from Venus then the person is ill-treated by his wife. if dispositor of Venus is in Kendra or Trikona from Venus the person gets wealth, vehicles and love from wife.
3. When the Karaka and the dispositor of a house are in Upchaya houses then the growth of house is assured.
4. Next, we check the condition of karaka in relevant divisional chart. If Venus is badly placed in Navamsha and have no benefic relation, then ill treatment is confirmed. Navamsha is

the relevant chart. We are not discussing divisional charts in this write up.

5. When the dispositor, Karaka and trine lords from house are in PAC then the house progresses.
6. Karaka shows the inner beauty and character.
7. Another method is to check the Nakshatra dispositor of Karaka. The placement of Nakshatra dispositor is checked from Moon. If the Nakshatra dispositor is well placed, then we get the good significations of the karaka.
8. We will apply this rule on three Karaka. These are Venus, Sun and Moon. Venus is for luxury of life; Sun is for father and Kind and Moon for mother.
9. We can face problems in case where a planet is Karaka of many significations. In such cases we cannot get a clear result. We can use the fixed Karaka of the house.

Nakshatra dispositor

Every sign consists of nine pada of three Nakshatra. If we consider a sign as a room, then the Nakshatra in the sign are the commodity stored. A planet placed in a Nakshatra is in that **commodity**. We can still further fine tune the commodity by the pada. The planet can offer the things available to him and these are the Nakshatra.

The Udu (Vimshottary) dasha lord of the Nakshatra is the Nakshatra dispositor of the planet. A planet has its significations which can be natural or acquired. When the commodity available with Nakshatra and the signification of planet is similar then the planet will happily accept it.

Next is to check the mutual placement of Nakshatra lord from the planet and also from lagna. If they are well placed, then the planet will provide its significations liberally.

A simple method to apply Nakshatra dispositor is given.

1. Note the Nakshatra of the planet.
2. Note the planet which is Udu dasha lord of Nakshatra.
3. Check the placement of Udu dasha lord from planet.
4. If this lord is well placed from planet, then good effects of the planet's significations are experienced.
5. Next is to check the lordship of Nakshatra lord from lagna. If the lordship is good and placement is good then we expect favourable results. The good placement is Kendra/ trikona/ eleventh house from planet.
6. For example, note the Udu dasha lord of Venus. Let us say that Venus is in the Revati Nakshatra. The lord is Mercury. See the placement of Mercury from lagna. If Mercury is in Kendra, Trikona or in eleventh house from Venus and also from lagna then the person gets all luxuries, vehicles and comforts of life.

Final dispositor

In Hindu Astrology dispositor is called **Poshaka** meaning nourisher. Dispositor of dispositor will nourish the nourisher of the planet. we can extend this chain till it stops at one planet. we can do this exercise for any planet. in this way we can have one planet or multiple planets which acts as final nourisher of the horoscope. This process is called "dispositor tree". We can construct dispositor tree for any planet. We can have the following situations in constructing a dispositor tree to arrive at final dispositor.

1. A planet is in its own sign then he is his final dispositor. For getting a final dispositor we must have planets in their own sign. Another condition is to have many planets in the sign of same planet.
2. Two planets are in exchange of sign then each is the final dispositor of other. This is called a loop.

3. For other situations we continue till a planet repeats in the process.

When the chain of dispositor is short then the effects are straight and defined. The dispositor planet will greatly modify the results and effects of the ruling planet of the house. The house effects will get modified by the final dispositor.

When the dispositor chain is long then the effects are intermingled, and the results are also not straight. Too many controlling planets will confuse the final outcome.

The extreme situation can also occur when no planet is the final dispositor. This becomes a committee of seven planets and decision making is difficult. This is a confused horoscope.

For better analysis we examine the final dispositor of each house. When we get only one planet as final dispositor of all houses, then it is a focussed horoscope, and the person is directed towards one goal. The same is also true when there are only two planets. When there are four or more than four planets becoming final dispositor of the houses then it is a confused horoscope.

Synthesis of results

We have noticed that most of the Yogas consider the dispositor of the dispositor of the planet and the Navamsha dispositor of the dispositor. When any of these two are in good status then the house flourishes. We can summarise this as follows.

1. Note the lord of a house. The lord is the dispositor of the house.
2. Note the dispositor of the dispositor (House lord).
3. Note the Navamsha dispositor of the dispositor.
4. Examine these two in the birth chart. When even one of them is exalted, in own sign, related to benefics, exalted in Navamsha or Vargottam then the good effects of the house are experienced.

5. For example, Jupiter is the lord of seventh house. Jupiter is in the sign of Sun and also in the Navamsha sign of Sun. Sun is exalted. The marriage will be very happy.
6. Their mutual placement should be good. They should not be in 6/ 8 to each other.
7. When these two dispositors are afflicted by malefic in birth chart, then the adverse results are expected.
8. In case a single planet becomes the dispositor of lord and also the Navamsha dispositor of the lord, then he becomes the main planet for that house. He should not be afflicted to give positive results.
9. We will apply this on example horoscopes for all twelfth houses.

Example Modi DOB 17 September 1950 TOB 10.10 POB Vadnagar

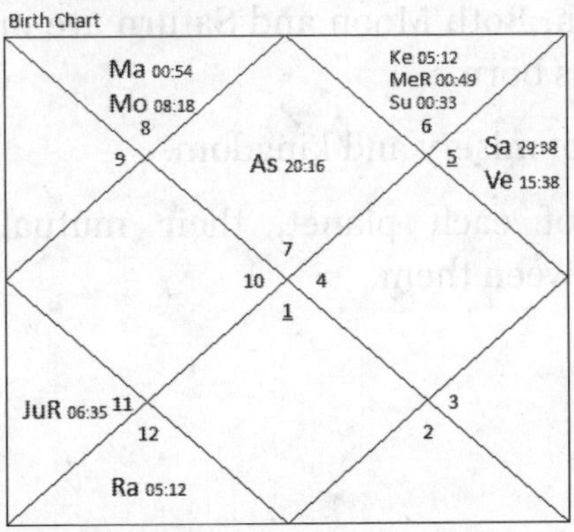

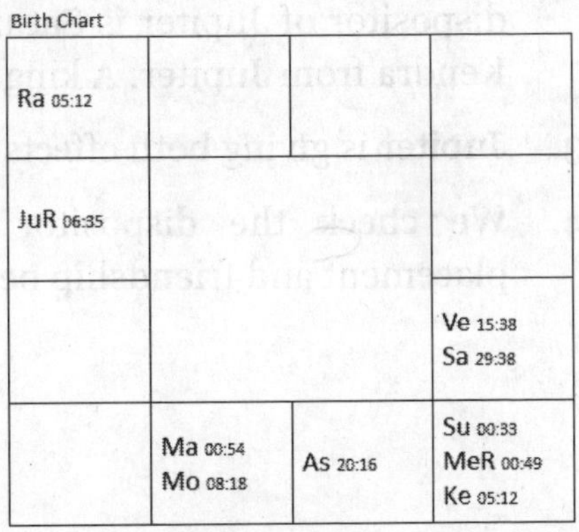

D9 Navamsha (spouse)

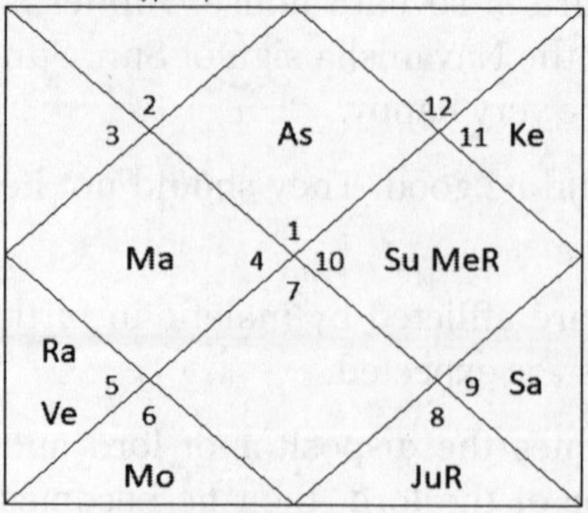

D9 Navamsha (spouse)

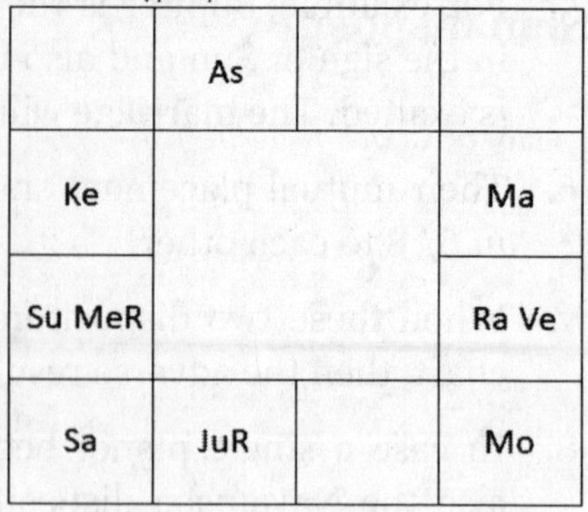

Classic rules

1. Sixth lord is Jupiter. Rahu is placed in sixth house. Jupiter is aspected by Mars and Saturn. The life of the person is miserable.
2. The exaltation dispositor of Jupiter is Moon. The debilitation dispositor of Jupiter is Saturn. Both Moon and Saturn are in Kendra from Jupiter. A king is born.
3. Jupiter is giving both effects of misery and kingdom.
4. We check the dispositor of each planet, their mutual placement and friendship between them.

Sign dispositor

Planet	Dispositor	Placement of dispositor from planet	Friendship	Remarks
Sun	Mercury	Kendra	Neutral	Being in Kendra is good. Mercury is exalted. Very good results.
Moon	Mars	Kendra	Neutral	Mars is in own sign. Good result
Mars	Mars	Own sign	self	Very good result
Mercury	Mercury	Own sign	self	Exalted. Very good result
Jupiter	Saturn	Kendra	Enemy	Saturn aspect give good result
Venus	Sun	Second	Neutral	Good result
Saturn	Sun	Second	Neutral	Good result
Rahu	Jupiter	Twelfth		Not good
Ketu	Mercury	Kendra		Good

1. The dispositors of all planets are in good placement from the planet except Rahu.
2. The sign dispositor of each house is checked to see the result of each house.

House dispositor

House	Lord	Dispositor	Placement of dispositor from house	Remarks
First	Venus	Sun	Twelfth	Sun is with exalted Mercury and Ketu.
Second	Mars	Mars	Same house	Promotes second house.
Third	Jupiter	Saturn	ninth	Gives courage, younger siblings
Fourth	Saturn	sun	trine	Very good for happiness and mother
Fifth	Saturn	Sun	eighth	Jeeva is damaged, intelligence is given.
Sixth	Jupiter	Saturn	sixth	Ill effect of sixth is destroyed.
Seventh	Mars	Mars	eighth	Jeeva of seventh is destroyed.
Eighth	Venus	Sun	Fifth	Long life, intuition.
Ninth	Mercury	Mercury	fourth	Luck is present.
Tenth	Moon	Mars	Trine	Promotes tenth house.
Eleventh	Sun	Mercury	Second	Gains, elder sibling.
Twelfth	Mercury	Mercury	Same house	Strong enemy, foreign relation.

Nodes dispositor

1. The dispositor of Rahu is in twelfth from Rahu. This is not good and can give bad results. Rahu dasha will give bad effects.

2. Ketu is with its dispositor and is good.

Navamsha dispositor

1. Moon is waxing. Navamsha dispositor of Moon is Mercury. Mercury is exalted and the birth is in daytime. The Garuda Yoga is present. The person is respected by pious, feared by enemies and faces danger from poison in thirty fourth year.

2. The Navamsha dispositor of fourth lord is Jupiter. Jupiter is placed in trine and the mother is long lived.

3. Navamsha lord of fifth lord is Jupiter. Jupiter is in trine and the person is very intelligent.

4. Now we check the Navamsha dispositor of each house.

House	lord	Dispositor in D9	Placement from Lagan	Placement from house
First	Venus	Sun	Twelfth	Twelfth
Second	Mars	Moon	Second	Same house
Third	Jupiter	Mars	Second	Twelfth
Fourth	Saturn	Jupiter	Trine	Second
Fifth	Saturn	Jupiter	Trine	In the house
Sixth	Jupiter	Mars	Second	Trine
Seventh	Mars	Moon	Second	Eighth
Eighth	Venus	Sun	Twelfth	Fifth
Ninth	Mercury	Mercury	Twelfth	Kendra
Tenth	Moon	Mercury	Twelfth	Third
Eleventh	Sun	Saturn	Eleventh	Same house
Twelfth	Mercury	Mercury	Twelfth	Same house

The dispositor of seventh lord is the worst placed. All other dispositor are well placed.

Karaka dispositor

1. Dispositor of Moon is Mars. Mars is with Moon. Long life to mother.

2. Dispositor of Sun is Mercury and Mercury is exalted in twelfth house which is fourth from ninth house. Happiness from father but twelfth house placement with Ketu is not good.
3. Dispositor of Venus is Sun. Sun is in twelfth house which is sixth from seventh house.

Nakshatra dispositor

The placement of Nakshatra dispositor is very important and is of great help in understanding the results of Udu dasha.

We give the Nakshatra dispositor placement for all planets in a tabular form.

Planet	Nakshatra Dispositor	Placement of Nakshatra dispositor from lagna	Placement of Nakshatra dispositor from Planet	Remarks
Sun	Sun	Twelfth	Same sign	Sun dasha gives secret enemy. Happiness to father is denied.
Moon	Saturn	Eleventh	Tenth	Gains in Profession. Mind is strong.
Mars	Jupiter	Trine	Fourth	Raj Yoga
Mercury	Sun	Twelfth	Same sign	intelligent
Jupiter	Mars	Second	Tenth	Maraca/ Family
Venus	Venus	Eleventh	Same	Gains. Gives luxury of Venus
Saturn	Sun	Twelfth	Second	Foreign
Rahu	Saturn	Eleventh	Seventh	Recognition
Ketu	Sun	Twelfth	Same sign	Expenses and wandering

Dispositor of Karaka

1. Venus is in the sign of Sun. Sun is placed in second house from Venus. Luxury is present.

2. Sun is in the sign of Mercury who is with Sun and is exalted. Father and king is favourable.

3. Moon is in the sign of Mars and is placed with Mars. Mother is favourable.

4. Venus occupies its own Nakshatra. Venus is in tenth from Moon giving luxuries of life.

5. Sun is also in its own Nakshatra and is placed in eleventh from Moon. Father and king is favourable.

6. Moon is in the Nakshatra of Saturn. Saturn is in tenth from Moon. Mother is favourable.

Final dispositor

The final dispositor of each house is worked out.

House	lord	Next dispositor	Next dispositor	Next dispositor	Final Dispositor
First	Venus	Sun	Mercury		Mercury
Second	Mars	Mars			Mars
Third	Jupiter	Saturn	Sun	Mercury	Mercury
Fourth	Saturn	Sun	Mercury		Mercury
Fifth	Saturn	Sun	Mercury		Mercury
Sixth	Jupiter	Saturn	Sun	Mercury	Mercury
Seventh	Mars	Mars			Mars
Eighth	Venus	Sun	Mercury		Mercury
Ninth	Mercury	Mercury			Mercury
Tenth	Moon	Mars			Mars
Eleventh	Sun	Mercury			Mercury
Twelfth	Mercury	Mercury			Mercury

1. Two planets are final dispositor of all houses. Mars and Mercury are the governing planets.

2. Mercury is the final dispositor of fourth house and is in eighth from it.

3. Mars is the final dispositor of seventh house and is in eighth from it.

4. When there are a smaller number of planets as final dispositor, then there is no confusion in taking decisions.

Synthesis of Result

House	Lord	Dispositor of lord	Navamsha dispositor of lord	Remarks
First	Venus	Sun	Saturn	Saturn is aspected by benefics only. Sun and Saturn are 2/ 12 to each.
Second	Mars	Mars	Moon	Mars is in own sign. Both dispositors are conjoined. Good family samskara.
Third	Jupiter	Saturn	Mars	Mars is in own sign. Mars and Saturn are in Kendra to each other.
Fourth	Saturn	Sun	Jupiter	Sun and Jupiter are in 6/ 8 to each. No landed property.
Fifth	Saturn	Sun	Jupiter	Sun and Jupiter are in 6/ 8 to each.
Sixth	Jupiter	Saturn	Mars	Mars is in own sign. Saturn and Mars are in Kendra to each.
Seventh	Mars	Mars	Moon	Mars is in own sign. Both dispositor are conjoined in eighth from house.
Eighth	Venus	Sun	Saturn	Saturn is the decider of eighth house.
Ninth	Mercury	Mercury	Saturn	Mercury is exalted. Luck is present.
Tenth	Moon	Mars	Mercury	Mars is in own sign and Mercury is exalted. Highly placed in profession.

Eleventh	Sun	Mercury	Saturn	Mercury exalted. High ambition.
Twelfth	Mercury	Mercury	Saturn	Mercury is exalted. Strong secret enemy. Big expenses.

Example Obama DOB 4 August 1961 TOB 19.24 POB Honolulu

Birth Chart

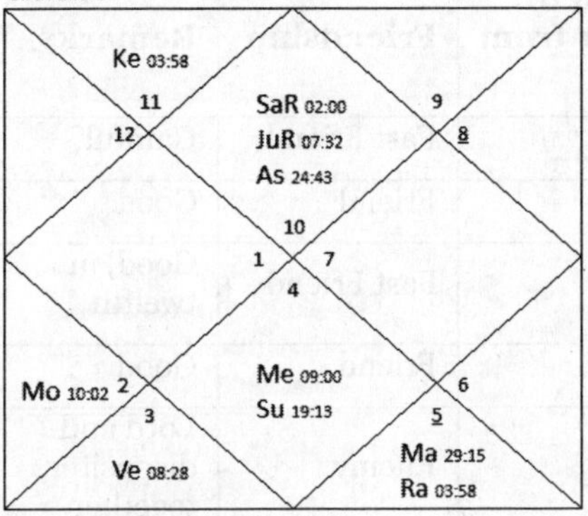

Birth Chart

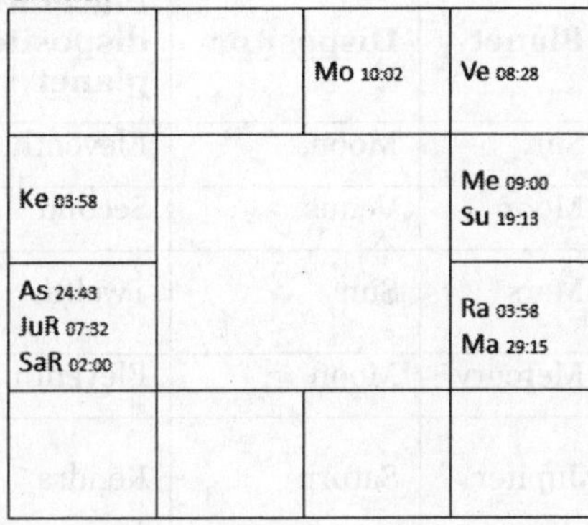

D9 Navamsha (spouse)

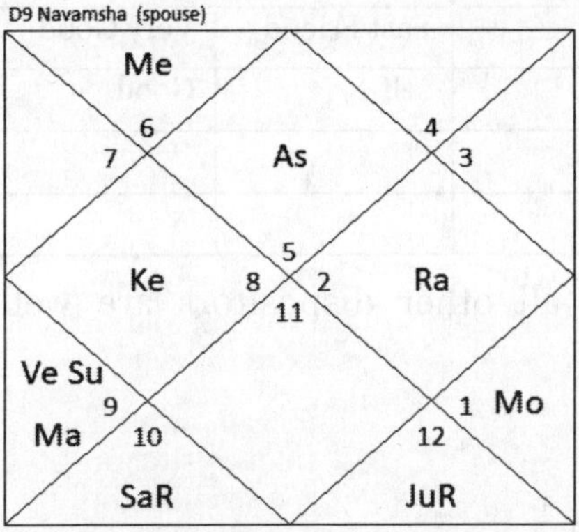

D9 Navamsha (spouse)

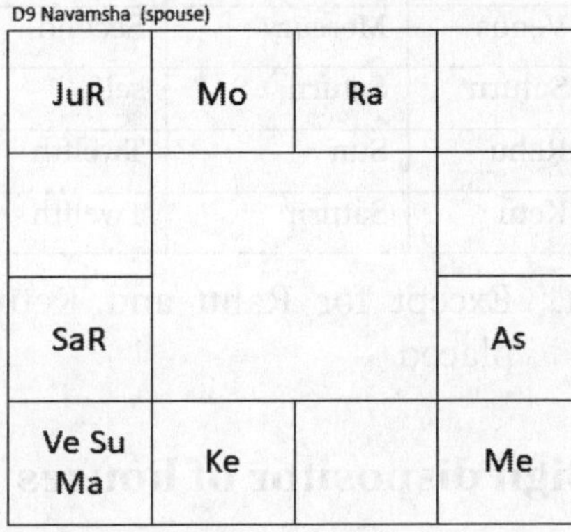

Classic Rules

1. Eighth house has two malefic. Eighth lord is Sun and Sun is placed in seventh house with Mercury. It is aspected by Jupiter and Saturn. As per classic, the person will have miserable life. The benefic relation is more than malefic relation. His early life was not good.

2. Lord of tenth house is Venus. The exaltation sign lord of Venus is Jupiter. Friends of Venus are Mercury and Saturn. All of them are in Kendra/ Trikona from tenth house. The tenth house will flourish.
3. Now we check the dispositor of each planet.

Dispositor of planets

Planet	Dispositor	Placement of dispositor from planet	Friendship	Remarks
Sun	Moon	Eleventh	Fast Friend	Gainful
Moon	Venus	Second	Friend	Good
Mars	Sun	Twelfth	Fast Friend	Good, in twelfth
Mercury	Moon	Eleventh	Friend	Good
Jupiter	Saturn	Kendra	Enemy	Lord and dispositor together
Venus	Mercury	Second	Fast Friend	Very Good
Saturn	Saturn	self	self	Good
Rahu	Sun	Twelfth		
Ketu	Saturn	Twelfth		

1. Except for Rahu and Ketu, all other dispositors are well placed

Sign dispositor of houses

House	Lord	Dispositor	Placement of dispositor from house	Remarks
First	Saturn	Saturn	Own house	First house is strong
Second	Saturn	Saturn	Twelfth	Away from family

Third	Jupiter	Saturn	Eleventh	Gains
Fourth	Mars	Sun	fourth	Comforts and happiness
Fifth	Venus	Mercury	Third	Intelligent
Sixth	Mercury	Moon	Twelfth	Loss of bad effects of sixth house
Seventh	Moon	Venus	Twelfth	Loss to seventh house
Eighth	Sun	Moon	Tenth	Long life, intuition
Ninth	Mercury	Moon	Ninth	Lucky
Tenth	Venus	Mercury	Tenth	Good profession
Eleventh	Mars	Sun	Ninth	Gains
Twelfth	Jupiter	Saturn	Second	Enemies are with you

1. The dispositor of the lord of three houses are in very good places. Dispositor of lord of fourth house is in fourth from the house. Dispositor of lord of ninth house is in ninth from the house. Dispositor of lord of tenth house is in tenth from the house.
2. These three houses gain strength.

Dispositor of Nodes

1. The dispositor of Rahu is Sun. Sun is in Kendra from Ascendant but is in twelfth from Sun.
2. Same is the case with Ketu. Saturn is in Kendra but is in twelfth from Ketu.

Navamsha dispositor

House	lord	Dispositor in D9	Placement from lagna	Placement from house
First	Saturn	Saturn	Kendra	Vargottam
Second	Saturn	Saturn	Kendra	Twelfth
Third	Jupiter	Jupiter	Kendra	Eleventh
Fourth	Mars	Jupiter	Kendra	Tenth
Fifth	Venus	Jupiter	Kendra	Trine
Sixth	Mercury	Mercury	Kendra	Second
Seventh	Moon	Mars	Eighth	Second
Eighth	Sun	Jupiter	Kendra	Sixth
Ninth	Mercury	Mercury	Kendra	Eleventh
Tenth	Venus	Jupiter	Kendra	Fourth
Eleventh	Mars	Jupiter	Kendra	Third
Twelfth	Jupiter	Jupiter	Kendra	Second

Navamsha dispositor of house lords are well placed except for second house. The Navamsha dispositor of eighth is in sixth from house and is considered good for a Vipreet house.

Nakshatra dispositor

Planet	Nakshatra Dispositor	Placement of Nakshatra dispositor from lagna	Placement of Nakshatra dispositor from Planet	Remarks
Sun	Mercury	Kendra	With Sun	Very Good
Moon	Moon	Kendra	Own Nakshatra	Gives strong mental strength
Mars	Sun	Kendra	Twelfth	Problem
Mercury	Saturn	Lagna	Kendra	Maraca

				house
Jupiter	Sun	Kendra	Kendra	Very Good
Venus	Rahu	Eighth	Third	Difficult time
Saturn	Sun	Kendra	Kendra	Very Good
Rahu	Ketu	Second	Kendra	Maraca house
Ketu	Mars	Eighth	Seventh	Not good

The Nakshatra dispositor of Saturn, Jupiter, Sun and Moon are very well placed and will promote their results. Venus is not well placed.

Dispositor of Karaka

1. Venus is in the sign of Mercury which is placed in second house from Venus. He has luxury of life.
2. Sun is in the sign of Moon. Moon is exalted in eleventh house from Sun. father and king is highly favourable.
3. Moon is in the sign of Venus placed in second from Moon. Mother is supportive.
4. The Nakshatra dispositor of Venus is Rahu. Rahu is in fourth from Moon with Mars. Luxury is present.
5. Sun is in the Nakshatra of Mercury. Mercury is in third from Moon. Father and king is favourable but needs efforts to make them favourable.
6. Moon is in own Nakshatra and mother is supportive.

Final Dispositor

House	lord	Next dispositor	Next dispositor	Next dispositor	Next dispositor	Next dispositor	Next dispositor	Final dispositor	Remarks
First	Saturn	Saturn						Saturn	
Second	Saturn	Saturn						Saturn	
Third	Jupiter	Saturn						Saturn	
Fourth	Mars	Sun	Moon	Venus	Mercury	Moon	Venus		Loop
Fifth	Venus	Mercury	Moon	Venus	Mercury				Loop
Sixth	Mercury	Moon	Venus	Mercury					Loop
Seventh	Moon	Venus	Mercury	Moon				Moon	
Eighth	Sun	Moon	Venus	Mercury	Moon	Venus			Loop
Ninth	Mercury	Moon	Venus	Mercury				Mercury	
Tenth	Venus	Mercury	Moon	Venus	Mercury				Loop
Eleventh	Mars	Sun	Moon	Venus	Mercury	Moon	Venus		Loop
Twelfth	Jupiter	Saturn						Saturn	

Saturn is the final dispositor of four houses. It is the final dispositor of first house and is very good to give a balanced self.

Synthesis of Result

House	Lord	Dispositor of lord	Navamsha dispositor of lord	Remarks
First	Saturn	Saturn	Saturn	Saturn is in own sign.
Second	Saturn	Saturn	Saturn	Saturn is in own sign.
Third	Jupiter	Saturn	Jupiter	Saturn is in own sign.
Fourth	Mars	Sun	Jupiter	Sun and Jupiter are in Kendra.
Fifth	Venus	Mercury	Jupiter	Mercury and Jupiter are in Kendra.
Sixth	Mercury	Moon	Mercury	Moon is exalted. Moon is aspected by Jupiter.
Seventh	Moon	Venus	Mars	Venus and Mars are well placed from each other.
Eighth	Sun	Moon	Jupiter	Moon is exalted and aspected by Jupiter.
Ninth	Mercury	Moon	Mercury	Moon is exalted and aspected by Jupiter.
Tenth	Venus	Mercury	Jupiter	Mercury and Jupiter are in Kendra.
Eleventh	Mars	Sun	Jupiter	Sun and Jupiter are in Kendra.
Twelfth	Jupiter	Saturn	Jupiter	Saturn and Jupiter are together.

1. The two dispositors of all houses are well placed.
2. Moon exalted and Saturn is in own sign have improved the horoscope and taken it to a great height.
3. The dispositor of lord and the Navamsha dispositor of first and second house is the same planet. Saturn is the main ruling planet.
4. Jupiter is the Navamsha dispositor of seven houses. Jupiter is with main planet, Saturn, and assumes high importance.

Example Sage of Kochhi DOB 20 May 1894 TOB 13.16 POB Villupuram

Birth Chart

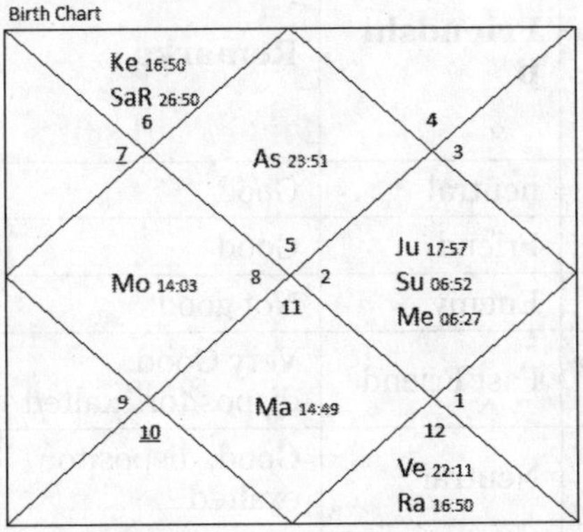

Birth Chart

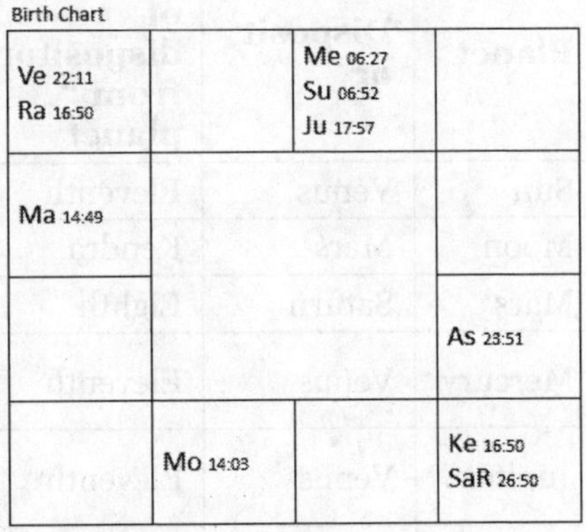

D9 Navamsha (spouse)

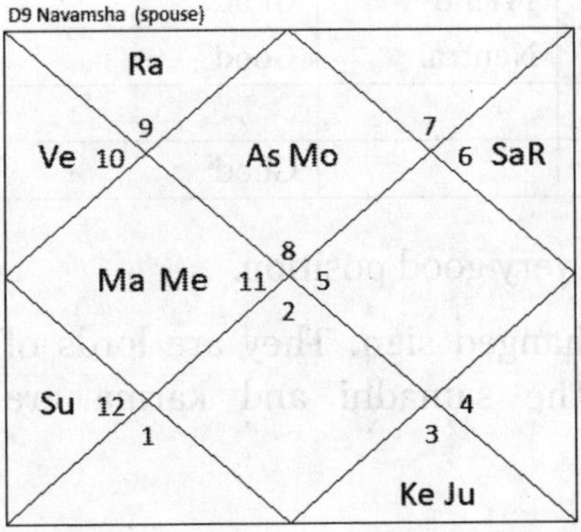

D9 Navamsha (spouse)

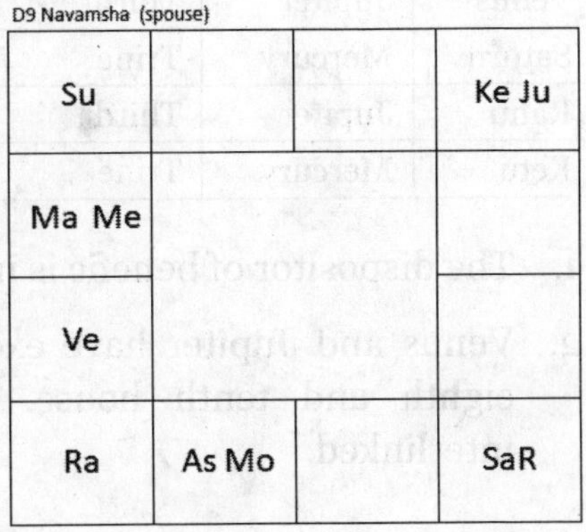

Classic

1. Rahu is in eighth house. The dispositor of eighth house is Jupiter. Jupiter is with Sun and Mercury. Jupiter is aspected by Moon and Mars. The life of the person is miserable. This is not applicable since Venus is in eighth house and Jupiter also have benefic association.

2. Moon is Vargottam.

Planets dispositor

Planet	Dispositor	Placement of dispositor from planet	Friendship	Remarks
Sun	Venus	Eleventh	neutral	Good
Moon	Mars	Kendra	Friend	Good
Mars	Saturn	Eighth	Enemy	Not good
Mercury	Venus	Eleventh	Fast Friend	Very Good, dispositor exalted
Jupiter	Venus	Eleventh	Neutral	Good, dispositor exalted
Venus	Jupiter	Third	Friend	Good.
Saturn	Mercury	Trine	Neutral	Good
Rahu	Jupiter	Third		
Ketu	Mercury	Trine		Good

1. The dispositor of benefic is in very good position.

2. Venus and Jupiter have exchanged sign. They are lords of eighth and tenth house. The samadhi and karma are interlinked.

Sign dispositor of house

House	Lord	Dispositor	Placement of dispositor from house	Remarks
First	Sun	Venus	eighth	Hard life
Second	Mercury	Venus	Kendra	Dispositor is aspecting house.
Third	Venus	Jupiter	eighth	Extra efforts
Fourth	Mars	Saturn	Eleventh	Saturn is aspecting house.
Fifth	Jupiter	Venus	Kendra	Growth of fifth house
Sixth	Saturn	Mercury	Trine	Good signification of sixth are present
Seventh	Saturn	Mercury	Kendra	
Eighth	Jupiter	Venus	Same house	Long life, Samadhi
Ninth	Mars	Saturn	sixth	Religion followed with determination
Tenth	Venus	Jupiter	Same house	Strong Karma
Eleventh	Mercury	Venus	Kendra	With Rahu
Twelfth	Moon	Mars	Eighth	No enemy

1. Second, fourth, eighth and tenth house are very strong.

Navamsha dispositor

House	lord	Dispositor in D9	Placement from lagna	Placement from house
First	Sun	Jupiter	Kendra	Tenth
Second	Mercury	Saturn	Second	In the house. Second house is strong.
Third	Venus	Saturn	Second	Twelfth
Fourth	Mars	Saturn	Second	Eleventh. Saturn is aspecting fourth house.
Fifth	Jupiter	Mercury	Kendra	Sixth
Sixth	Saturn	Mercury	Kendra	Trine
Seventh	Saturn	Mercury	Kendra	Kendra
Eighth	Jupiter	Mercury	Kendra	Third
Ninth	Mars	Saturn	Second	Sixth
Tenth	Venus	Saturn	Second	Trine
Eleventh	Mercury	Saturn	Second	Kendra
Twelfth	Moon	Mars	Kendra	Eighth

1. Venus is exalted. Navamsha dispositor of Venus is Saturn. Saturn is in sign of a friend and is aspected by two benefic. This is Mridang Yoga. The person is respected by rulers, famous, attractive and commands much influence.
2. The Navamsha dispositor of all house lords are placed in good houses.

Nakshatra dispositor

Planet	Nakshatra Dispositor	Placement of Nakshatra dispositor from lagna	Placement of Nakshatra dispositor from Planet	Remarks
Sun	Sun	Tenth house	Same	Gives authority
Moon	Saturn	Second	Eleventh	Strong mind. Saturn is aspecting Moon.
Mars	Rahu	Eighth	Second	Not good
Mercury	Sun	Tenth	Together	High intelligence
Jupiter	Moon	Kendra	Kendra	Wisdom
Venus	Mercury	Kendra	Third	Efforts
Saturn	Mars	Kendra	Sixth	Hard work
Rahu	Mercury	Kendra	Third	Efforts
Ketu	Moon	Fourth	Third	Family/ Home

1. The Nakshatra dispositor of Sun is Sun.
2. The Nakshatra dispositor of Moon is aspecting Moon.
3. Nakshatra dispositor of Mercury is with Mercury.
4. Nakshatra dispositor of Jupiter is in mutual aspect with Jupiter.
5. Saturn is aspected by its Nakshatra dispositor.

Dispositor of Karaka

1. Venus is in the sign of Jupiter. Jupiter is in third from Venus. Luxuries are present.
2. Sun is in the sign of Venus which is in eleventh house from Sun. father and King is favourable.
3. Moon occupies sign of Mars placed in fourth from Moon. Mother is favourable.
4. Nakshatra dispositor of Venus is Mercury. Mercury is in seventh from Moon. Luxury is present.
5. Sun is in the Nakshatra of Sun. Sun is in seventh from Moon. Father and king is favourable.
6. The Nakshatra lord of Moon is Saturn. Saturn is in eleventh house from Moon. Mother is favourable.

Final dispositor

House	lord	Next D	Next D	Next D	Next D	Next D	Next D	Final D	Remark
First	Sun	Venus	Jupiter	Venus				Venus	Exchange
Second	Mercury	Venus	Jupiter	Venus				Venus	Exchange
Third	Venus	Jupiter	Venus					Venus	Exchange
Fourth	Mars	Saturn	Mercury	Venus	Jupiter	Venus		Venus	Exchange
Fifth	Jupiter	Venus	Jupiter					Jupiter	Exchange
Sixth	Saturn	Mercury	Venus	Jupiter	Venus			Venus	Exchange
Seventh	Saturn	Mercury	Venus	Jupiter	Venus			Venus	Exchange
Eighth	Jupiter	Venus	Jupiter					Jupiter	Exchange
Ninth	Mars	Saturn	Mercury	Venus	Jupiter	Venus		Venus	Exchange
Tenth	Venus	Jupiter	Venus					Venus	Exchange
Eleventh	Mercury	Venus	Jupiter	Venus				Venus	Exchange
Twelfth	Moon	Mars	Saturn	Mercury	Venus	Jupiter	Venus	Venus	Exchange

In this table, I use 'D" instead of Dispositor to make the words fit.

1. The final dispositors of every house is ending in Venus and Jupiter. The final results are controlled by two great benefics. This is only possible for a great saint.

Synthesis of Result

House	Lord	Dispositor of lord	Navamsha dispositor of lord	Remarks
First	Sun	Venus	Jupiter	Venus is exalted.
Second	Mercury	Venus	Saturn	Venus is exalted. Saturn is Vargottam.
Third	Venus	Jupiter	Saturn	Jupiter and Saturn are in trine to each other. Saturn is Vargottam.
Fourth	Mars	Saturn	Saturn	Saturn is aspected by Venus and Jupiter. Saturn is Vargottam.
Fifth	Jupiter	Venus	Mercury	Venus is exalted.
Sixth	Saturn	Mercury	Mercury	Mercury rules sixth house. Intelligence controls enemy.
Seventh	Saturn	Mercury	Mercury	
Eighth	Jupiter	Venus	Mercury	Venus is exalted.
Ninth	Mars	Saturn	Saturn	Saturn is Vargottam.
Tenth	Venus	Jupiter	Saturn	Saturn is Vargottam. Jupiter and Saturn are in trine to each.
Eleventh	Mercury	Venus	Saturn	Venus is exalted and Saturn is Vargottam.
Twelfth	Moon	Mars	Mars	Moon and Mars are in Kendra.

1. When any one of the dispositor of lord or the Navamsha dispositor of the lord is exalted, in own house, Vargottam or in good position it causes great Yoga.

Example HR Bachchan DOB 27 November 1907 TOB 05.24.54 POB Allahabad

Birth Chart

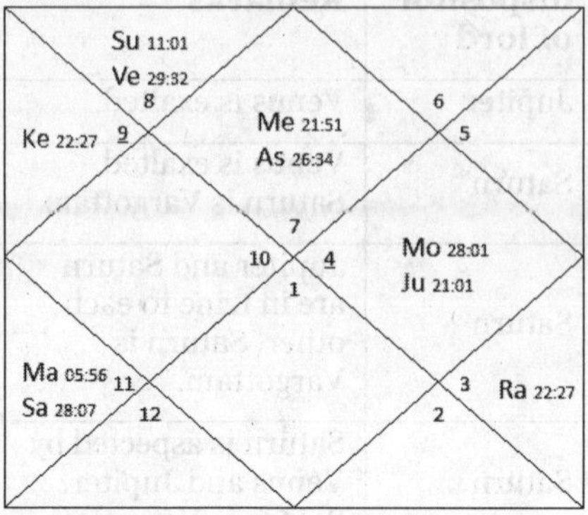

Birth Chart

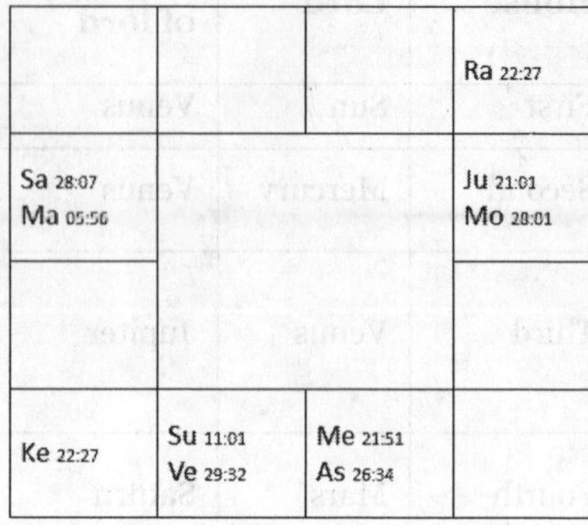

D9 Navamsha (spouse)

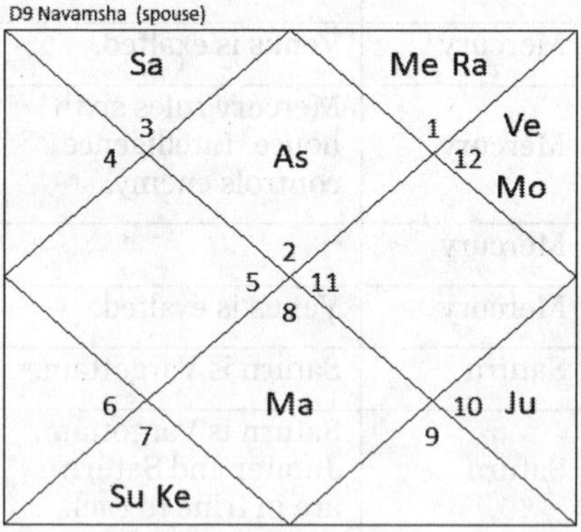

D9 Navamsha (spouse)

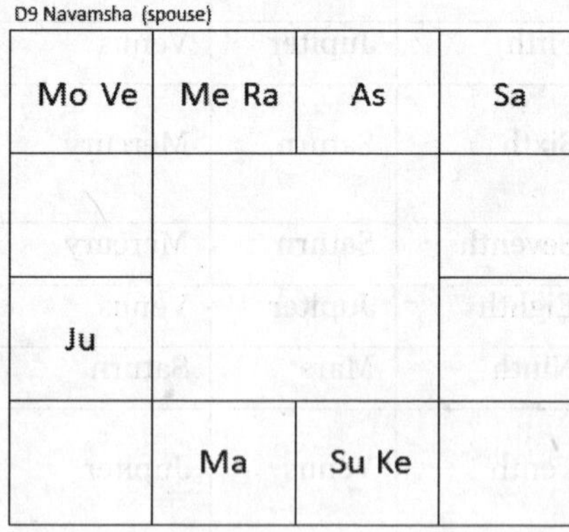

Classic results

1. No malefic is placed in trik house.
2. The dispositor of Mars is Saturn. The exaltation and debilitation lords of Saturn are Mars and Venus. Both are in Kendra from Mars. A king is born. Mars is boosted.
3. The dispositor of Mercury is Venus. The exaltation and debilitation lord of Venus are Mercury and Jupiter. Both are in Kendra from Mercury. The significations of Mercury are getting strong. He was a good poet.

4. Saturn is own dispositor. Mars and Venus are in Kendra from Saturn.

Dispositor of Planets

Planet	Dispositor	Placement of dispositor from planet	Friendship	Remarks
Sun	Mars	Kendra	Fast Friend	Very Good
Moon	Moon	self	self	Very Good
Mars	Saturn	Kendra	Enemy	Mars is with dispositor.
Mercury	Venus	Second	Fast Friend	Very Good
Jupiter	Moon	Kendra	Friend	Good. Jupiter and Moon conjoined
Venus	Mars	Kendra	Friend	Good
Saturn	Saturn	self	self	Good
Rahu	Mercury	Trine		Good
Ketu	Jupiter	Eighth		Not Good

1. Except Ketu, all planets are well connected with dispositor.

Sign dispositor of house

House	Lord	Dispositor	Placement of dispositor from house	Remarks
First	Venus	Mars	Trine	Good
Second	Mars	Saturn	Kendra	Saturn is aspecting house and is with house lord.
Third	Jupiter	Moon	Eighth	Jupiter and Moon conjoined in eighth from house.
Fourth	Saturn	Saturn	Second	Lord in own sign. Saturn will promote

				fourth house.
Fifth	Saturn	Saturn	Same house	Fifth house is strong
Sixth	Jupiter	Moon	Trine	Jupiter and Moon conjoined in fifth from house.
Seventh	Mars	Saturn	Eleventh	Saturn is aspecting seventh house and promotes it.
Eighth	Venus	Mars	tenth	Mars and Venus are aspecing house. Long life
Ninth	Mercury	Venus	Sixth	Not good for ninth house
Tenth	Moon	Moon	Same house	Tenth house is strong
Eleventh	Sun	Mars	Kendra	Mars is aspecting the house
Twelfth	Mercury	Venus	Third	expenses

1. All house dispositors are well placed except ninth house.

Navamsha dispositor

1. Jupiter is exalted. The Navamsha dispositor of Jupiter is Saturn. Saturn is placed in own sign in a trine. Lagna lord is strong. Mridang Yoga is present.
2. The Navamsha dispositor of sixth lord is Saturn and the Navamsha dispositor of ninth lord is Mars. Saturn and Mars are conjoined but Sun is not there. We cannot term it as Chandika Yoga.
3. The Navamsha dispositor of fourth lord is in trine. His mother is long lived.
4. The Navamsha dispositor of fifth lord is strong in a trine. The person is intelligent.

House	lord	Dispositor in D9	Placement from lagna	Placement from house
First	Venus	sun	Second	Second.
Second	Mars	Saturn	Trine	Kendra

Third	Jupiter	Saturn	Trine	Third
Fourth	Saturn	Mars	Trine	Second
Fifth	Saturn	Mars	Trine	In the house
Sixth	Jupiter	Saturn	Trine	Trine
Seventh	Mars	Saturn	Trine	Eleventh
Eighth	Venus	Sun	Second	Seventh. Dispositor aspecting house
Ninth	Mercury	Mars	Trine	Trine
Tenth	Moon	Mars	Trine	Eighth. Loss of job
Eleventh	Sun	Saturn	Trine	Kendra, dispositor aspecting house
Twelfth	Mercury	Mars	Trine	Sixth

Navamsha dispositor of all houses are well placed. The houses aspected by Navamsha dispositor becomes strong.

Nakshatra dispositor

Planet	Nakshatra Dispositor	Placement of Nakshatra dispositor from lagna	Placement of Nakshatra dispositor from Planet	Remarks
Sun	Saturn	Trine	Kendra	Very Good
Moon	Mercury	Lagna	Fourth	Very Good and strong mind
Mars	Mars	Trine	Same	Strong logic
Mercury	Jupiter	Tenth House	Tenth House	Good for Profession
Jupiter	Mercury	Lagna	Fourth	Happiness
Venus	Mercury	Lagna	Twelfth	Loss
Saturn	Jupiter	Tenth house	Sixth	Struggle
Rahu	Jupiter	Tenth house	Second	Wealth and Maraca
Ketu	Venus	Second	Twelfth	Not good

1. Jupiter is exalted and is the Nakshatra dispositor of Mercury, Saturn and Rahu. Jupiter is in tenth house and dasha of these planets give recognition of work. Mercury and Jupiter are in mutual Nakshatra and is good.
2. Sun is in the Nakshatra of Saturn. Saturn is in own sign in fifth house. The Sun dasha gave deep thinking and hard work. He completed Madhushala in dasha of Moon. The seed was planted in Sun dasha.

Dispositor of Karaka

1. Venus is placed in the sign of Mars. Mars is in Kendra from Venus with Saturn. He gets luxuries of life.
2. Sun is with Venus in the sign of Mars. His father and king is favourable.
3. Moon occupies his own sign Cancer. Mother is supportive.
4. The Nakshatra dispositor of Venus is Mercury. Mercury is in fourth from Moon. Luxuries are present.
5. Sun is in the Nakshatra of Saturn. Saturn is in eighth from Moon. Father and king is not supportive.
6. Moon is in Nakshatra of Mercury who is placed in fourth from Moon. Mother is favourable.

Final Dispositor

House	lord	Next D	Next D	Next D	Next D	Next D	Next D	Final D
First	Venus	Mars	Saturn					Saturn
Second	Mars	Saturn						Saturn
Third	Jupiter	Moon						Moon
Fourth	Saturn	Saturn						Saturn
Fifth	Saturn	Saturn						Saturn
Sixth	Jupiter	Moon						Moon
Seventh	Mars	Saturn						Saturn
Eighth	Venus	Mars	Saturn					Saturn
Ninth	Mercury	Venus	Mars	Saturn				Saturn
Tenth	Moon	Moon						Moon

Elevzenth	Sun	Mars	Saturn					Saturn
Twelfth	Mercury	Venus	Mars	Saturn				Saturn

In this table, I use 'D" instead of Dispositor to make the words fit.

1. Saturn is the final dispositor of nine houses. Moon is final dispositor of three houses. The results are streamlined and there is no confusion in decision making.

Synthesis of Result

House	Lord	Dispositor of lord	Navamsha dispositor of lord	Remarks
First	Venus	Mars	Jupiter	Jupiter is exalted. Mars and Jupiter are in 6/ 8 to each other.
Second	Mars	Saturn	Mars	Saturn is in own sign. Mars and Saturn are together in fifth house.
Third	Jupiter	Moon	Saturn	Moon and Saturn are in own sign but are in 6/ 8 to each.
Fourth	Saturn	Saturn	Mercury	Saturn is in own sign. Saturn and Mercury are in trine.
Fifth	Saturn	Saturn	Mercury	Saturn in own sign. Saturn and Mercury are in trine.
Sixth	Jupiter	Moon	Saturn	Moon and Saturn are in own sign but are in 6/ 8 to each.
Seventh	Mars	Saturn	Mars	Saturn is in own sign. Mars and Saturn are together in fifth house.
Eighth	Venus	Mars	Jupiter	Jupiter is exalted. Mars and Jupiter are in 6/ 8 to each other.
Ninth	Mercury	Venus	Mars	Venus and Mars are in Kendra to each other.
Tenth	Moon	Moon	Jupiter	Moon is in own sign with Jupiter.
Eleventh	Sun	Mars	Venus	Mars and Venus are in Kendra from each other.
Twelfth	Mercury	Venus	Mars	Venus and Mars are in Kendra to each other.

1. Jupiter is the Navamsha dispositor of first and eighth house. Long life is granted.

2. Saturn is Navamsha dispositor of two houses and promotes these houses.

3. Saturn is the dispositor of lord of four houses and they are also promoted.

4. Saturn and Jupiter are causing Parijata Yoga.

Example Prince Charles DOB 14 November 1948 TOB 21.14 POB London

Birth Chart

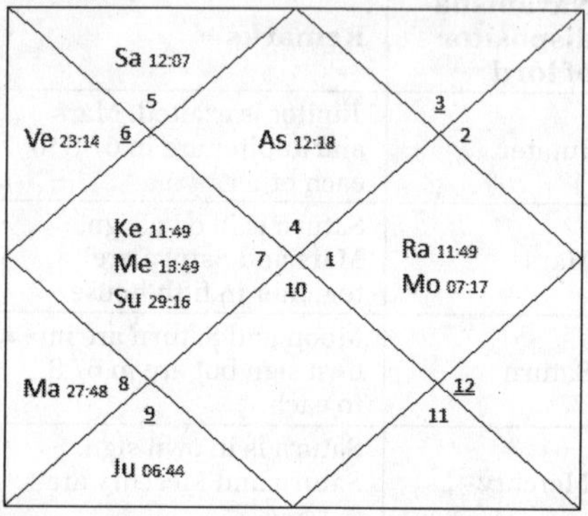

Birth Chart

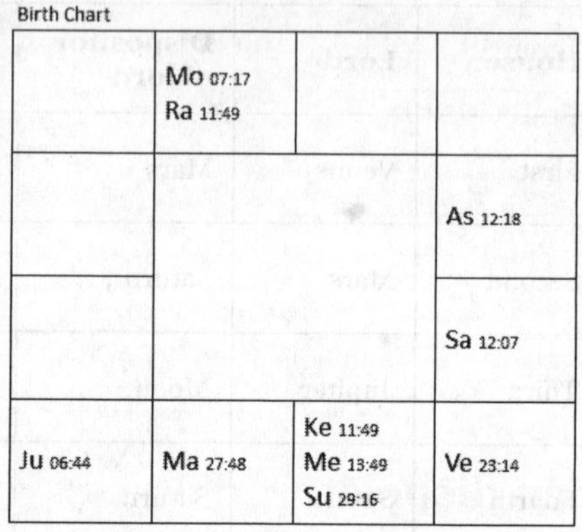

D9 Navamsha (spouse)

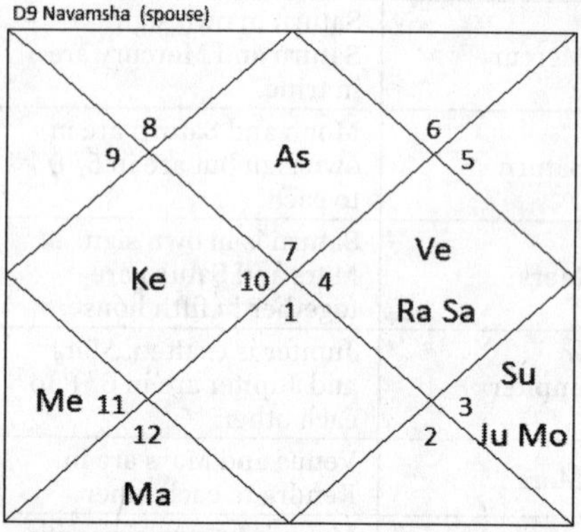

D9 Navamsha (spouse)

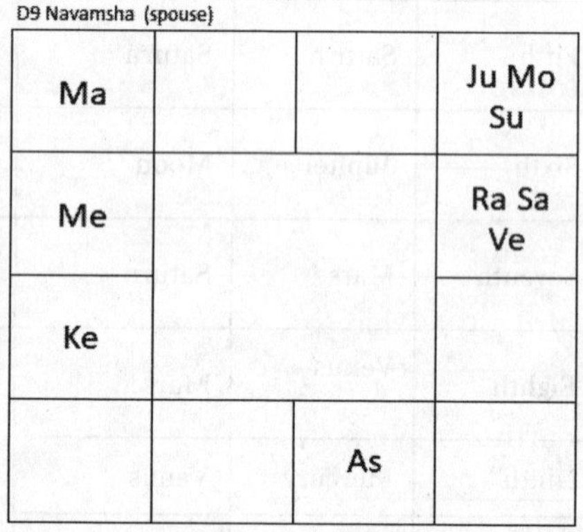

Classic rules

1. There is no malefic in trik houses.

2. Sun is debilitated in Kendra, but Jupiter is not in Kendra.

Sign dispositor of planets

Planet	Dispositor	Placement of dispositor from planet	Friendship	Remarks
Sun	Venus	Twelfth	Neutral	Not good
Moon	Mars	Eighth	neutral	Not good
Mars	Mars	self	self	Good
Mercury	Venus	Twelfth	Fast Friend	Good
Jupiter	Jupiter	self	self	Good
Venus	Mercury	Second	Fast Friend	Very Good
Saturn	Sun	Third	Neutral	
Rahu	Mars	Eighth		Not Good
Ketu	Venus	Twelfth		Not Good

Sign dispositor of house

House	Lord	Dispositor	Placement of dispositor from house	Remarks
First	Moon	Mars	Trikona	Good
Second	Sun	Venus	second	Venus is debilitated.
Third	Mercury	Venus	Same house	Dispositor is in the house.
Fourth	Venus	Mercury	Same house	Dispositor in same house will promote fourth house.
Fifth	Mars	Mars	Same house	Fifth house is strong
Sixth	Jupiter	Jupiter	Same house	Jupiter will promote sixth house
Seventh	Saturn	Sun	Tenth	
Eighth	Saturn	Sun	ninth	Saturn is aspecting house. Long life
Ninth	Jupiter	Jupiter	Tenth	Very good for ninth house

Tenth	Mars	Mars	eighth	Tenth house is not strong
Eleventh	Venus	Mercury	sixth	Not good for eleventh house
Twelfth	Mercury	Venus	fourth	expenses

1. Third, fourth, fifth, sixth and ninth house are strong.

Dispositor of nodes

1. Rahu is in the sign of Mars. Mars is not a lord of trik or trishadaya house. Mars is in own sign. Mars is not a functional malefic. The drawback is the placement of Mars in eighth from Rahu.
2. Ketu is in the sign of Venus. Venus is lord of eleventh house also. Venus is placed in twelfth from Ketu. The dispositor of Ketu is badly placed.

Navamsha dispositor

1. Venus is debilitated. The Navamsha dispositor of Venus is Moon. Moon is in tenth house in a movable sign and the Ascendant is also a movable sign. This confers raj Yoga.
2. The Navamsha dispositor of sixth lord and of ninth lord are in mutual aspect with Sun. lagna is not a fixed sign and is not aspected by sixth lord. Chandika Yoga is not present.
3. The Navamsha dispositor of fourth lord is Moon. Moon is in Kendra and his mother will be long lived.
4. The Navamsha lord of fifth lord is Jupiter. Jupiter is in own sign without any other aspect and the person is intelligent.

House	lord	Dispositor in D9	Placement from lagan	Placement from house
First	Moon	Mercury	Kendra	Kendra
Second	Sun	Mercury	Kendra	Third
Third	Mercury	Saturn	Second	Twelfth
Fourth	Venus	Moon	Kendra	Kendra
Fifth	Mars	Jupiter	Sixth	Second
Sixth	Jupiter	Mercury	Fourth	Eleventh
Seventh	Saturn	Moon	Kendra	Kendra
Eighth	Saturn	Moon	Kendra	Third
Ninth	Jupiter	Mercury	Kendra	Eighth
Tenth	Mars	Jupiter	Sixth	Trine
Eleventh	Venus	Moon	Kendra	Twelfth
Twelfth	Mercury	Saturn	Second	Third

1. The Navamsha dispositor position of good houses is not favourable.

Karaka dispositor

1. Dispositor of Venus is Mercury. Mercury is in second house from Venus and is in RKA. Venus is afflicted in Navamsha. The marriage experience is not good.
2. Dispositor of Sun is Venus. Venus is in twelfth from Sun. Sun is with benefics in Navamsha. The Sun is favourable and gives good treatment from father.
3. Dispositor of Moon is Mars. Mars is in eighth house from Sun. Moon is with benefic in Navamsha and gets love from mother.
4. Venus is in the Nakshatra of Moon. He enjoys luxuries of life.
5. Nakshatra dispositor of Sun is Jupiter. Jupiter is in ninth house from Moon. He has father and king in his favour.

6. Moon is in the Nakshatra of Ketu. Ketu is in seventh from Moon. Mother favours him.

Nakshatra dispositor

Planet	Nakshatra Dispositor	Placement of Nakshatra dispositor from lagna	Placement of Nakshatra dispositor from Planet	Remarks
Sun	Jupiter	Sixth	Third	Efforts
Moon	Ketu	Fourth	Seventh	Family affairs
Mars	Mercury	Kendra	Twelfth	Not Good
Mercury	Rahu	Tenth	Seventh	Family Issues
Jupiter	Ketu	Fourth	Eleventh	Sudden event
Venus	Moon	Tenth	Eighth	Venus suffers
Saturn	Ketu	Fourth	Third	Family matters
Rahu	Ketu	Fourth	Seventh	Again Kendra
Ketu	Rahu	Tenth	Seventh	Family/ Profession

Final Dispositor

House	lord	Next D	Next D	Next D	Next D	Next D	Next D	Final D	Remarks
First	Moon	Mars	Mars					Mars	
Second	Sun	Venus	Mercury	Venus					Exchange
Third	Mercury	Venus	Mercury						Exchange
Fourth	Venus	Mercury	Venus						Exchange
Fifth	Mars	Mars						Mars	
Sixth	Jupiter	Jupiter						Jupiter	
Seventh	Saturn	Sun	Venus	Mercury	Venus				Exchange
Eighth	Saturn	Sun	Venus	Mercury	Venus				Exchange
Ninth	Jupiter	Jupiter						Jupiter	
Tenth	Mars	Mars						Mars	
Eleventh	Venus	Mercury	Venus						Exchange
Twelfth	Mercury	Venus	Mercury						Exchange

In this table, I use 'D" instead of Dispositor to make the words fit.

1. The final dispositor of five houses are Mars and Jupiter. There is no confusion about these houses.
2. The final dispositor of rest of the houses are ending in loop of Mercury and Venus. The decisions of matters in regard to these houses are influenced by these two planets. This creates a sense of indecision.

Synthesis of Result

House	Lord	Dispositor of lord	Navamsha dispositor of lord	Remarks
First	Moon	Mars	Mercury	Mars is in own sign. Moon and Mercury are in Kendra to each other.
Second	Sun	Venus	Mercury	
Third	Mercury	Venus	Saturn	
Fourth	Venus	Mercury	Moon	Moon and Mercury are in Kendra to each other.
Fifth	Mars	Mars	Jupiter	Mars is in own sign. Jupiter is in own sign.
Sixth	Jupiter	Jupiter	Mercury	Jupiter is in own sign.
Seventh	Saturn	Sun	Moon	Sun and Moon are in Kendra to each other.
Eighth	Saturn	Sun	Moon	Sun and Moon are in Kendra to each other.
Ninth	Jupiter	Jupiter	Mercury	Jupiter is in own sign.
Tenth	Mars	Mars	Jupiter	Mars and Jupiter are in own sign.
Eleventh	Venus	Mercury	Moon	Moon and Mercury are in Kendra to each other.
Twelfth	Mercury	Venus	Saturn	

1. Mars and Jupiter are in own sign. The houses whose Navamsha lords are these planets will prosper because of Yoga conferred. These houses are fifth and tenth.
2. These two lords will promote the houses lorded by them. The promotional effects can be good or bad depending on the house. Mars will promote tenth house. Jupiter will give results of sixth and ninth. Ninth house is promoted by Jupiter.

Example Charan Singh DOB 23 December 1902 TOB 7.23 POB Bagpat

Birth Chart

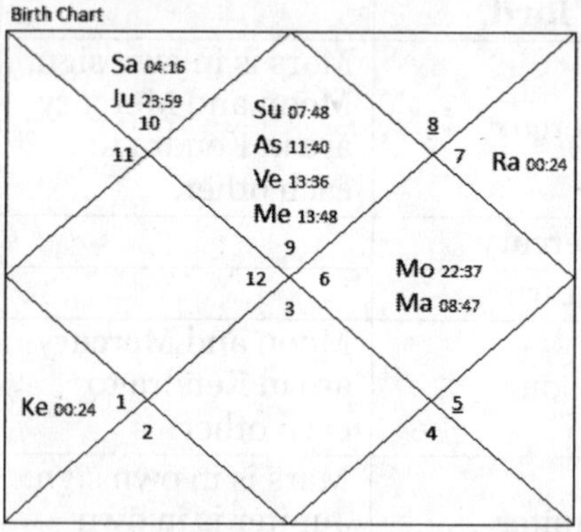

Birth Chart

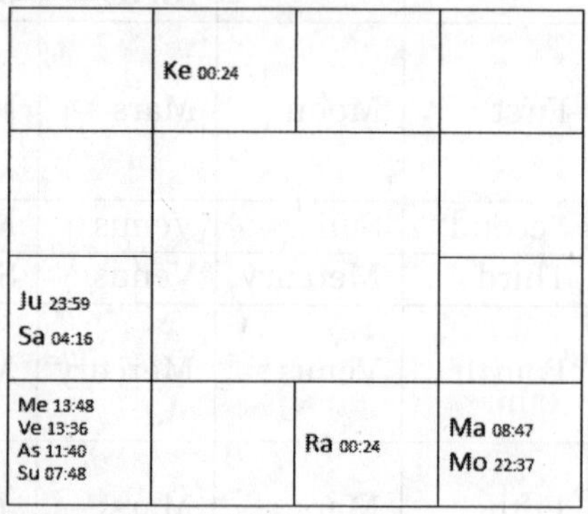

D9 Navamsha (spouse)

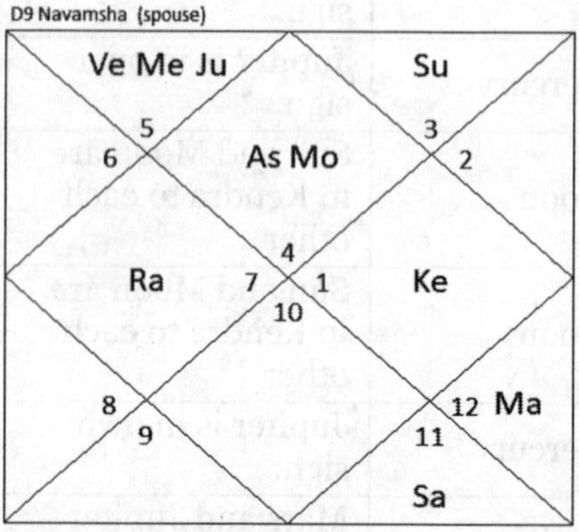

D9 Navamsha (spouse)

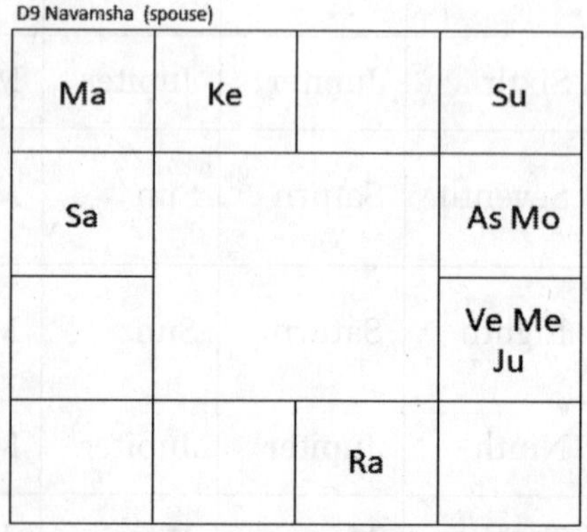

Classic rules

1. There is no malefic in trik house.

2. Venus is in lagna. Jupiter is the lord of exaltation sign of Venus. Saturn is a friend of Venus. Jupiter and Saturn are placed in second house from Venus. Venus becomes strong.

Sign dispositor of planets

Planet	Dispositor	Placement of dispositor from planet	Friendship	Remarks
Sun	Jupiter	Second	Fast Friend	Very Good
Moon	Mercury	Kendra	Fast Friend	Very Good
Mars	Mercury	Kendra	Neutral	
Mercury	Jupiter	Second	Friend	Good
Jupiter	Saturn	Kendra	Enemy	
Venus	Jupiter	Second	Friend	Good
Saturn	Saturn	self	self	Good
Rahu	Venus	Third		
Ketu	Mars	Sixth		

1. The sign dispositor of all planets except Rahu/ Ketu are well placed from the planet.

Sign dispositor of house

House	Lord	Dispositor	Placement of dispositor from house	Remarks
First	Jupiter	Saturn	Second	
Second	Saturn	Saturn	Same house	Dispositor is in the house
Third	Saturn	Saturn	Twelfth	
Fourth	Jupiter	Saturn	Eleventh	Dispositor is aspecting house

Fifth	Mars	Mercury	Ninth	Lord is aspecting the house
Sixth	Venus	Jupiter	Ninth	Dispositor is aspecting the house
Seventh	Mercury	Jupiter	Eighth	
Eighth	Moon	Mercury	Sixth	
Ninth	Sun	Jupiter	Sixth	
Tenth	Mercury	Jupiter	Fifth	Dispositor is aspecting house
Eleventh	Venus	Jupiter	Fourth	
Twelfth	Mars	Mercury	Second	

1. Second, fourth, fifth, sixth and tenth house are strong.

Dispositor of Nodes

1. The dispositor of Rahu is Venus. Venus is in third from Rahu and gives effort to Rahu.
2. The dispositor of Ketu is Mars. Mars is in sixth from Ketu and is aspecting Ketu thus gives strength to Ketu.
3. Venus and Mars are in Ascendant and tenth house. Mars is aspecting Venus. The dispositor of Ketu is influencing the dispositor of Rahu and as such Ketu is stronger than Rahu.

Navamsha dispositor

1. Jupiter is debilitated and the Navamsha dispositor of Jupiter is Sun. sun is placed in Kendra but not in a movable sign.
2. The Navamsha dispositor of sixth lord is Sun. the Navamsha dispositor of ninth lord is Mercury. Both are in Kendra in fixed sign along with Sun. sixth lord Venus is in lagna. This is Chandika Yoga. The person is aggressive, charitable, wealthy, minister and enjoys long life of fame.

3. The Navamsha dispositor of fourth lord is Sun. Sun is in Kendra. Mother is long lived.

4. Fifth lord is Mars. Jupiter is the Navamsha dispositor of fifth lord. Jupiter is strong and aspects Mars. The person is intelligent.

House	lord	Dispositor in D9	Placement from lagna	Placement from house
First	Jupiter	Sun	Kendra	Kendra with two benefic.
Second	Saturn	Saturn	Second	In the house
Third	Saturn	Saturn	Second	Twelfth
Fourth	Jupiter	Sun	Kendra	Kendra
Fifth	Mars	Jupiter	Second	Kendra
Sixth	Venus	Sun	Kendra	Eighth
Seventh	Mercury	Sun	Kendra	Kendra
Eighth	Moon	Moon	Kendra	Third
Ninth	Sun	Mercury	Kendra	Trine
Tenth	Mercury	Sun	Kendra	Kendra
Eleventh	Venus	Sun	Kendra	Third
Twelfth	Mars	Jupiter	Second	Third

1. The Navamsha dispositor of third and sixth house are placed in trik house from lagna.
2. For all other houses Navamsha dispositor is well placed.

Karaka dispositor

1. The dispositor of Venus is Jupiter. Jupiter is placed in second house with Saturn. Jupiter considers Saturn as neutral, and the luxuries are normal.
2. Dispositor of Sun is also Jupiter.

3. Dispositor of Moon is Mercury. Mercury is placed in Kendra from Moon. The blessings of mother are present.
4. Nakshatra dispositor of Venus is Venus. Venus is in fourth from Moon. He has luxuries of life.
5. Nakshatra dispositor of Sun is Ketu. Ketu is in eighth from Moon. He faces opposition from father and king.
6. Moon is in own Nakshatra and his mother is favourable.

Nakshatra dispositor

Planet	Nakshatra Dispositor	Placement of Nakshatra dispositor from lagna	Placement of Nakshatra dispositor from Planet	Remarks
Sun	Ketu	Trine	Trine	Good period
Moon	Moon	Tenth	Same	Mentally sound
Mars	Sun	Lagna	Fourth	Good
Mercury	Venus	Lagna	Together	Good Intelligence
Jupiter	Mars	Tenth	Trine	Very Good
Venus	Venus	Lagna	Same	All luxury
Saturn	Sun	Lagna	Twelfth	Expenses
Rahu	Mars	Tenth	Twelfth	Losses
Ketu	Ketu	Trine	Same	Very Good

1. The Nakshatra dispositor of Rahu is not well placed.
2. All other planets have their Nakshatra lords well placed and are favourable.

Final Dispositor

House	lord	Next D	Next D	Next D	Next D	Next D	Next D	Final D
First	Jupiter	Saturn	Saturn					Saturn
Second	Saturn	Saturn						Saturn
Third	Saturn	Saturn						Saturn
Fourth	Jupiter	Saturn	Saturn					Saturn
Fifth	Mars	Mercury	Jupiter	Saturn	Saturn			Saturn
Sixth	Venus	Jupiter	Saturn	Saturn				Saturn
Seventh	Mercury	Jupiter	Saturn	Saturn				Saturn
Eighth	Moon	Mercury	Jupiter	Saturn	Saturn			Saturn
Ninth	Sun	Jupiter	Saturn	Saturn				Saturn
Tenth	Mercury	Jupiter	Saturn	Saturn				Saturn
Eleventh	Venus	Jupiter	Saturn	Saturn				Saturn
Twelfth	Venus	Jupiter	Saturn	Saturn				Saturn

In this table, I use 'D" instead of Dispositor to make the words fit.

1. Saturn is the final dispositor of all houses. The life is governed by Saturn. There is no confusion in decision making.

Synthesis of Result

House	Lord	Dispositor of lord	Navamsha dispositor of lord	Remarks
First	Jupiter	Saturn	Sun	Saturn is in own sign. Navamsha dispositor is in the house.
Second	Saturn	Saturn	Saturn	Saturn in own sign. Saturn is the main planet. wealthy.
Third	Saturn	Saturn	Saturn	Saturn in own sign. Saturn is the main planet.
Fourth	Jupiter	Saturn	Sun	Saturn in own sign.

Fifth	Mars	Mercury	Jupiter	
Sixth	Venus	Jupiter	Sun	
Seventh	Mercury	Jupiter	Sun	Sun is aspecting house.
Eighth	Moon	Mercury	Moon	Moon and Mercury together long life.
Ninth	Sun	Jupiter	Mercury	
Tenth	Mercury	Jupiter	Sun	Jupiter is aspecting house.
Eleventh	Venus	Jupiter	Sun	
Twelfth	Mars	Mercury	Jupiter	

1. Saturn is the controller of the horoscope.
2. Most of the two dispositor are in 2/12 to each other. This is a gain and loss situation. It gives up and down in life. He faces hurdles.

Example Rock Hudson DOB 17 November 1925 TOB 02.15 POB Winnetka IL

Birth Chart

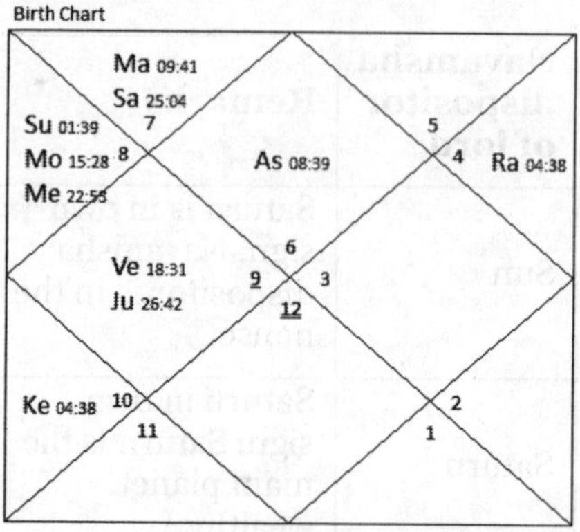

Birth Chart

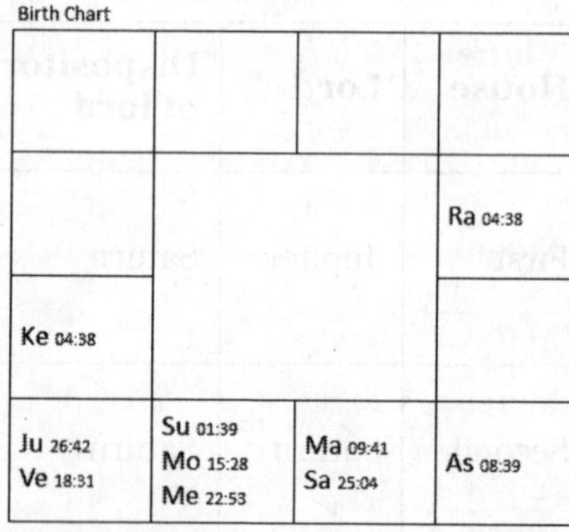

D9 Navamsha (spouse)

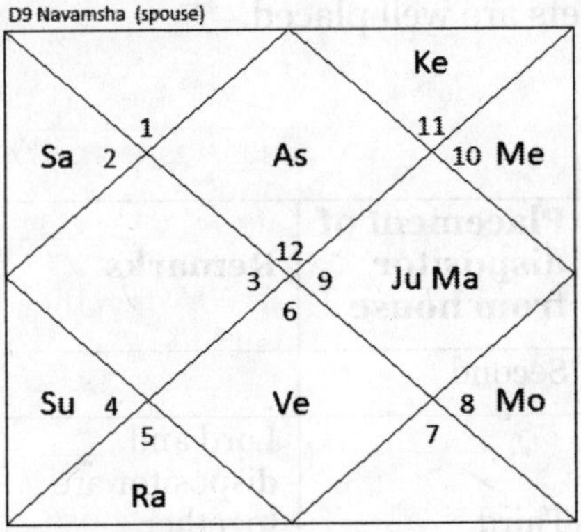

D9 Navamsha (spouse)

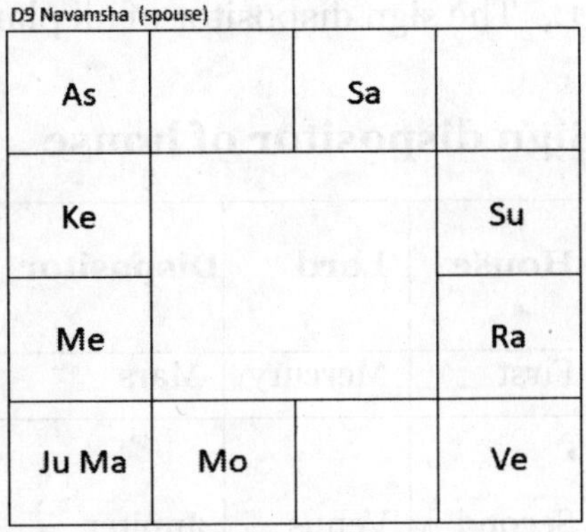

Classic results

1. There is no malefic in trik house.
2. Lord of Ascendant is Mercury. Mercury, Saturn are in third and second house. The first house will progress.
3. Jupiter and Moon are Vargottam.

Sign dispositor of planets

Planet	Dispositor	Placement of dispositor from planet	Friendship	Remarks
Sun	Mars	Twelfth	Fast Friend	Very Good
Moon	Mars	Twelfth	Fast Friend	Very Good
Mars	Venus	Third	Friend	Good
Mercury	Mars	Twelfth	Friend	Good
Jupiter	Jupiter	self	self	Good
Venus	Jupiter	Kendra	Enemy	
Saturn	Venus	Third	Fast Friend	Very Good
Rahu	Moon	Trine		Good
Ketu	Saturn	Kendra		Good

1. The sign dispositor of all planets are well placed.

Sign dispositor of house

House	Lord	Dispositor	Placement of dispositor from house	Remarks
First	Mercury	Mars	Second	
Second	Venus	Jupiter	Third	Lord and dispositor are together. House to progress.
Third	Mars	Venus	Second	
Fourth	Jupiter	Jupiter	Same house	House will progress
Fifth	Saturn	Venus	Twelfth	Not good
Sixth	Saturn	Venus	Eleventh	Competition
Seventh	Jupiter	Jupiter	Tenth	House to progress
Eighth	Mars	Venus	Trine	Long life
Ninth	Venus	Jupiter	Eighth	Adherence to religion is not there.
Tenth	Mercury	Mars	Fifth	Good for house
Eleventh	Moon	Mars	Fourth	Good for house
Twelfth	Sun	Mars	Third	

1. The first house gains strength and the quality of horoscope improves.
2. Except for twelfth house, the good things of other trik house will be experienced.
3. The progress of seventh house can give multiple affair or marriages.

Dispositor of nodes

1. Dispositor of Rahu is Moon. Moon is debilitated in third house. Debilitated of eleventh lord is welcome and gives strength to Rahu.
2. Dispositor of Ketu is Saturn. Saturn is exalted in tenth house from Ketu. Ketu will be good for profession and wealth.

Navamsha dispositor

1. Saturn is exalted. Navamsha dispositor of Saturn is placed in a Kendra in a neutral sign. Lagna lord is not strong. It is partial Mridang Yoga. The person is respected by rulers, famous, attractive and commands influence.
2. The Navamsha lord of fourth lord is Jupiter. Jupiter is in own sign in Kendra. His mother will be long lived.
3. The Navamsha lord of fifth lord is Venus. Venus is with a benefic. The person is intelligent.

House	lord	Dispositor in D9	Placement from lagna	Placement from house
First	Mercury	Saturn	Second	Second. Saturn is exalted.
Second	Venus	Mercury	Third	Second. Good for wealth.
Third	Mars	Jupiter	Kendra	Second. Lord and Navamsha dispositor are together.
Fourth	Jupiter	Jupiter	Kendra	Vargottam
Fifth	Saturn	Venus	Kendra	Twelfth. Saturn exalted and aspecting Venus.
Sixth	Saturn	Venus	Kendra	Eleventh. Saturn exalted and aspecting Venus.
Seventh	Jupiter	Jupiter	Kendra	Kendra.
Eighth	Mars	Jupiter	Kendra	Trine. Jupiter is aspecting house.

Ninth	Venus	Mercury	Third	Kendra
Tenth	Mercury	Venus	Kendra	Kendra. Navamsha dispositor aspecting house.
Eleventh	Moon	Mars	Second	Kendra
Twelfth	Sun	Moon	Third	Kendra

1. Relation of Navamsha dispositor with the house grants strength to house.

2. The Navamsha dispositor of all house lords is well placed. It promotes good results of all houses.

Dispositor of Karaka

1. Dispositor of Venus is Jupiter. Jupiter is in own sign with Venus. All luxuries of life are promised.
2. Dispositor of Sun is Mars. Mars is in twelfth from Sun. Sun is not favourable.
3. Dispositor of Moon is Mars and is placed in twelfth from Moon. Moon is not favourable.
4. Venus is in own Nakshatra. Venus is in second from Moon and with benefic. He has luxury of life.
5. Nakshatra dispositor of Sun is Jupiter. Jupiter is in second from Moon. Father and king is favourable.
6. Nakshatra dispositor of Moon is Saturn. Saturn is in twelfth from Moon. No favour from mother.

Nakshatra dispositor

Planet	Nakshatra Dispositor	Placement of Nakshatra dispositor from lagna	Placement of Nakshatra dispositor from Planet	Remarks
Sun	Jupiter	Fourth	Second	Family happiness. Jupiter is lord of Kendra.
Moon	Saturn	Second	Twelfth	Loss/ Mental disturbance. Saturn is sixth lord.
Mars	Rahu	Eleventh	Tenth	Professional gain
Mercury	Mercury	Third	Same	Efforts. Mercury is lagna and tenth lord
Jupiter	Sun	Third	Twelfth	Efforts and loss
Venus	Venus	Fourth	Same	All luxuries
Saturn	Jupiter	Fourth	Third	Professional happiness/ effort
Rahu	Saturn	Second	Fourth	Family/ Wealth
Ketu	Sun	Third	Eleventh	Gain from effort

1. Moon and Rahu are placed in Nakshatra of Saturn. Saturn is sixth lord also. The placement of Saturn from Moon is not good, and Moon will give illness. Placement of Saturn from Rahu is good.

Final Dispositor

House	lord	Next D	Next D	Next D	Next D	Next D	Next D	Final D
First	Mercury	Mars	Venus	Jupiter	Jupiter			Jupiter
Second	Venus	Jupiter	Jupiter					Jupiter
Third	Mars	Venus	Jupiter	Jupiter				Jupiter
Fourth	Jupiter	Jupiter						Jupiter
Fifth	Saturn	Venus	Jupiter	Jupiter				Jupiter
Sixth	Saturn	Venus	Jupiter	Jupiter				Jupiter
Seventh	Jupiter	Jupiter						Jupiter
Eighth	Mars	Venus	Jupiter	Jupiter				Jupiter
Ninth	Venus	Jupiter	Jupiter					Jupiter
Tenth	Mercury	Mars	Venus	Jupiter	Jupiter			Jupiter
Eleventh	Moon	Mars	Venus	Jupiter	Jupiter			Jupiter
Twelfth	Sun	Mars	Venus	Jupiter	Jupiter			Jupiter

In this table, I use 'D" instead of Dispositor to make the words fit.

1. The final dispositor of all houses is Jupiter. A balanced thinking and no confusion is there in decision making. Jupiter is in own sign and gives rise in life.

Synthesis of Result

House	Lord	Dispositor of lord	Navamsha dispositor of lord	Remarks
First	Mercury	Mars	Saturn	Saturn is exalted. Mars and Saturn are in conjunction.
Second	Venus	Jupiter	Mercury	Jupiter in own sign and Vargottam.
Third	Mars	Venus	Jupiter	Jupiter in own sign with Venus.
Fourth	Jupiter	Jupiter	Jupiter	Jupiter in own sign. Jupiter is main planet for fourth house.
Fifth	Saturn	Venus	Venus	Venus is the decider.
Sixth	Saturn	Venus	Venus	Venus is the decider.
Seventh	Jupiter	Jupiter	Jupiter	Jupiter in own sign

				and is the main planet for seventh house.
Eighth	Mars	Venus	Jupiter	Jupiter in own sign. Jupiter and Venus conjoined. Jupiter is Vargottam. Long life.
Ninth	Venus	Jupiter	Mercury	Jupiter in own sign.
Tenth	Mercury	Mars	Saturn	Saturn exalted.
Eleventh	Moon	Mars	Mars	High gains in Moon
Twelfth	Sun	Mars	Moon	Moon is Vargottam.

Example Prince Williams DOB 21 June 1982 TOB 21.30 POB London

Birth Chart

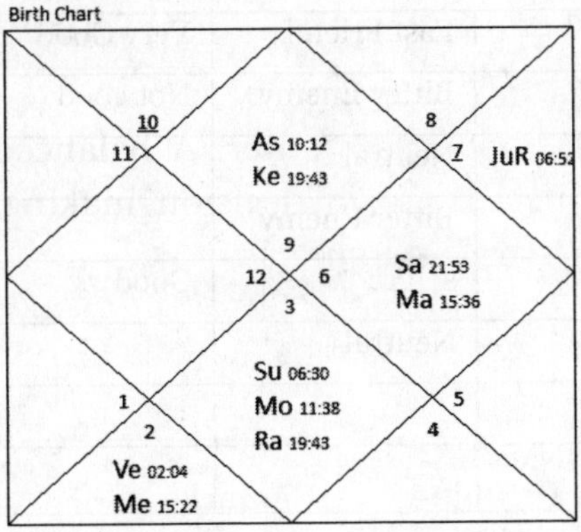

Birth Chart

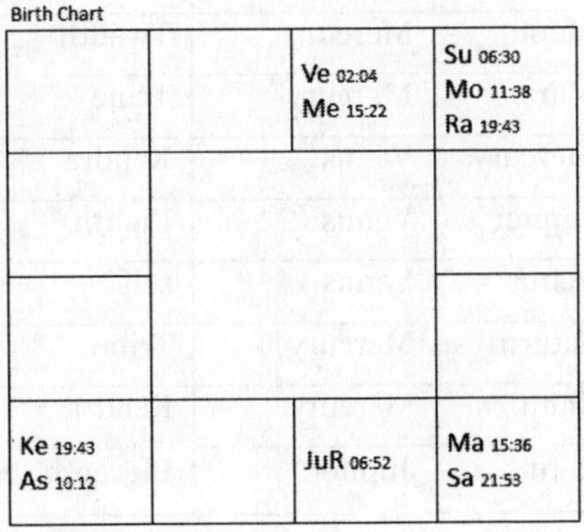

D9 Navamsha (spouse)

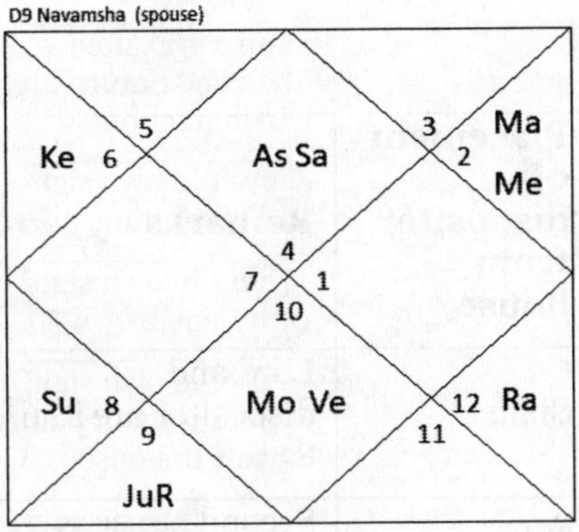

D9 Navamsha (spouse)

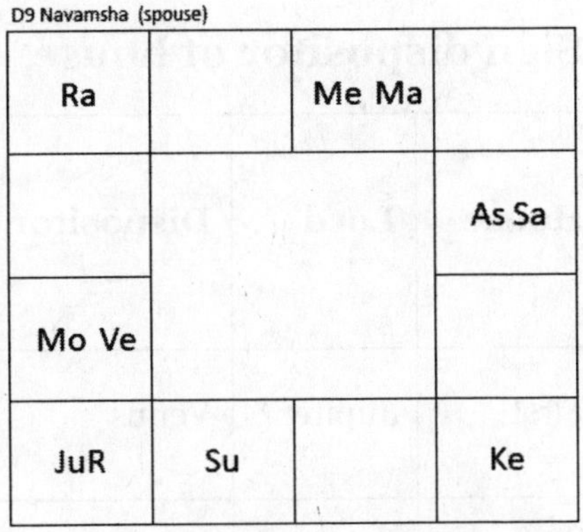

Classic rules

1. There is no malefic in trik house.
2. Sun is the lord of ninth house. Moon, Mars and Jupiter are friends of Sun. Mars is the lord of exaltation sign of Sun. All of these are placed in second, third and eleventh house from ninth house. Ninth house is very strong.

Sign dispositor of planets

Planet	Dispositor	Placement of dispositor from planet	Friendship	Remarks
Sun	Mercury	Twelfth	Friend	Good
Moon	Mercury	Twelfth	Fast Friend	Very Good
Mars	Mercury	Trine	Bitter Enemy	Not good
Mercury	Venus	Kendra	Neutral	
Jupiter	Venus	Eighth	Bitter Enemy	
Venus	Venus	self	self	Good
Saturn	Mercury	Trine	Neutral	
Rahu	Mercury	Kendra		
Ketu	Jupiter	Eleventh		

Sign dispositor of house

House	Lord	Dispositor	Placement of dispositor from house	Remarks
First	Jupiter	Venus	Sixth	Lord and dispositor are in 6/ 8
Second	Saturn	Mercury	Trine	Second house is strong
Third	Saturn	Mercury	Kendra	Good

Fourth	Jupiter	Venus	Third	Efforts
Fifth	Mars	Mercury	Second	Mars is aspecting house. Good
Sixth	Venus	Venus	same	Sixth house is strong
Seventh	Mercury	Venus	Twelfth	Lord and dispositor conjoined in twelfth from house. Not good
Eighth	Moon	Mercury	Eleventh	Long life
Ninth	Sun	Mercury	Kendra	Ninth gets strength
Tenth	Mercury	Venus	Trine	Lord and dispositor conjoined in ninth from house.
Eleventh	Venus	Venus	Eighth	Jeeva of eleventh suffers
Twelfth	Mars	Mercury	Seventh	Very good

Navamsha dispositor

1. No planet is exalted or debilitated.
2. Fourth lord is Jupiter. Jupiter is in its own Navamsha. Jupiter is placed in eleventh from fourth house. Mother is not having long life.
3. Navamsha dispositor of fifth lord is Venus. Venus is with Mercury. The person is intelligent.

House	**lord**	**Dispositor in D9**	**Placement from lagna**	**Placement from house**
First	Jupiter	Jupiter	Eleventh	Eleventh First house gains strength
Second	Saturn	Moon	Kendra	Sixth

Third	Saturn	Moon	Kendra	Trine
Fourth	Jupiter	Jupiter	Eleventh	Eighth. Not good for mother.
Fifth	Mars	Venus	Sixth	Second
Sixth	Venus	Saturn	Kendra	Trine
Seventh	Mercury	Venus	Sixth	Twelfth. Seventh house suffers
Eighth	Moon	Saturn	Kendra	Third
Ninth	Sun	Mars	Kendra	Second
Tenth	Mercury	Venus	Sixth	Trine
Eleventh	Venus	Saturn	Kendra	Twelfth
Twelfth	Mars	Venus	Sixth	Kendra

Dispositor of nodes

1. Rahu is in the sign of Mercury. Mercury is placed in twelfth house from Rahu and in sixth from lagna. Rahu may not give good results.

2. Jupiter is the dispositor of Ketu. Jupiter is in eleventh from Ketu and lagna. Ketu gives good results.

Dispositor of Karaka

1. The dispositor of Venus is Venus. The person gets wealth, vehicles and love from wife.

2. The dispositor of Sun and Moon is Mercury. Mercury is in twelfth from Sun and Moon. Both are not favourable.

3. Venus is in the Nakshatra of Sun. sun is with Moon. He has luxuries of life.

4. Nakshatra dispositor of Sun is Mars. Mars is in fourth from Moon. He has favours from father and King.

5. Nakshatra dispositor of Moon is Rahu. Rahu is with Moon. Mother favour him.

Nakshatra dispositor

Planet	Nakshatra Dispositor	Placement of Nakshatra dispositor from lagna	Placement of Nakshatra dispositor from Planet	Remarks
Sun	Mars	Tenth	Fourth	Mars is trine lord in tenth. Good position.
Moon	Rahu	Seventh	Together	Partnership
Mars	Moon	Seventh	Tenth	Professional happiness. Moon is eighth lord
Mercury	Moon	Seventh	Second	Family affairs gets boost. Moon is eighth lord
Jupiter	Rahu	Seventh	Trine	Good period
Venus	Sun	Seventh	Second	Luxury from family
Saturn	Moon	Seventh	Tenth	Good for Profession
Rahu	Rahu	Seventh	Same	Partner matters
Ketu	Venus	Sixth	Sixth	Not Good

Mars, Mercury and Saturn are in the Nakshatra of Moon. Moon is eighth lord and can create obstacles in the dasha of these planets. No planet is placed in the Nakshatra of tenth lord.

Final Dispositor

House	lord	Next D	Next D	Next D	Next D	Next D	Next D	Final D
First	Jupiter	Venus	Venus					Venus
Second	Saturn	Mercury	Venus	Venus				Venus
Third	Saturn	Mercury	Venus	Venus				Venus

Fourth	Jupiter	Venus	Venus					Venus
Fifth	Mars	Mercury	Venus	Venus				Venus
Sixth	Venus	Venus						Venus
Seventh	Mercury	Venus	Venus					Venus
Eighth	Moon	Mercury	Venus	Venus				Venus
Ninth	Sun	Mercury	Venus	Venus				Venus
Tenth	Mercury	Venus	Venus					Venus
Eleventh	Venus	Venus						Venus
Twelfth	Mars	Mercury	Venus	Venus				Venus

In this table, I use 'D" instead of Dispositor to make the words fit.

Venus is the final dispositor of all houses. Venus governs the decision making. Here Venus is not a functional benefic and the end results are not happy.

Synthesis of Result

House	Lord	Dispositor of lord	Navamsha dispositor of lord	Remarks
First	Jupiter	Venus	Jupiter	Venus is in own sign. Jupiter and Venus are in 6/ 8 and is not good.
Second	Saturn	Mercury	Moon	Mercury and Moon are in 2/ 12 and not good
Third	Saturn	Mercury	Moon	Mercury and Moon are in 2/ 12 and not good
Fourth	Jupiter	Venus	Jupiter	Venus is in own sign. Jupiter and Venus are in 6/ 8 and is not good.
Fifth	Mars	Mercury	Venus	Venus and Mercury conjoined. Venus is in own sign. Fifth house is strong.
Sixth	Venus	Venus	Saturn	Venus is in own sign.
Seventh	Mercury	Venus	Venus	Venus is in own sign and is the main planet for seventh house.
Eighth	Moon	Mercury	Saturn	Saturn and Mercury are

				in trine to each other.
Ninth	Sun	Mercury	Mars	Mars and Mercury are in trine to each other.
Tenth	Mercury	Venus	Venus	Venus is in own sign and is the main planet for tenth house.
Eleventh	Venus	Venus	Saturn	Venus in own sign.
Twelfth	Mars	Mercury	Venus	Venus is in own sign with Mercury.

1. Venus is the planet ruling many houses. Venus is also the final dispositor of all houses.

Example Rishikesh DOB 13 May 1955 TOB 21.15 POB Rishikesh

Birth Chart

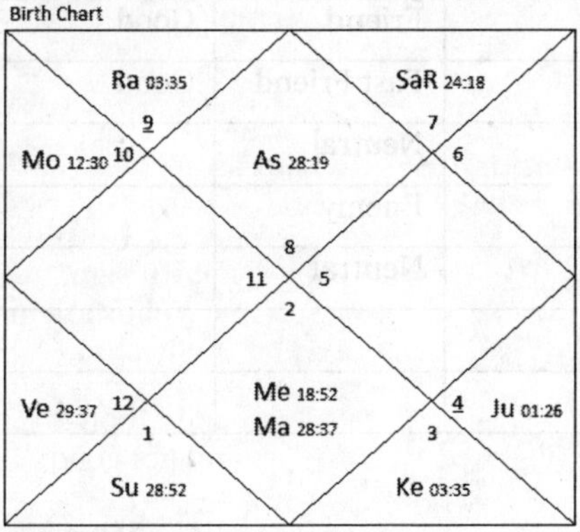

Birth Chart

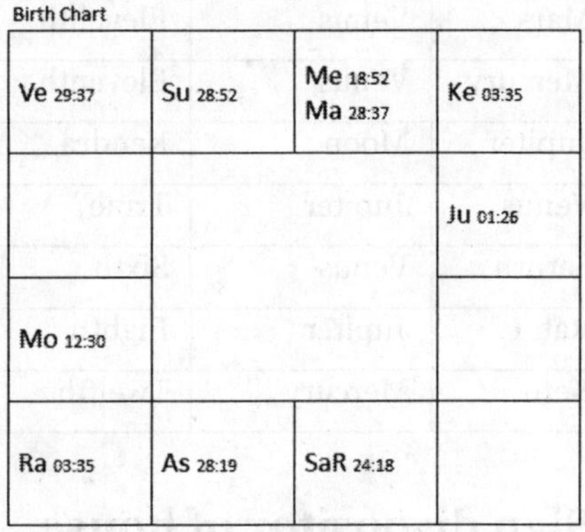

D9 Navamsha (spouse)

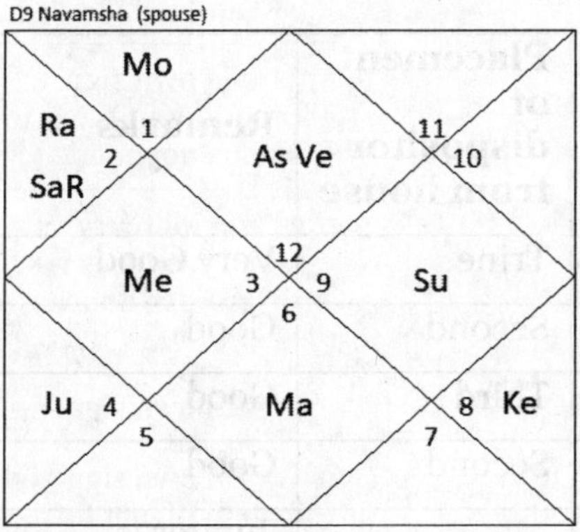

D9 Navamsha (spouse)

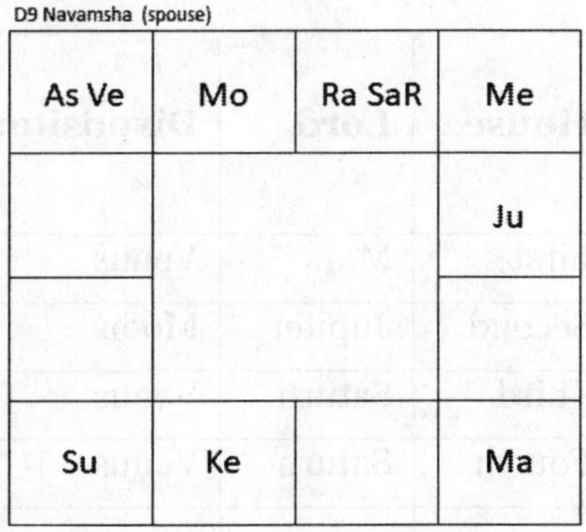

Classic rules

1. Malefic is placed in trik houses.
2. Lord of eighth house is Mercury. Mercury is with Mars and Ketu is placed in eighth house. The life of the person is miserable.

Sign dispositor of planets

Planet	Dispositor	Placement of dispositor from planet	Friendship	Remarks
Sun	Mars	Second	Fast Friend	Very Good
Moon	Saturn	Kendra	Friend	Good
Mars	Venus	Eleventh	Friend	Good
Mercury	Venus	Eleventh	Fast Friend	Good
Jupiter	Moon	Kendra	Neutral	
Venus	Jupiter	Trine	Enemy	
Saturn	Venus	Sixth	Neutral	
Rahu	Jupiter	Eighth		
Ketu	Mercury	Twelfth		

Sign dispositor of house

House	Lord	Dispositor	Placement of dispositor from house	Remarks
First	Mars	Venus	Trine	Very Good
Second	Jupiter	Moon	Second	Good
Third	Saturn	Venus	Third	Good
Fourth	Saturn	Venus	Second	Good
Fifth	Jupiter	Moon	Eleventh	Jupiter is aspecting Moon. Fifth

				house is strong
Sixth	Mars	Venus	Twelfth	Sixth house suffers
Seventh	Venus	Jupiter	Third	Jupiter aspects lord. seventh house is strong
Eighth	Mercury	Venus	Kendra	Eighth has Ketu. Long term disease
Ninth	Moon	Saturn	Fourth	Saturn aspects house.
Tenth	Sun	Mars	Tenth	Dispositor is aspecting house.
Eleventh	Mercury	Venus	Seventh	Dispositor is aspecting house.
Twelfth	Venus	Jupiter	Tenth	Expenses and enemy

Dispositor of nodes

1. Rahu is in the sign of Jupiter. Jupiter is placed in eighth from Rahu. This is not a good placement.
2. Dispositor of Ketu is Mercury. Mercury is in twelfth from Ketu. This is also not good.

Navamsha dispositor

1. Sun is exalted. The Navamsha dispositor of Sun is Jupiter. Jupiter is exalted in a trine.
2. Saturn is exalted. The Navamsha dispositor of Saturn is Venus. Venus is exalted in a trine.
3. Venus is exalted. The Navamsha dispositor of Venus is Jupiter. Jupiter is exalted in a trine.

4. These three are causing Mridang Yoga. The person will be respected by rulers, famous, attractive and commands much influence. He never felt the result of Mridang Yoga.
5. The Navamsha dispositor of fourth lord is Venus. Venus is exalted and placed in a trine. His mother was long lived.
6. The Navamsha dispositor of fifth lord is Moon. Moon is aspected by Jupiter. He is intelligent.

House	lord	Dispositor in D9	Placement from lagna	Placement from house
First	Mars	Mercury	Kendra	Kendra. Mercury is aspecting lagna.
Second	Jupiter	Moon	Third	Second. Moon and Jupiter are in mutual aspect.
Third	Saturn	Venus	Trine	Third
Fourth	Saturn	Venus	Trine	Second
Fifth	Jupiter	Moon	Third	Eleventh. Fifth house gets gains
Sixth	Mars	Mercury	Kendra	Second. Mars and Mercury conjoined. Sixth house is strong
Seventh	Venus	Jupiter	Trine	Third. Seventh house is strong.
Eighth	Mercury	Mercury	Kendra	Twelfth. Loss of life
Ninth	Moon	Mars	Kendra	Eleventh. Gain from ninth house
Tenth	Sun	Jupiter	Trine	Twelfth. Loss in profession
Eleventh	Mercury	Mercury	Kendra	Trine. gains
Twelfth	Venus	Jupiter	Trine	Kendra. Expenses.

1. Gains are spent as both eleventh and twelfth are strong.
2. Strength of seventh house gives a dominating wife.
3. Eighth house gives medium life.

Dispositor of Karaka

1. Dispositor of Venus is Jupiter. Jupiter is placed in trine from Venus. He will have luxury of life.
2. Dispositor of Sun is Mars. Mars is in second house from Sun. The favour from father is good.
3. dispositor of Moon is Saturn who is in Kendra from Moon. Blessings of mother is present.
4. Nakshatra dispositor of Venus is Mercury. Mercury is in fifth from Moon. Mercury is with Mars. He has luxury of life.
5. Nakshatra dispositor of Sun is Sun. Sun is placed in fourth from Moon. Blessing of father is present.
6. Nakshatra dispositor of Moon is Moon. Mother is giving her blessings.

Nakshatra dispositor

Planet	Nakshatra Dispositor	Placement of Nakshatra dispositor from lagna	Placement of Nakshatra dispositor from Planet	Remarks
Sun	Sun	sixth	same	Sun is good
Moon	Moon	Third	Same	Efforts
Mars	Mars	Seventh	Same	Marriage is important
Mercury	Moon	Third	Trine	Lot of efforts
Jupiter	Jupiter	Trine	Same	Religious
Venus	Mercury	Seventh	Third	Efforts for seventh
Saturn	Jupiter	Trine	Kendra	Good but expenses
Rahu	Ketu	Eighth	Seventh	Trouble/ maraca
Ketu	Mars	Seventh	Twelfth	losses

1. Five planets are placed in their own Nakshatra. This makes these planets give the results fully.

Final Dispositor

House	lord	Next D	Next D	Next D	Next D	Next D	Next D	Final D	Remarks
First	Mars	Venus	Jupiter	Moon	Saturn	Venus	Jupiter		Loop
Second	Jupiter	Moon	Saturn	Venus	Jupiter			Jupiter	
Third	Saturn	Venus	Jupiter	Moon	Saturn	Venus	Jupiter		Loop
Fourth	Saturn	Venus	Jupiter	Moon	Saturn	Venus	Jupiter		Loop
Fifth	Jupiter	Moon	Saturn	Venus	Jupiter			Jupiter	
Sixth	Mars	Venus	Jupiter	Moon	Saturn	Venus	Jupiter		Loop
Seventh	Venus	Jupiter	Moon	Saturn	Venus	Jupiter			Loop
Eighth	Mercury	Venus	Jupiter	Moon	Saturn	Venus	Jupiter		Loop
Ninth	Moon	Saturn	Venus	Jupiter					Loop
Tenth	Sun	Mars	Venus	Jupiter	Moon	Saturn	Venus		Loop
Eleventh	Mercury	Venus	Jupiter	Moon	Saturn	Venus	Jupiter		Loop
Twelfth	Venus	Jupiter	Moon	Saturn	Venus	Jupiter			Loop

In this table, I use 'D" instead of Dispositor to make the words fit.

The final dispositor of ten houses are ending in loop. There is no firmness in any of these houses. The final dispositor of second and fifth house is Jupiter. The life is full of indecision and uncertain.

Synthesis of Result

House	Lord	Dispositor of lord	Navamsha dispositor of lord	Remarks
First	Mars	Venus	Mercury	Both are in seventh house.
Second	Jupiter	Moon	Moon	Moon is the main planet.
Third	Saturn	Venus	Venus	Saturn and Venus are exalted but are in 6/ 8 to each other.
Fourth	Saturn	Venus	Venus	Saturn and Venus are exalted but are in 6/ 8 to each other.

Fifth	Jupiter	Moon	Moon	Moon is the main planet.
Sixth	Mars	Venus	Mercury	Venus is exalted.
Seventh	Venus	Jupiter	Jupiter	Jupiter is exalted and is the governing planet.
Eighth	Mercury	Venus	Mercury	Venus is exalted.
Ninth	Moon	Saturn	Mars	Mars and Saturn are in 6/8. Saturn is exalted.
Tenth	Sun	Mars	Jupiter	Jupiter is exalted.
Eleventh	Mercury	Venus	Mercury	Venus is exalted.
Twelfth	Venus	Jupiter	Jupiter	Jupiter is exalted and is the main planet for twelfth house.

1. Venus, Moon and Jupiter are the main planets of six houses.
2. The dispositor and Navamsha dispositor of two major houses are not well placed. These are fourth and ninth house. The happiness and the dharma are not present. This has spoiled a good life.

Example James Ray DOB 10 March 1928 TOB 15.00 POB Alton IL

Birth Chart

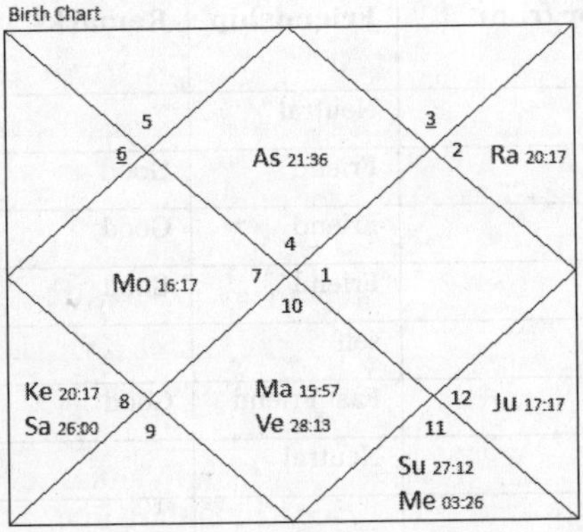

Birth Chart

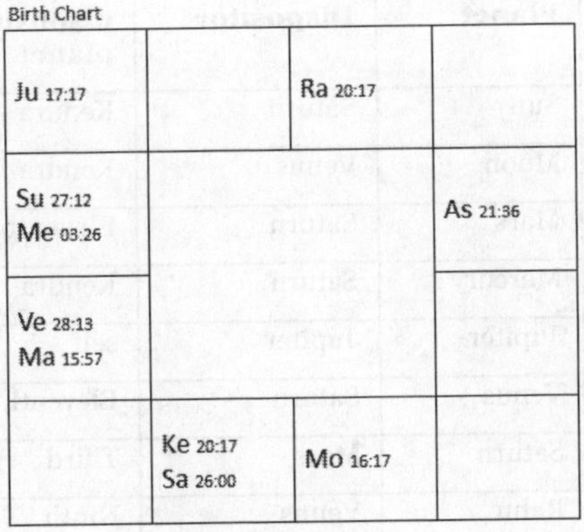

D9 Navamsha (spouse)

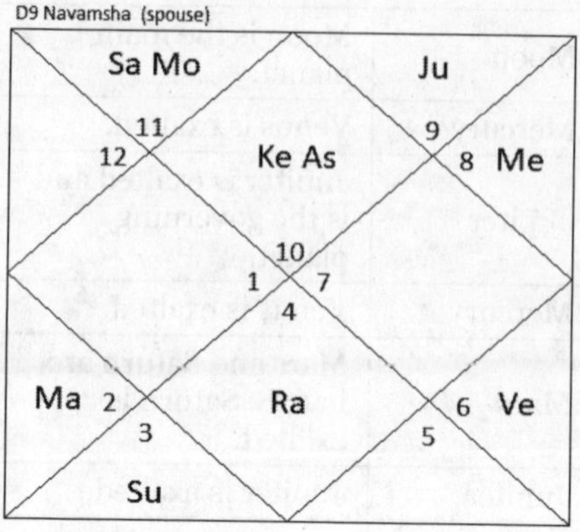

D9 Navamsha (spouse)

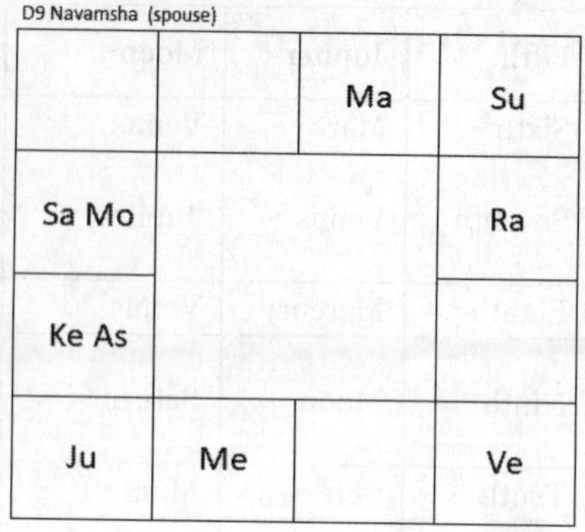

Classic rules

1. A malefic is placed in eighth house. Eighth lord is with Ketu. The life is full of miseries.
2. Dispositor of Mars is Saturn. The exaltation lord of Saturn is Venus and debilitation lord of Saturn is Mars. Both are in Kendra from Mars. A king is born.
3. No planet is debilitated.

Sign dispositor of planets

Planet	Dispositor	Placement of dispositor from planet	Friendship	Remarks
Sun	Saturn	Kendra	Neutral	
Moon	Venus	Kendra	Friend	Good
Mars	Saturn	Eleventh	Friend	Good
Mercury	Saturn	Kendra	Friend	Good
Jupiter	Jupiter	self	self	
Venus	Saturn	Eleventh	Fast Friend	Good
Saturn	Mars	Third	Neutral	
Rahu	Venus	Ninth		
Ketu	Mars	Third		

Sign dispositor of house

House	Lord	Dispositor	Placement of dispositor from house	Remarks
First	Moon	Venus	Fourth	Good. happiness
Second	Sun	Saturn	Fourth	Happiness of second house.
Third	Mercury	Saturn	Third	Traits of third are strong
Fourth	Venus	Saturn	Second	
Fifth	Mars	Saturn	In the house	Fifth house is strong
Sixth	Jupiter	Jupiter	Kendra	Strong determination
Seventh	Saturn	Mars	In the house	Partner is strong
Eighth	Saturn	Mars	Twelfth	Loss of longevity
Ninth	Jupiter	Jupiter	Same house	Strongly religious
Tenth	Mars	Saturn	eighth	Bad deeds
Eleventh	Venus	Saturn	Seventh	Desires fulfilled
Twelfth	Mercury	Saturn	Sixth	No expenses.

The dispositor of tenth house is in eighth from house and is with Ketu. Karma is spoiled. The journey of crime started in Saturn dasha.

Dispositor of nodes

1. Rahu is in the sign of Venus. Venus is in ninth from Rahu. Venus is badly afflicted.
2. Dispositor of Ketu is Mars. Mars is in third house from Ketu.
3. Both dispositor of nodes are conjoined and is not good.

Navamsha dispositor

1. No planet is debilitated.
2. The Navamsha dispositor of Mars is Venus. Venus is placed in Kendra and lagna lord is strong. Mridang Yoga is formed. The person will be respected by rulers, famous, attractive and commands much influence.
3. The Navamsha dispositor of fourth lord is Mercury. Mercury is placed in eighth house. He will have no property and mother will not live long.
4. Fifth lord is Mars. The Navamsha dispositor of Mars is Venus. Venus is not having any benefic relation. The person is not intelligent.

House	lord	Dispositor in D9	Placement from lagna	Placement from house
First	Moon	Saturn	Trine	Trine. Saturn is with Ketu
Second	Sun	Mercury	Eighth	Kendra. Aspecting house
Third	Mercury	Mars	Kendra	Trine
Fourth	Venus	Mercury	Eighth	Trine
Fifth	Mars	Venus	Kendra	Third
Sixth	Jupiter	Jupiter	Trine	Kendra. Sixth is strong
Seventh	Saturn	Saturn	Trine	Eleventh. Saturn aspect house gives strength
Eighth	Saturn	Saturn	Trine	Kendra. longevity
Ninth	Jupiter	Jupiter	Trine	Same house. Ninth house is strong
Tenth	Mars	Venus	Kendra	Kendra. Karma gets support
Eleventh	Venus	Mercury	Eighth	Kendra
Twelfth	Mercury	Mars	Kendra	Eighth

Navamsha dispositor confirms the determined attitude of the person.

Dispositor of Karaka

1. Dispositor of Venus is Saturn. Saturn is in eleventh from Venus and is with Ketu. He has luxury of life but quality is not good.
2. Sun is in the sign of Saturn. Saturn is in tenth from Sun. Father is supportive.
3. Moon is in the sign of Venus. Venus is in fourth from Moon. Mother is supportive.
4. The dispositor of all three are with malefic and support can be for bad cause.
5. Venus is in the Nakshatra of Mars. Mars is in fourth from Moon. Has amenities of life.
6. Nakshatra dispositor of Sun is Jupiter. Jupiter is placed in sixth from Moon. Father and King is not favourable.
7. Moon is in the Nakshatra of Rahu. Rahu is placed in eighth from Moon. Not favourable.

Nakshatra dispositor

Planet	Nakshatra Dispositor	Placement of Nakshatra dispositor from lagna	Placement of Nakshatra dispositor from Planet	Remarks
Sun	Jupiter	Trine	Second	Family and religion
Moon	Rahu	Eleventh	Eighth	Mental Problems
Mars	Moon	Kendra	Tenth	Action of Mars
Mercury	Mars	Seventh	Twelfth	Loss of intelligence
Jupiter	Mercury	Eighth	Twelfth	Loss of Dharam

Venus	Mars	Seventh	Together	Family concerns
Saturn	Mercury	Eighth	Fourth	Bad for family
Rahu	Moon	Fourth	Sixth	Accident, loss of home
Ketu	Mercury	Eighth	Fourth	Fatal accident

1. The Nakshatra dispositor of Sun is Jupiter and promotes Sun.
2. Mars is the Nakshatra dispositor of Mercury and Venus. Mars is the lord if fifth and tenth house and is Yoga karaka. Houses ruled by Mercury and Venus gains strength.

Final Dispositor

House	lord	Next D	Next D	Next D	Next D	Next D	Next D	Final D	Remark
First	Moon	Venus	Saturn	Mars	Saturn				Exchange
Second	Sun	Saturn	Mars	Saturn					Exchange
Third	Mercury	Saturn	Mars	Saturn					Exchange
Fourth	Venus	Saturn	Mars	Saturn					Exchange
Fifth	Mars	Saturn	Mars	Saturn					Exchange
Sixth	Jupiter	Jupiter						Jupiter	
Seventh	Saturn	Mars	Saturn						Exchange
Eighth	Saturn	Mars	Saturn						Exchange
Ninth	Jupiter	Jupiter						Jupiter	
Tenth	Mars	Saturn	Mars	Saturn					Exchange
Eleventh	Venus	Saturn	Mars	Saturn					Exchange
Twelfth	Mercury	Saturn	Mars	Saturn					Exchange

In this table, I use 'D" instead of Dispositor to make the words fit.

Only two houses are having final dispositor as Jupiter. These are sixth and ninth house. The person has no confusion regarding these two houses. It is revenge/ competition and religion. For other houses there is exchange of Mars and Saturn. Mars is Yoga karaka and Saturn is malefic.

Synthesis of Result

House	Lord	Dispositor of lord	Navamsha dispositor of lord	Remarks
First	Moon	Venus	Saturn	Saturn and Venus are afflicted.
Second	Sun	Saturn	Mercury	Mercury and Sun are in eighth house.
Third	Mercury	Saturn	Mars	Mars is exalted.
Fourth	Venus	Saturn	Mercury	Saturn and Mercury are afflicted.
Fifth	Mars	Saturn	Venus	Saturn and Venus are afflicted.
Sixth	Jupiter	Jupiter	Jupiter	Jupiter is the main planet of sixth house.
Seventh	Saturn	Mars	Saturn	Mars and Saturn are related to seventh house. Mars is exalted.
Eighth	Saturn	Mars	Saturn	Mars is exalted. Mars is serious maraca.
Ninth	Jupiter	Jupiter	Jupiter	Jupiter is the main planet. Very strongly attached to religion.
Tenth	Mars	Saturn	Venus	Both Saturn and Venus are afflicted.
Eleventh	Venus	Saturn	Mercury	Saturn and Mercury afflicted.
Twelfth	Mercury	Saturn	Mars	Saturn is afflicted. Mars is exalted.

1. Jupiter is the governing planet of sixth and ninth house.

In this chart ten houses are having Mars and Saturn as the dispositor of house lord and the Navamsha lord of the house lord. He was a criminal who assassinated Martin Luther King in April 1968. The reason was his hatred for black people and upholding his religion.

Chapter 3
Shakat Yoga

It is normally said that presence of Shakat Yoga in a horoscope will cancel all other Yoga. Will it cancel good Yoga or bad Yoga? If it cancels a good Yoga, then why it is a Yoga and not a Dosha? When it cancels bad Yoga then only it can be a Yoga. It is also said that a stronger Yoga will suffer more with the presence of Shakat Yoga.

Formation of Yoga

Shakat Yoga is formed when Jupiter is in sixth or eighth house from Moon.

Another version is placement of all planets in Ascendant and seventh house. This is rarely found.

In a lunar month Jupiter will be in sixth or eighth house from Moon for appx. 4.5 days in 27.5 days of the month. All births in the world during these 4.5 days will have Shakat Yoga in their horoscopes. This is about 16 percent of all horoscopes.

In formation of this Yoga only Jupiter is considered and not any other natural benefic like Venus or Mercury is considered.

Classic results

1. Person born in Shakat Yoga will have a bad childhood, will suffer mental stress and will be unlucky.

2. He will have a bad wife, suffer hatred from relations and is unpopular among friends.
3. All other Yoga will be cancelled.

   Shakat means a cart. Some classic says that a person with Shakat Yoga will be a cart driver. In present days it can mean a pilot. **He can be a driving force for the society. He can be a leader of the masses.**

Cancellation

1. When Mars is aspecting Moon then it is cancelled.
2. Moon or Jupiter is in Kendra from Ascendant.
3. Moon is in conjunction with Venus.
4. Mercury and Venus are in third, sixth, seventh, eighth, tenth or eleventh house from Moon.
5. Moon is in the signs of Mercury or Venus and Mercury and Venus are in Cancer.
6. When Rahu/ Ketu is with Jupiter.

Discussion

1. The potency of Shakat Yoga will depend on the Paksha Bala of Moon. The Moon can be waxing or waning.
2. When Moon is conjoined with a planet and is aspected by a planet then the significations of Moon get modified. For example, if Mercury is with Moon and aspected by Mars, can give perverted intelligence.
3. Association of Rahu/ Ketu in Shakat Yoga gives problems to child and wife.
4. The strength of Moon and Jupiter is of prime importance. When Jupiter and/or Moon are in their exaltation or in own

sign then this is no longer Shakat Yoga. **This is now a Mukut Yoga.** Mukut Yoga is very beneficial and gives all achievements in life. The strength of Mukut Yoga depends on the strength of Jupiter and Moon. When both are strong then it is best form of Mukut Yoga.

5. Mukut Yoga is found in the horoscopes of great saints and highly placed achievers. Jupiter or Moon is found associated with Saturn in the horoscope of saints. Relation of Saturn gives detachment.

6. The next important consideration is the condition of dispositor of Jupiter and Moon. A strong dispositor will boost the results of the planet. When the dispositor is same planet for both, then the results are uniform. When the dispositors are not friendly to each other then, the results are not uniform and tends to give bad results.

7. Presence of Shakat Yoga will enhance the bad effects of bad Yoga. The effects of good Yoga are not experienced fully. When it is cancelled then these are not experienced.

   We examine the Shakat Yoga for different placement of Moon and Jupiter. The remarks given are subjected to cancellation or modification in the horoscope.

Table

Sr. No.	Sign of Moon	Sign of Jupiter	Remarks
1	Aries	Virgo	Shakat
2	Aries	Scorpio	Shakat
3	Taurus	Libra	Shakat
4	Taurus	Sagittarius	Mukut
5	Gemini	Scorpio	Shakat
6	Gemini	Capricorn	Shakat
7	Cancer	Sagittarius	Mukut
8	Cancer	Aquarius	Mukut
9	Leo	Capricorn	Shakat
10	Leo	Pisces	Mukut
11	Virgo	Aquarius	Shakat
12	Virgo	Aries	Shakat
13	Libra	Pisces	Mukut
14	Libra	Taurus	Shakat
15	Scorpio	Aries	Shakat
16	Scorpio	Gemini	Shakat
17	Sagittarius	Taurus	Shakat
18	Sagittarius	Cancer	Mukut
19	Capricorn	Gemini	Shakat
20	Capricorn	Leo	Shakat
21	Aquarius	Cancer	Mukut
22	Aquarius	Virgo	Shakat
23	Pisces	Leo	Shakat
24	Pisces	Libra	Shakat

Example Ma Anandmayi DOB 1 May 1896 TOB 03.02 POB Kheora Bangla Desh

Birth Chart

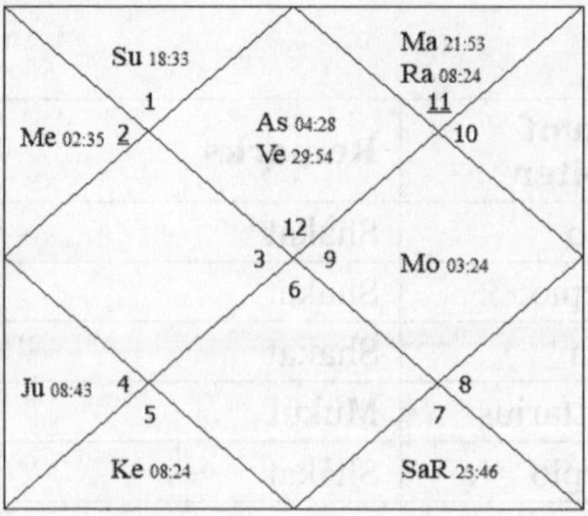

Birth Chart

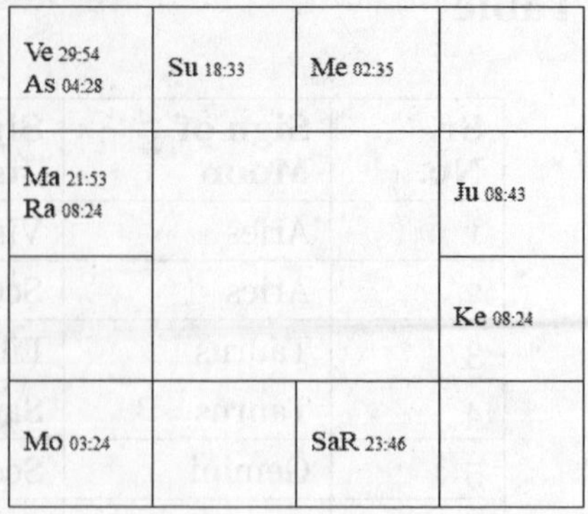

1. Jupiter is exalted.
2. Moon and Jupiter have exchanged sign.
3. Moon is strong in Paksha Bala.
4. Moon is in Kendra and Shakat Yoga is cancelled.
5. This Yoga is now Mukut Yoga.
6. Saturn is aspecting Jupiter and Moon. She was a great saint.
7. Five planets are Karaka planets.

Example Paramhans Yoganand DOB 5 January 1893 TOB 20.38 POB Gorakhpur UP

Birth Chart

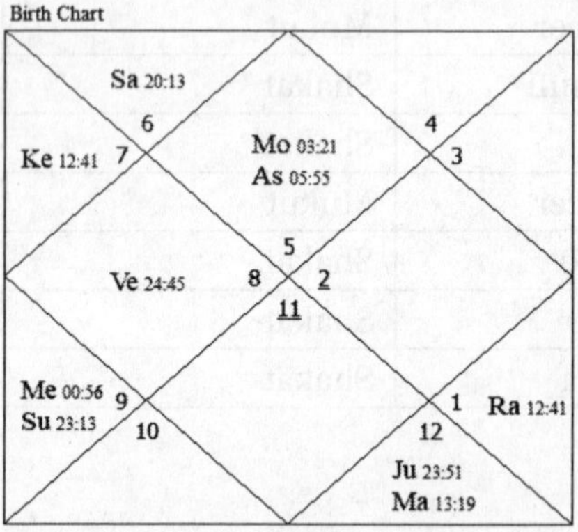

Birth Chart

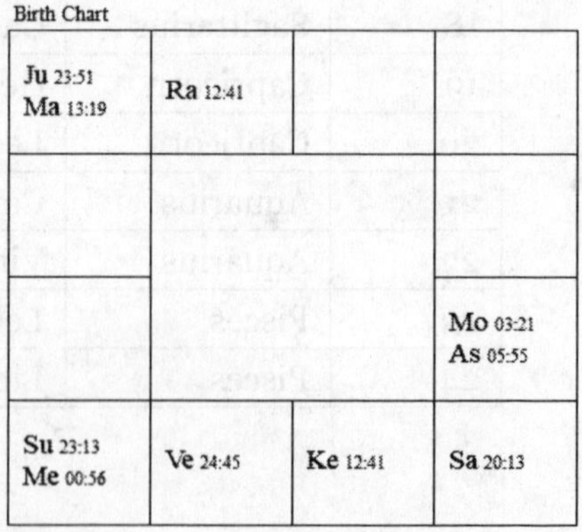

1. Jupiter is in own sign Pisces.

2. Moon is in sign of a friend.
3. Moon is having Paksha Bala.
4. Moon is in Kendra. Shakat Yoga is cancelled.
5. This is Mukut Yoga.
6. Saturn is aspecting Jupiter. He was a great saint.
7. Mars is conjunct with Jupiter.

Example Aurobindo DOB 15 August 1872 TOB 4.50 POB Calcutta

Birth Chart

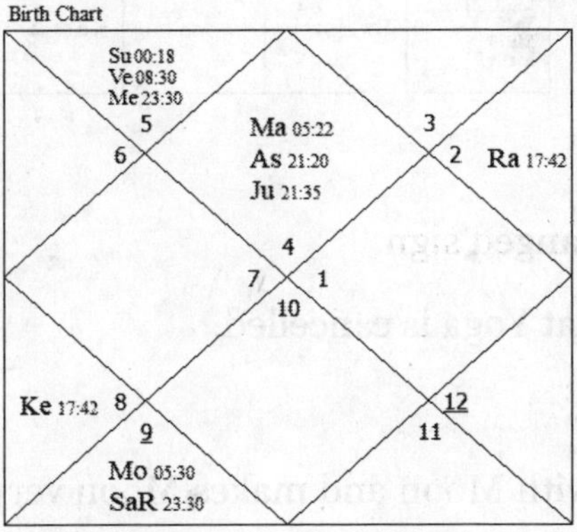

Birth Chart

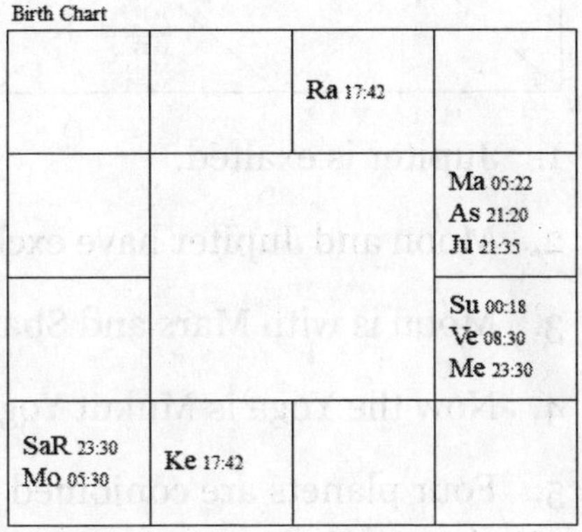

1. Jupiter and Moon have exchanged sign.
2. Jupiter is exalted.
3. Jupiter is in lagna. Shakat Yoga is cancelled.
4. This is Mukut Yoga.
5. Moon is having Paksha Bala.
6. Saturn is with Moon and Mars is with Jupiter.
7. Moon is with Saturn, but it is not aspected by any planet.
8. He was a great saint.

Example Rajneesh DOB 11 December 1931 TOB 17.19 POB Kuchwada

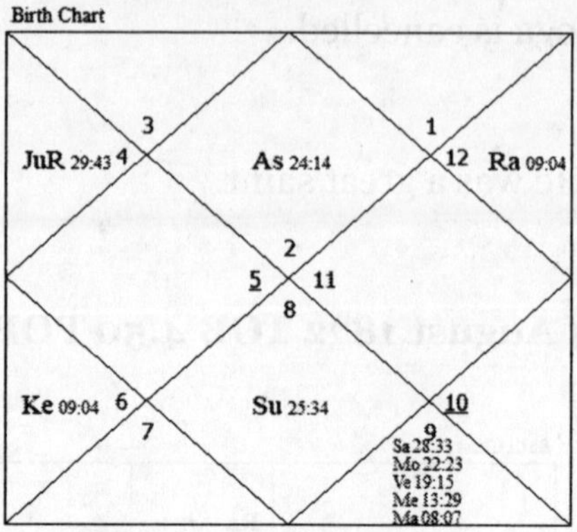

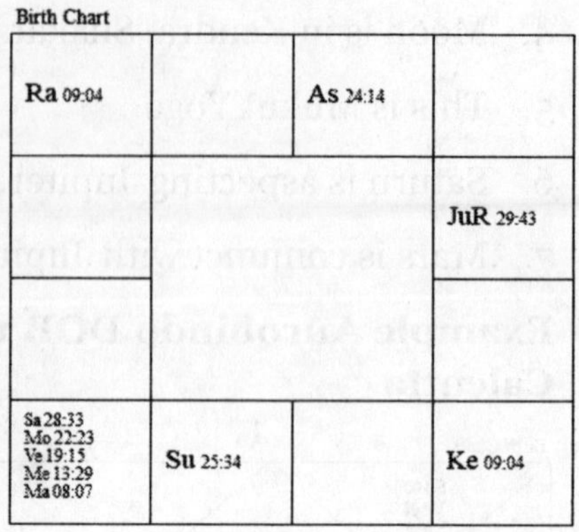

1. Jupiter is exalted.
2. Moon and Jupiter have exchanged sign.
3. Moon is with Mars and Shakat Yoga is cancelled.
4. Now the Yoga is Mukut Yoga.
5. Four planets are conjoined with Moon and makes Moon very strong.
6. Moon is not aspected by any planet. The association of planets with Moon and presence of Shakat Yoga gives some perversion about the signification of these planets.

Example Jawahar Lal Nehru DOB 14 November 1889 TOB 23.36 POB Allahabad

Birth Chart

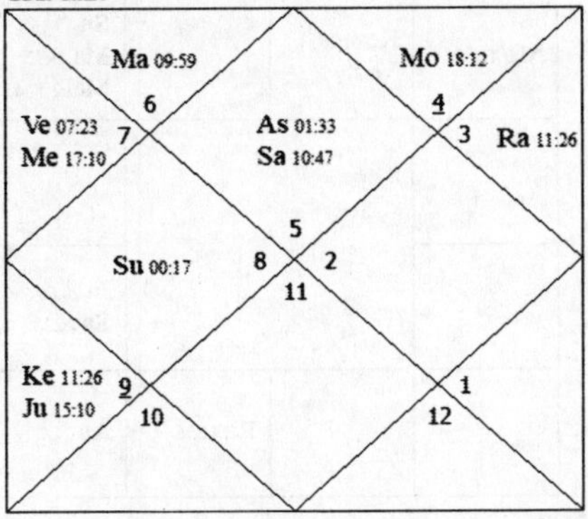

Birth Chart

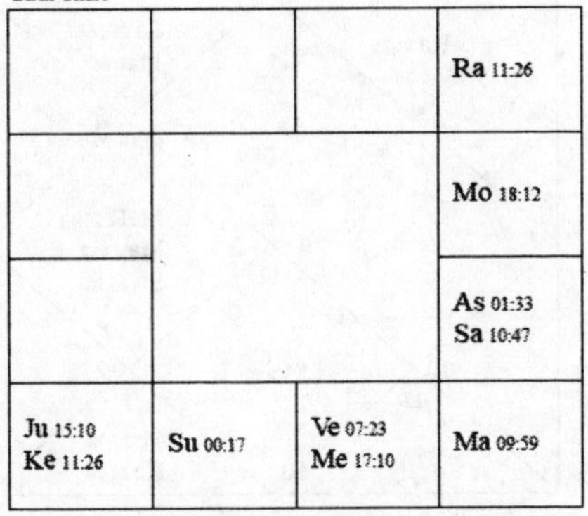

1. This horoscope is taken from Astro data bank. The most used lagna is cancer. The presence of Shakat is there from both lagna.

2. In this horoscope also, Moon and Jupiter are in own signs.

3. This is Mukut Yoga.

4. Moon is in Papa Kartari and Jupiter is with Ketu and aspected by Mars. It is cancellation of Shakat Yoga.

5. Saturn is not related to Moon or Jupiter. Therefore, it not a chart of a saint but a politician and a Prime Minister.

6. Ketu is with Jupiter in fifth house of intelligence and children.

7. Association of Rahu/ Ketu in Shakat Yoga gave problems to child and wife.

Example PVN Rao DOB 28 June 1921 TOB 13.02 POB Warangal

Birth Chart

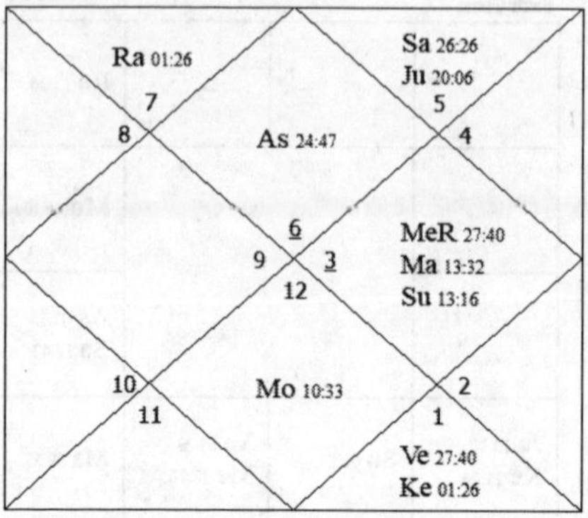

Birth Chart

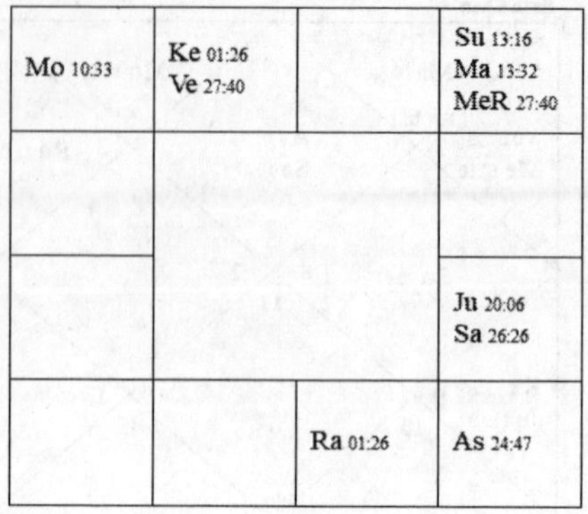

1. This is a chart of a Prime Minister.
2. Jupiter is with Saturn in a friendly sign.
3. Moon is in Kendra and Shakat Yoga is cancelled.
4. We can rate this as Mukut Yoga.
5. Rahu or Ketu are not related with Moon or Jupiter.

Example Mayavati DOB 15 January 1956 TOB 19.50 POB Delhi

Birth Chart

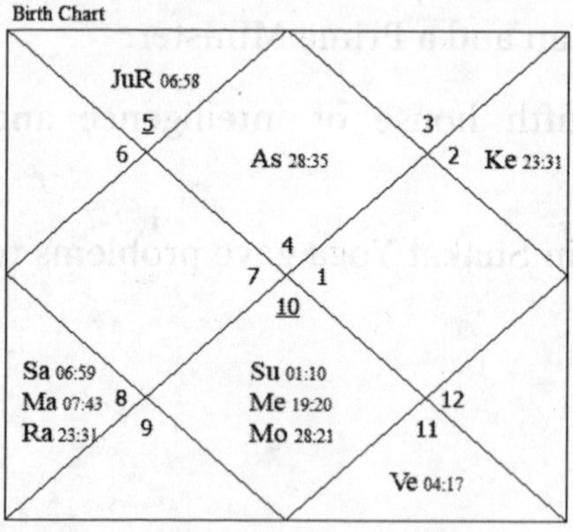

Birth Chart

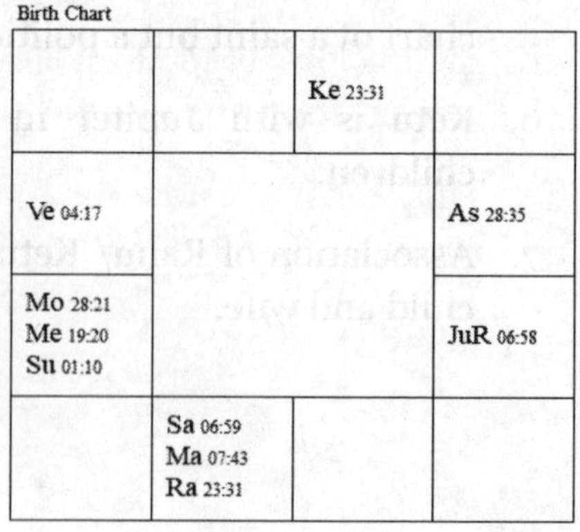

1. Moon is weak in Paksha Bala.
2. Shakat Yoga is cancelled by location of Moon in seventh house.
3. Moon is with Mercury and Sun. it is aspected by Saturn. The perversion of the traits of Sun and Mercury can be present.
4. Three malefic are in fifth house and makes third house very strong. This gives extra ordinary courage.

Example Jean Pierre Raffarin DOB 3 August 1948 TOB 03.00 POB Poitiers

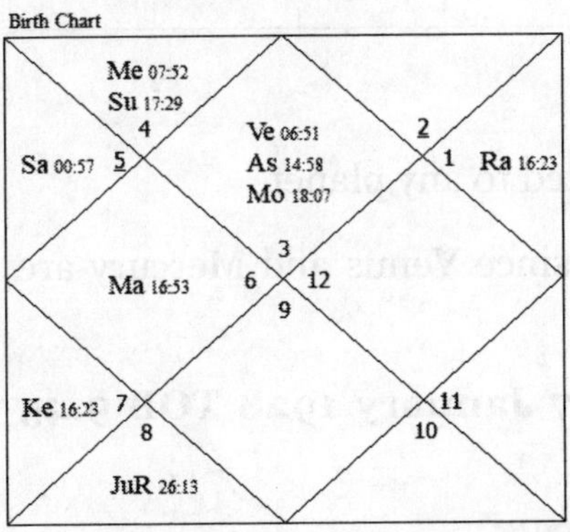

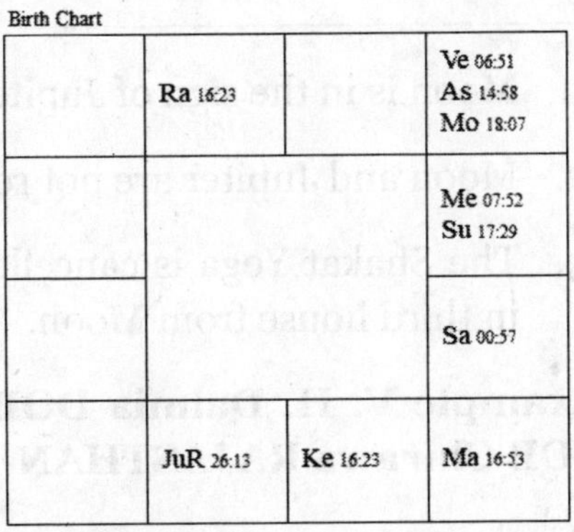

1. He was Prime Minister of France from 2002 to 2005.
2. Eighth lord is in third house and causes a strong Yoga to give position and wealth.
3. This was not hampered by the presence of Shakat Yoga as it is cancelled. Moon is in Kendra.
4. Moon is with Venus and Shakat Yoga is cancelled.

Example Guru Golwalkar DOB 19 February 1906 TOB 4.34 POB Nagpur

Birth Chart

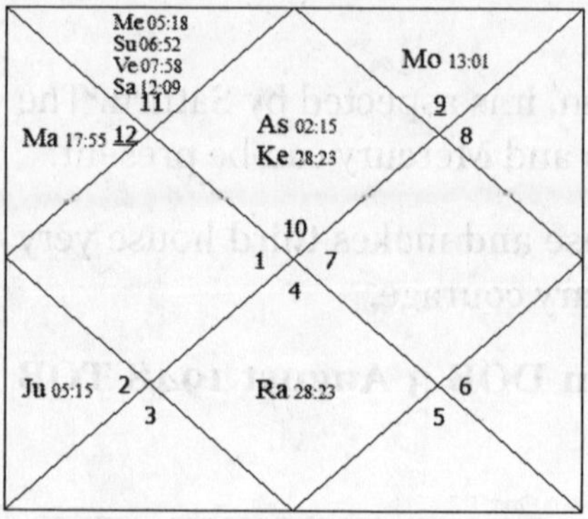

Birth Chart

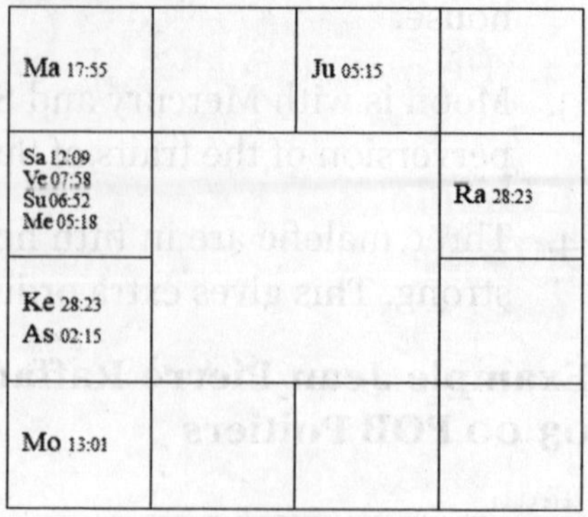

1. Moon is in the sign of Jupiter.
2. Moon and Jupiter are not related to any planet.
3. The Shakat Yoga is cancelled since Venus and Mercury are in third house from Moon.

Example V. H. Dalmia DOB 17 January 1928 TOB 9.45 POB Chirawa RAJASTHAN

Birth Chart

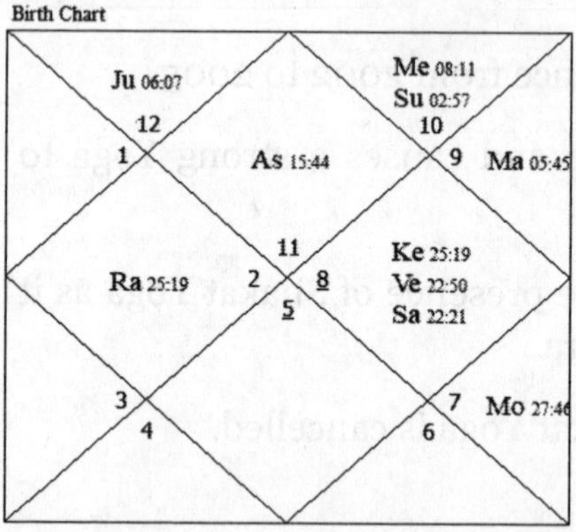

Birth Chart

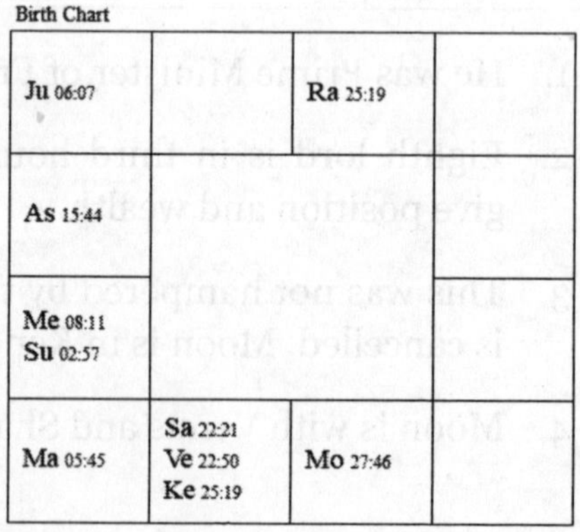

1. Jupiter is in own sign Pisces.

2. Jupiter and Mars are in mutual Kendra in the sign of Jupiter and is a Karaka Yoga.
3. Shakat Yoga has not destroyed Karaka Yoga.
4. He was an industrialist and established a big business empire.

Example Bill Gates DOB 28 October 1955 TOB 21.15 POB Seattle Washington

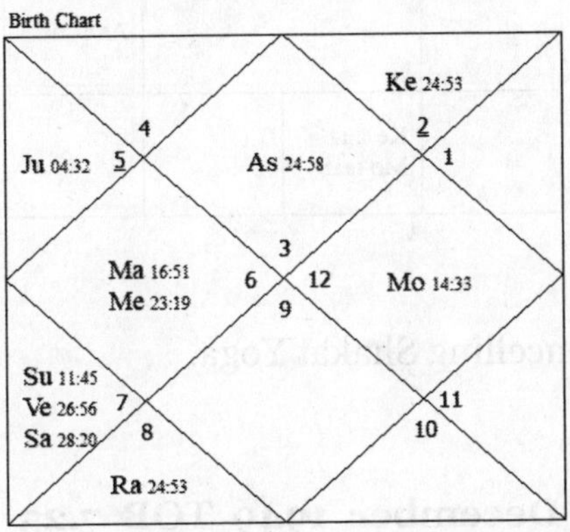

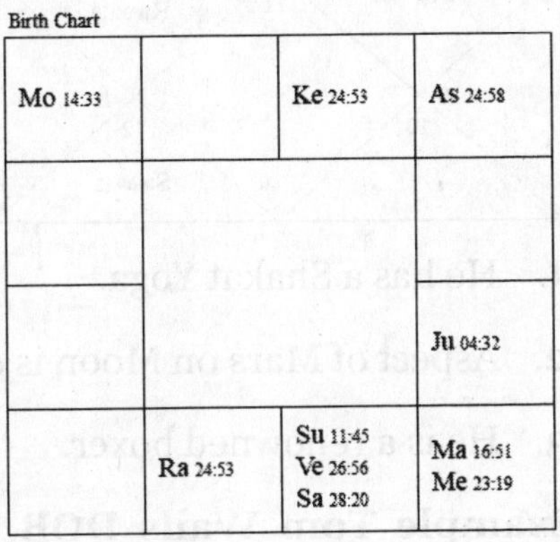

1. Moon is in the sign of Jupiter.
2. Jupiter is in Leo and have no aspect.
3. Moon is aspected by Mars and Mercury. The Shakat Yoga is cancelled.
4. He is the wealthiest person of world.

Example Mike Tyson DOB 30 June 1966 TOB 9.40 POB New York

Birth Chart

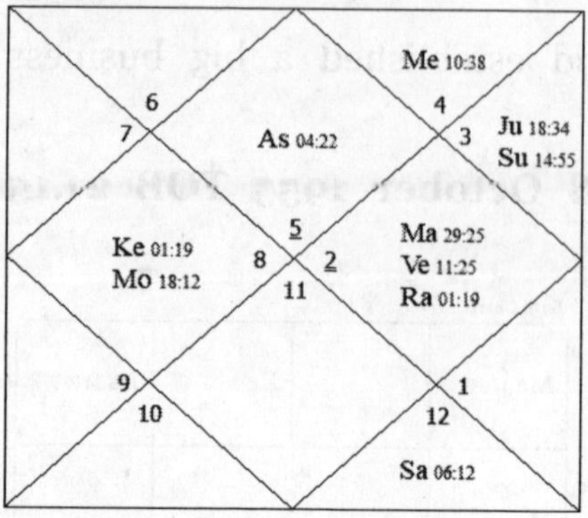

Birth Chart

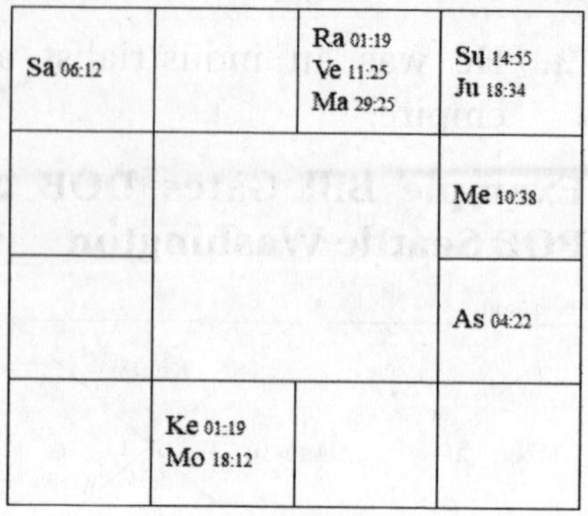

1. He has a Shakat Yoga.
2. Aspect of Mars on Moon is cancelling Shakat Yoga.
3. He is a renowned boxer.

Example Tom Wails DOB 7 December 1949 TOB 7.25 POB Pomona California

Birth Chart

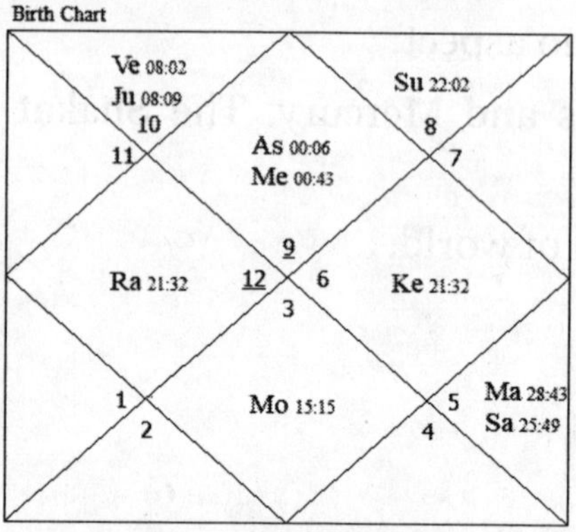

Birth Chart

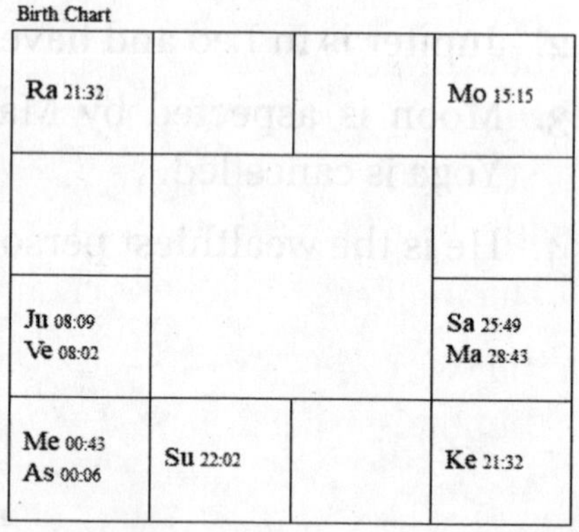

1. Jupiter is debilitated.
2. The debilitation of Jupiter is cancelled as Moon is in Kendra.

3. Mercury is in seventh and Venus is in eighth from Moon and the Shakat Yoga is cancelled.
4. Jupiter is with Venus.
5. He is an actor, singer and composer.

Example Surya Bonaly DOB 15 December 1973 TOB 0.25 POB Nice France

Birth Chart

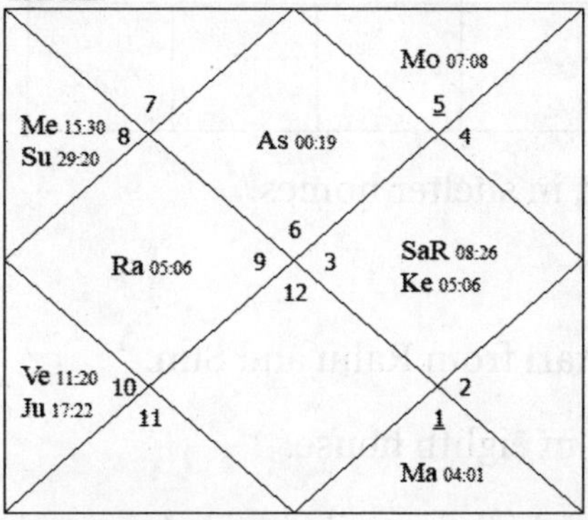

Birth Chart

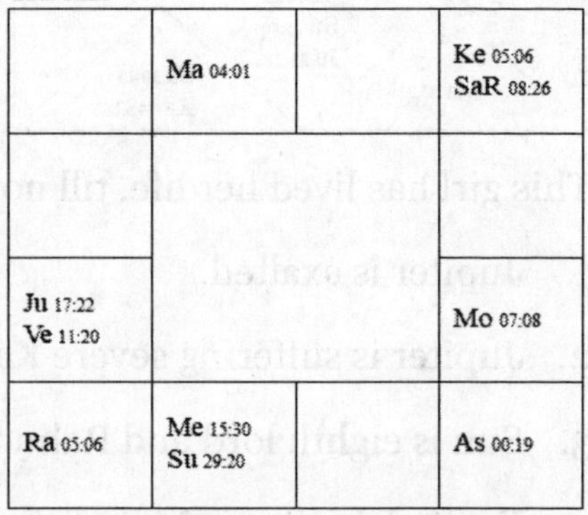

This chart belongs to an Olympic skater. She is the only athlete in the world who could perform back flip on one blade. She is five-time champion in world events.

She was left in an orphanage and was adopted at the age of eight months.

1. Her Jupiter is debilitated but with cancellation.
2. Jupiter is with Venus.
3. Jupiter is aspecting Ascendant causing a Yoga.
4. Moon is aspected by Saturn giving her concentration.

Example Name withheld DOB 9 August 1979 TOB 18.20 POB Sangli

Birth Chart

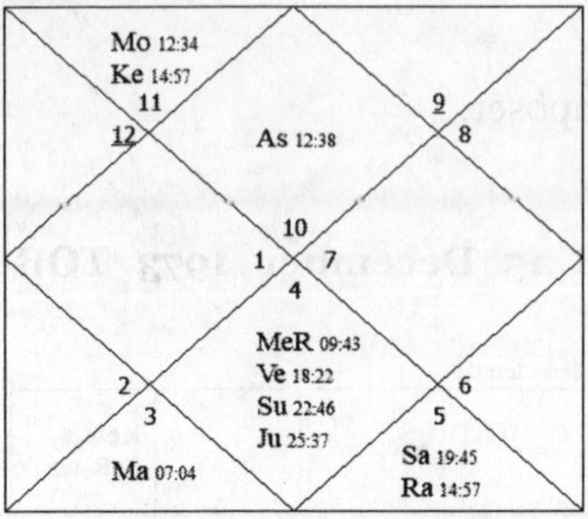

Birth Chart

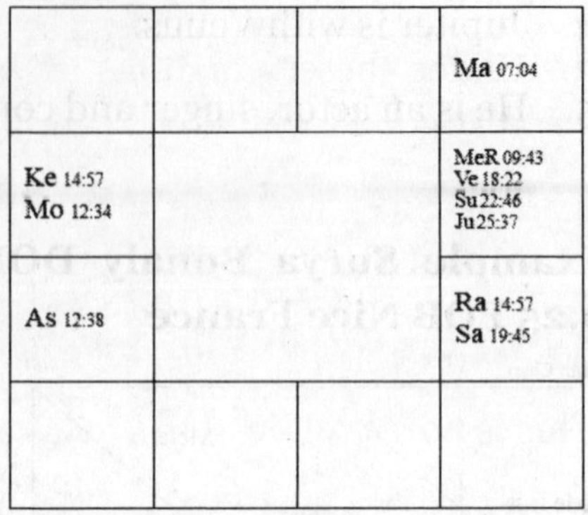

This girl has lived her life, till now, in shelter homes.

1. Jupiter is exalted.

2. Jupiter is suffering severe Kartari from Rahu and Sun.

3. Sun is eighth lord and Rahu is in eighth house.

4. Exalted Jupiter is Mukut Yoga which is spoiled.

5. Three benefics are in Kendra and Ketu is in second house is the reason of poverty.

Shakat Yoga in Divisional charts

Shakat Yoga finds a very useful application in divisional charts. The Paksha Bala and the strength of Jupiter is important.

1. We can check the Paksha Bala of Moon in a divisional chart. This is done by noting the position of Moon from Sun in the divisional chart. This will be specific for the chart under consideration.

2. Jupiter gains strength when it is exalted, in own sign, friendly sign or associated with its dispositor in divisional chart.

3. Under these situations, it becomes Mukut Yoga and gives very good results.

4. Dashamsha is seen for position and fame. The presence of Mukut Yoga will give good position and fame to the person.

5. We can consider this in other divisional charts also.

This is now explained in practical examples.

Example Barack Obama DOB 4 August 1961 TOB 19.24 POB Honolulu HI

Birth Chart

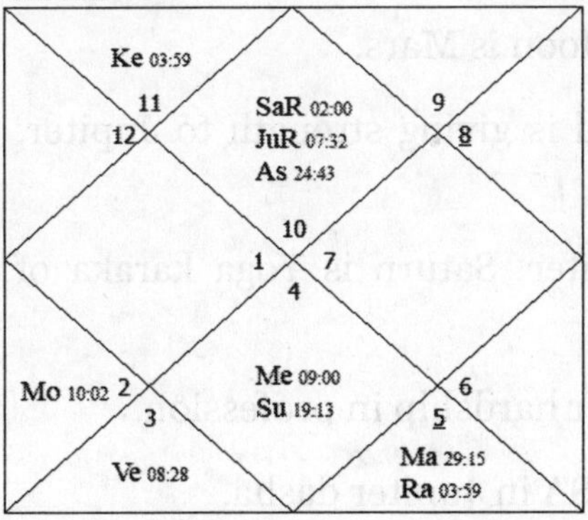

Birth Chart

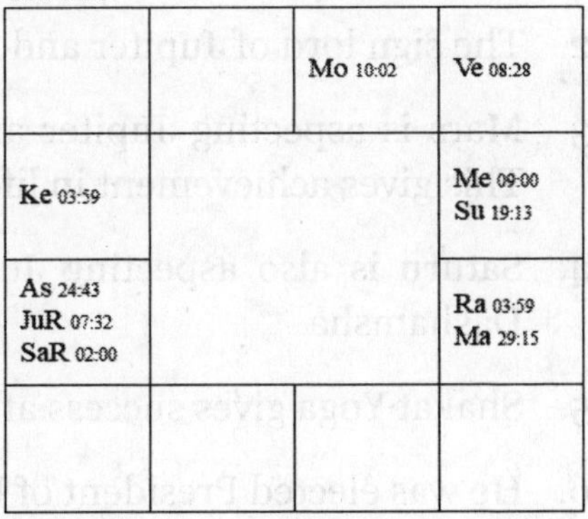

D10 Dashamsha (great successes)

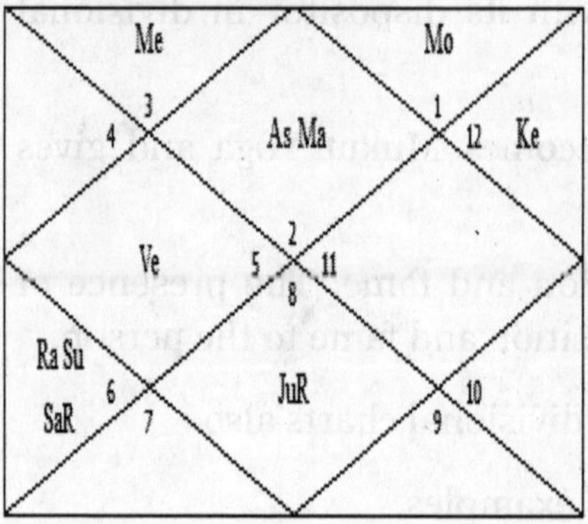

D10 Dashamsha (great successes)

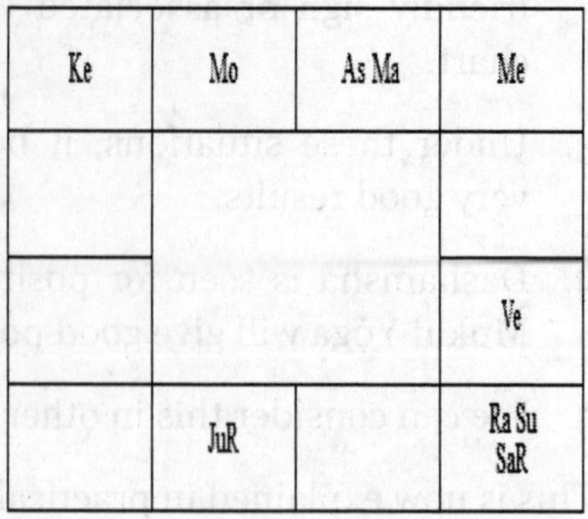

1. Shakat Yoga is not present in birth horoscope. It is present in Dashamsha.
2. The sign lord of Jupiter and Moon is Mars.
3. Mars is aspecting Jupiter and is giving strength to Jupiter. This gives achievement in life.
4. Saturn is also aspecting Jupiter. Saturn is Yoga karaka of Dashamsha.
5. Shakat Yoga gives success after hardship in profession.
6. He was elected President of USA in Jupiter dasha.

Example DOB 12 December 1940 TOB 7.31 POB Baramati

Birth Chart

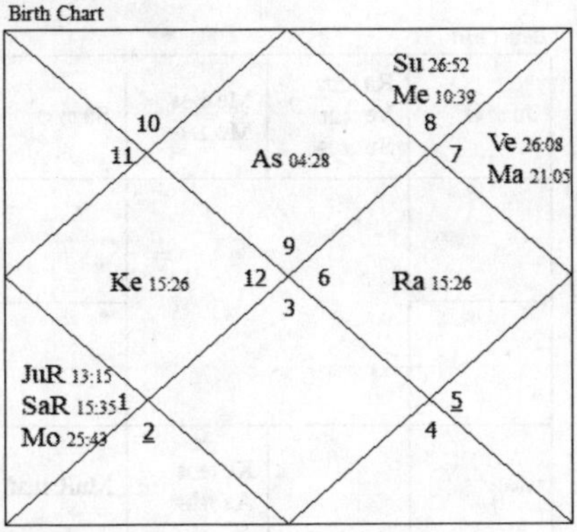

Birth Chart

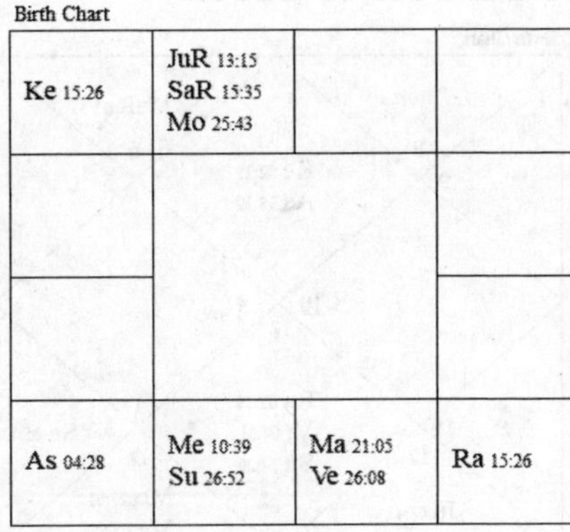

D12 Dwadashamsha (parents)

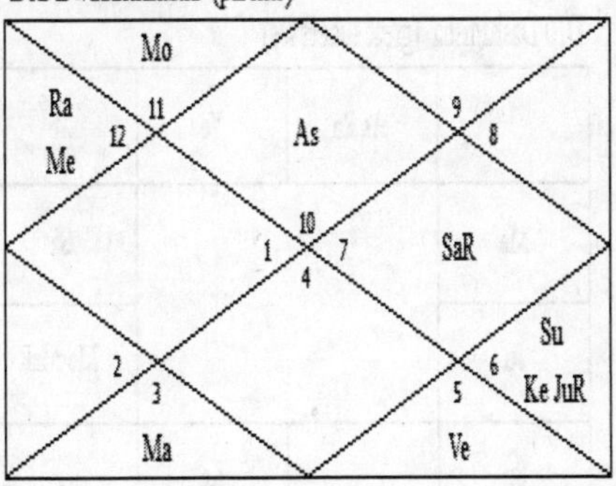

D12 Dwadashamsha (parents)

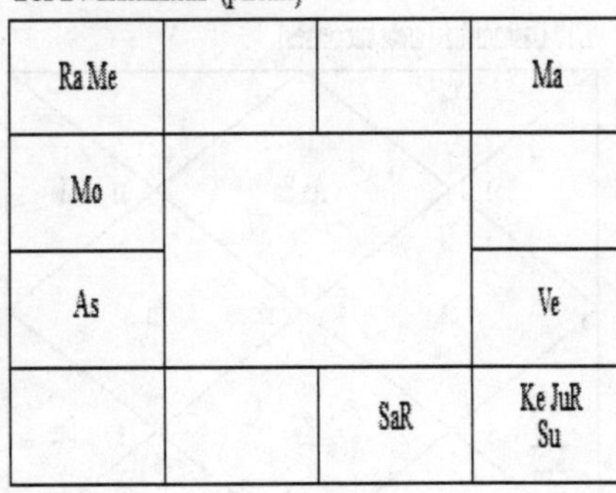

1. Shakat Yoga is present in Dwadamsha.
2. Sign lord of Moon is exalted.
3. Jupiter is with Sun and Ketu. The good thing is the aspect of Mercury on Jupiter. Mercury is the sign lord of Jupiter.
4. His father was an employee of a sugar cooperative in Maharashtra.
5. His parents were very religious.

Example Sigmond Freud DOB 6 May 1856 TOB 18.30 POB Pribor Czech

Birth Chart

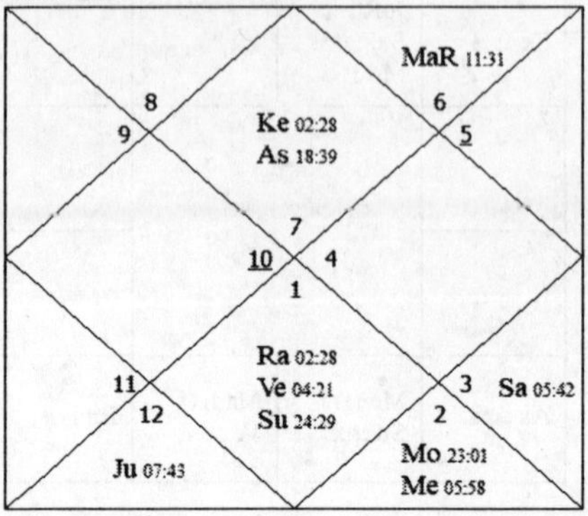

Birth Chart

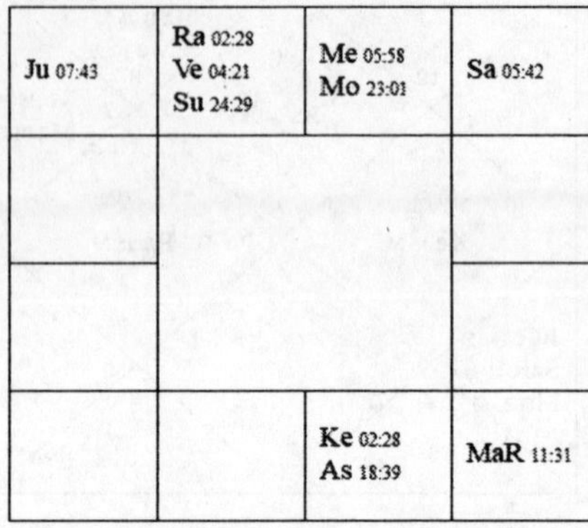

D10 Dashamsha (great successes)

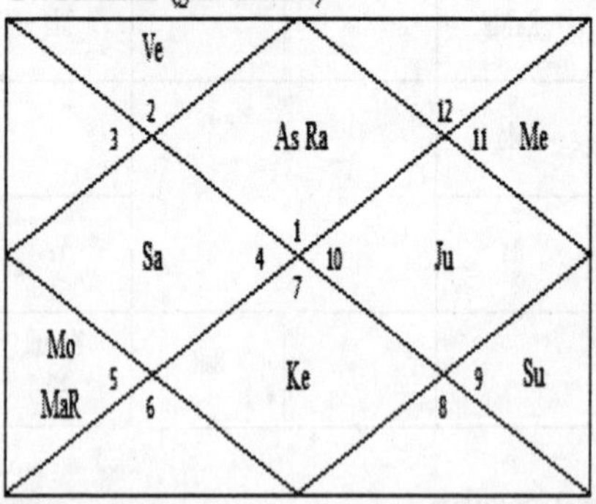

D10 Dashamsha (great successes)

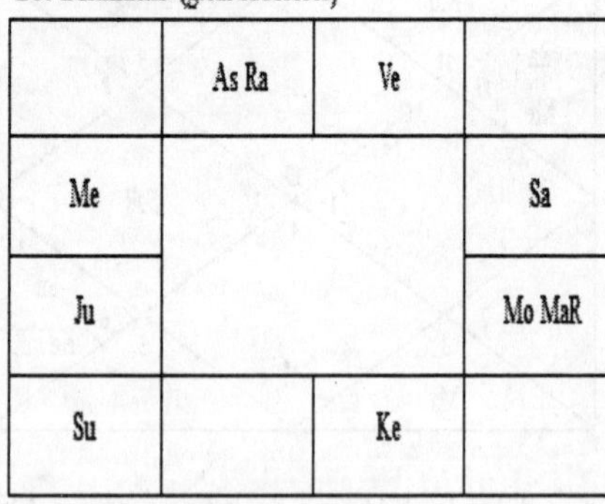

1. Shakat Yoga is present in Dashamsha and gives success after hard work.
2. Jupiter is aspected by its dispositor Saturn. This will give achievement in life.

Example Osho DOB 11 December 1931 TOB 17.19 POB Kuchwada

Birth Chart

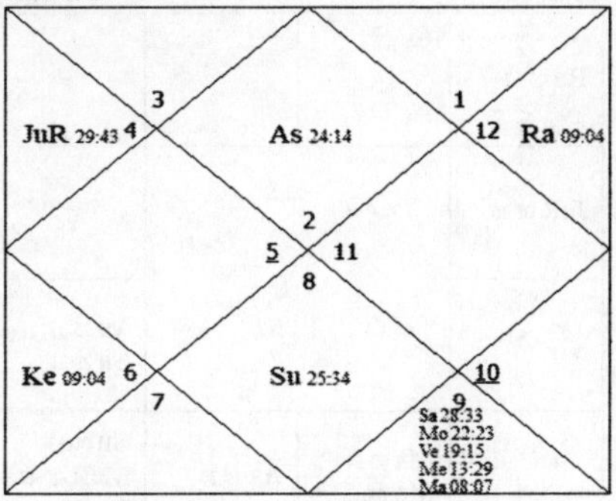

Birth Chart

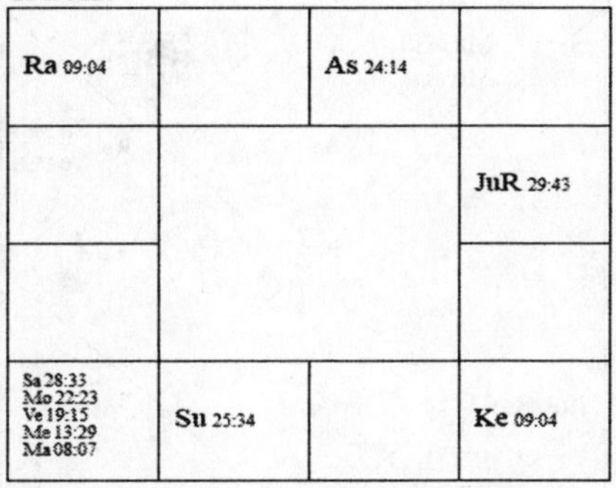

D9 Navamsha (spouse)

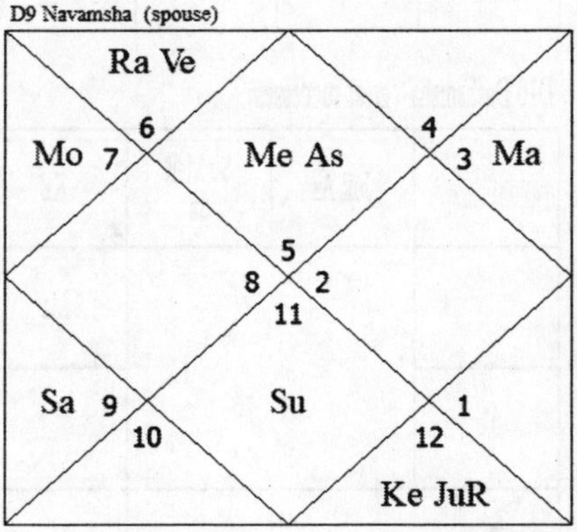

D9 Navamsha (spouse)

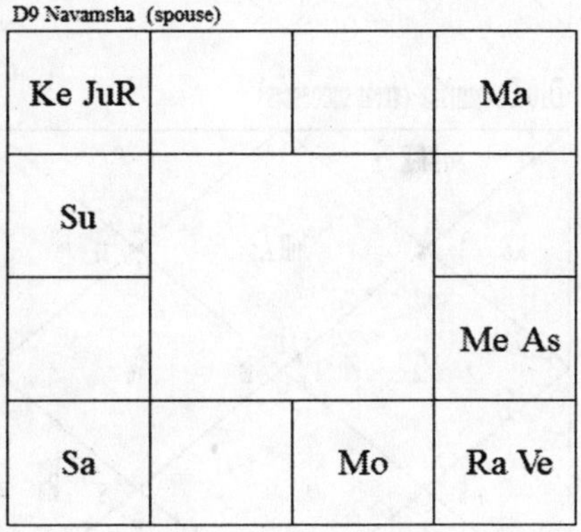

1. Shakat Yoga is in Navamsha.
2. Jupiter is placed in its own sign Pisces. It is with Ketu and aspected by debilitated Venus.
3. He was not married but progressed to create a new outlook of religion.
4. Venus is debilitated and Sun is aspecting lagna.

Example Modi DOB 17 September 1950 TOB 10.10 POB Vadnagar

Birth Chart

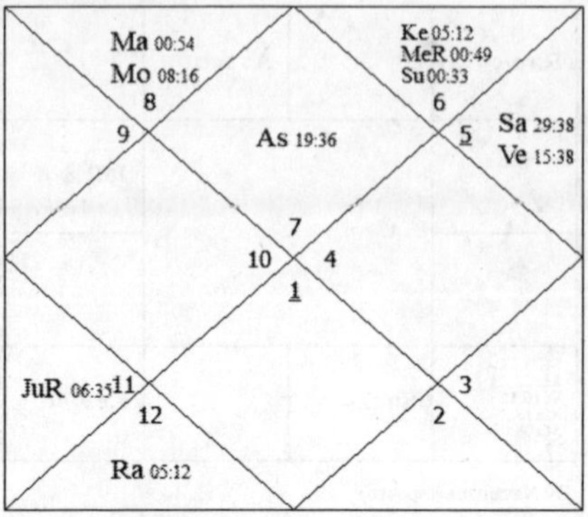

Birth Chart

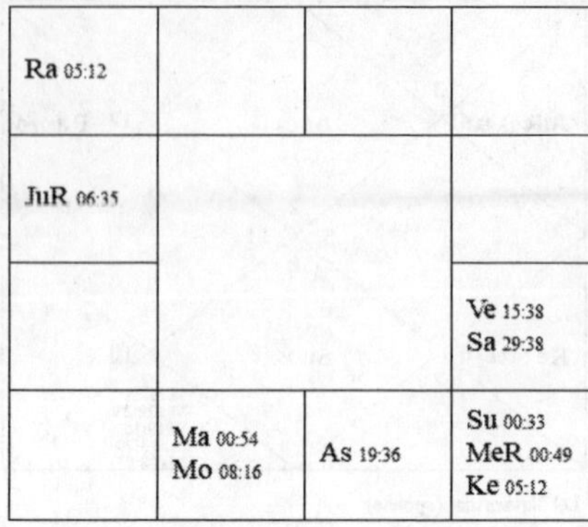

D10 Dashamsha (great successes)

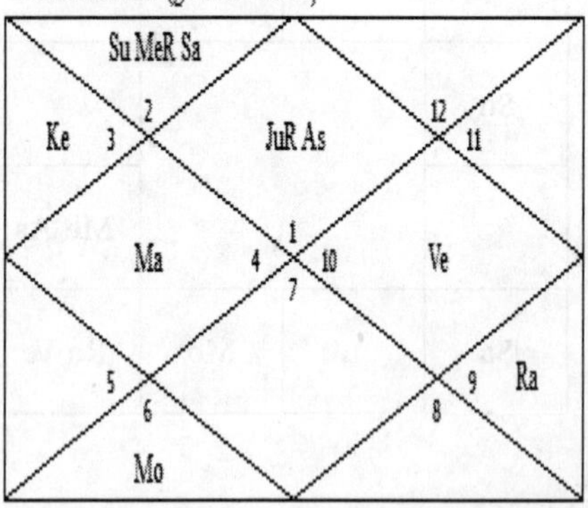

D10 Dashamsha (great successes)

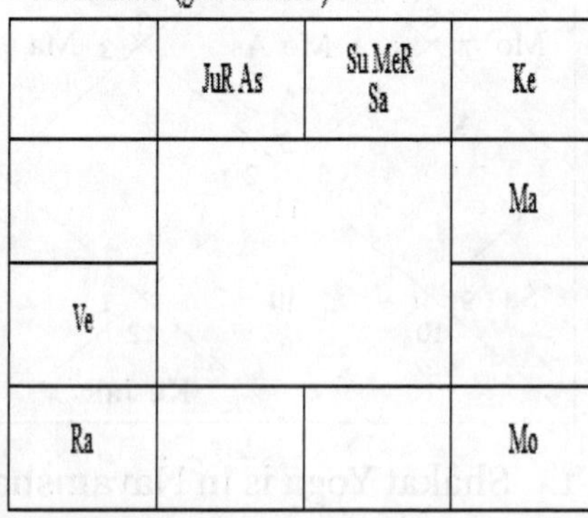

1. Presence of Shakat Yoga in Dashamsha gives success after hard work.
2. There is no malefic relation with Jupiter and the hardships can be overcome easily.
3. Moon is in the sign of Mercury. Moon also has no malefic relation, but Mercury is with malefic. This gives mental stress.

Example Donatella Versace DOB 2 May 1955 TOB 5.00 POB Reggio Di Calabria Italy

Birth Chart

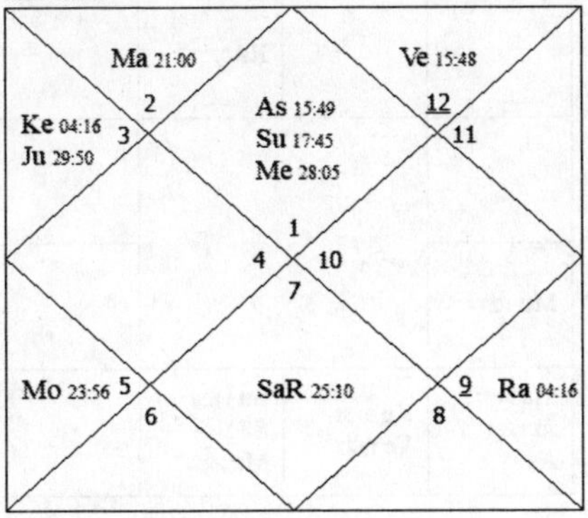

Birth Chart

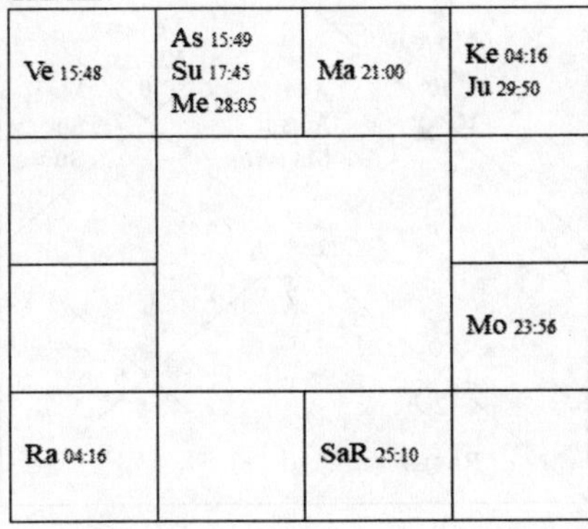

D9 Navamsha (spouse)

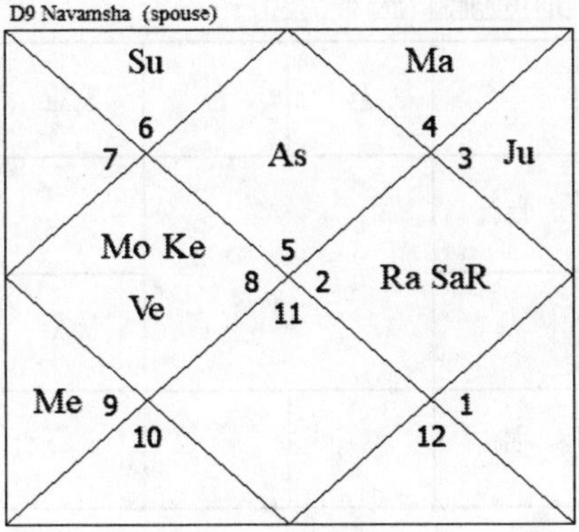

D9 Navamsha (spouse)

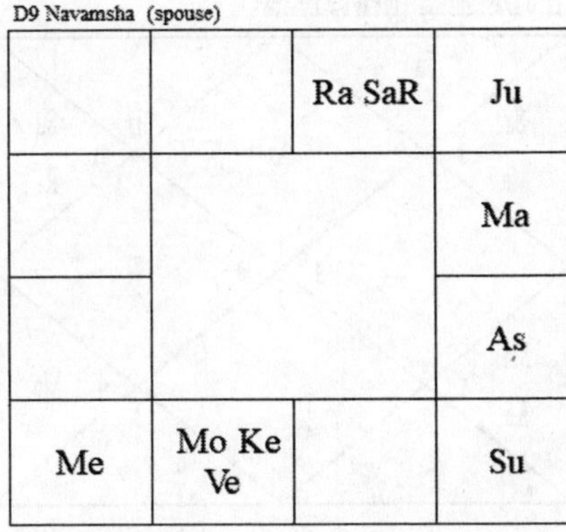

1. In Dashamsha, Jupiter is aspected by Mercury. It gives problems in relationship.

2. She was a renowned fashion designer.

3. Moon is with Ketu and aspected by Saturn. The dispositor of Moon is debilitated.

Example DOB 31 October 1984 TOB 11.05 POB Delhi

Birth Chart

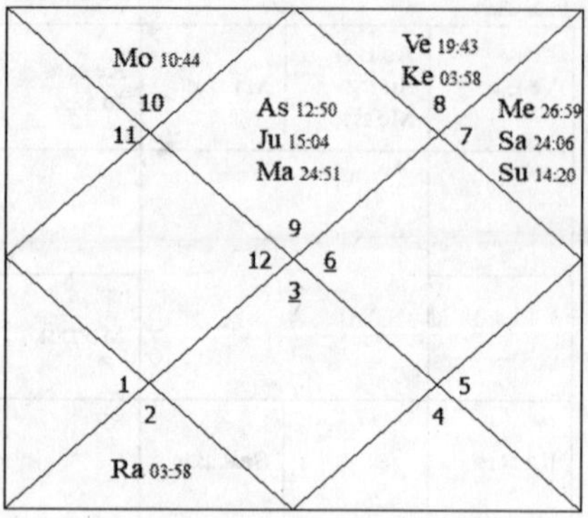

Birth Chart

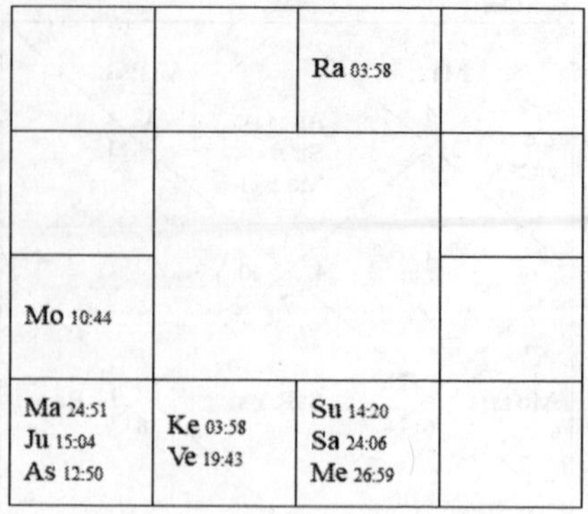

D10 Dashamsha (great successes)

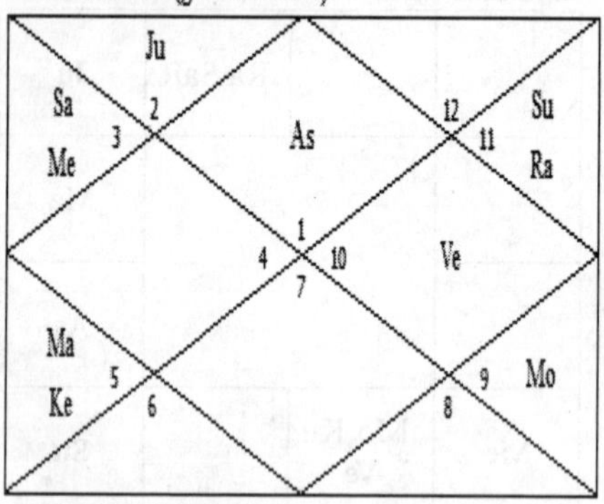

D10 Dashamsha (great successes)

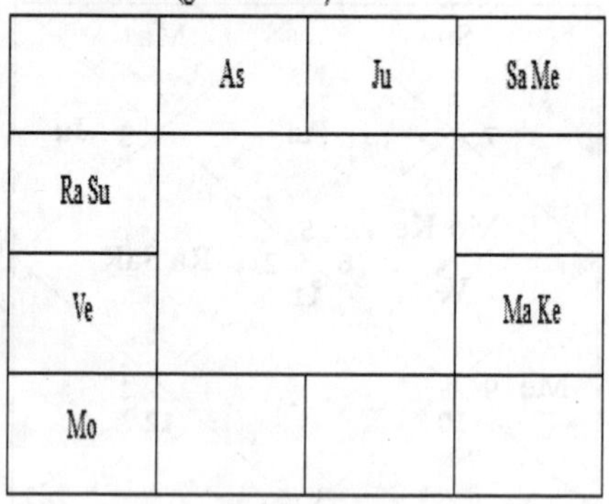

This horoscope belongs to a medical doctor. By his hard work he was selected for IPS and is a very senior officer.

1. Jupiter is the dispositor of Moon.
2. Jupiter is in sixth house from Moon and gives lot of effort.
3. Dispositor of Jupiter is well placed in tenth house.

Example Bose DOB 23 January 1897 TOB 12.00 POB Cuttack

Birth Chart

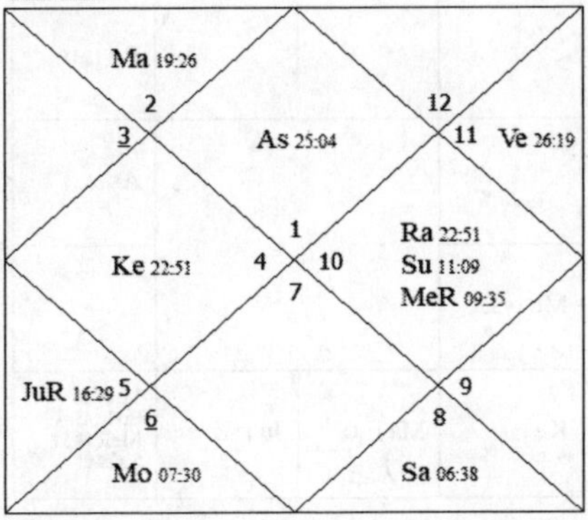

Birth Chart

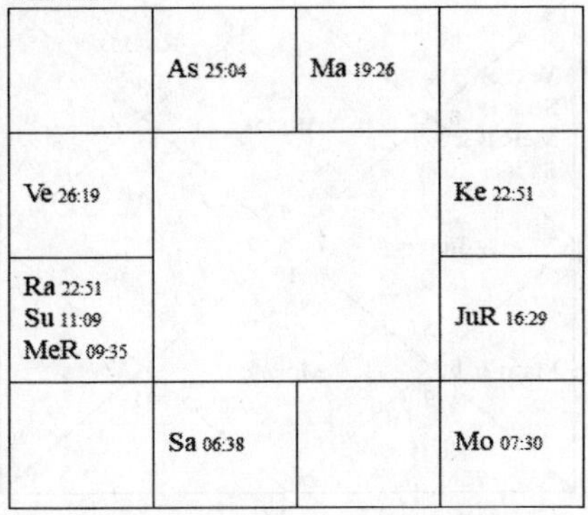

D7 Saptamsha (children)

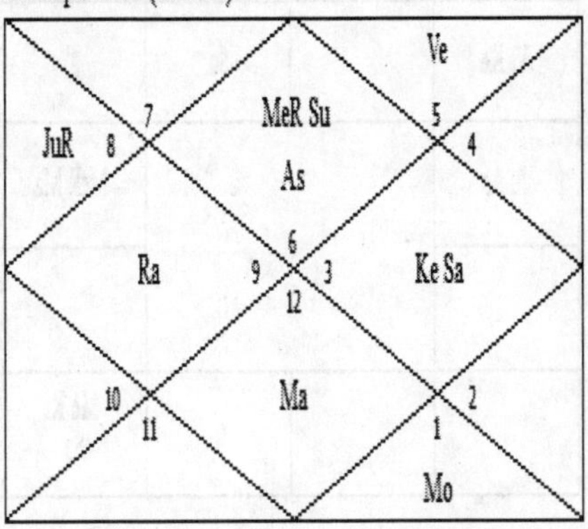

D7 Saptamsha (children)

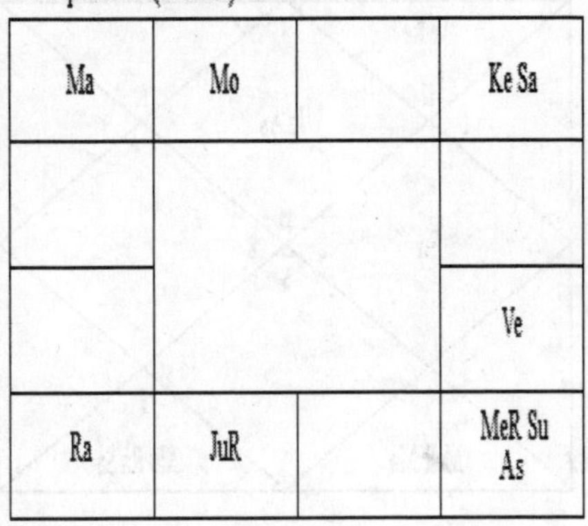

1. Shakat Yoga is in Saptamsha.
2. Mars is the sign lord of Jupiter and Moon.
3. It shows hard work for having children.
4. He had a daughter but could not meet her.

Example Bindra DOB 28 September 1982 TOB 01.10 POB Dehradun

Birth Chart

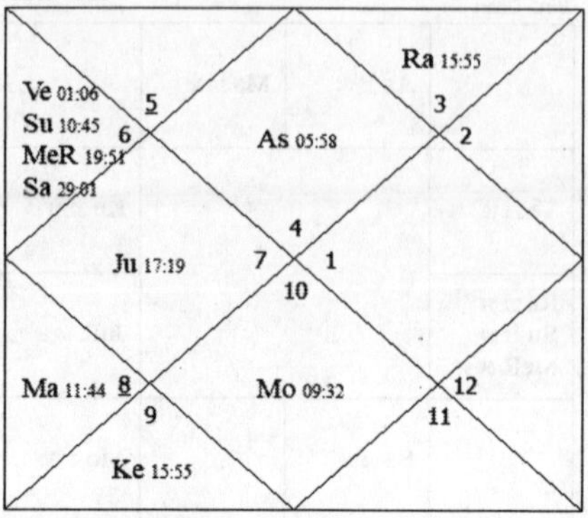

Birth Chart

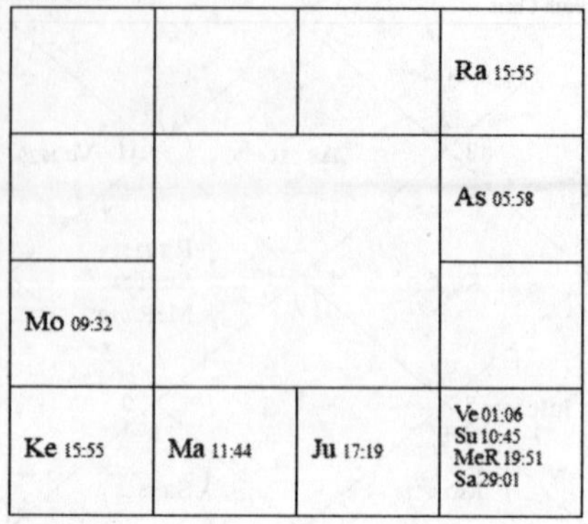

D7 Saptamsha (children)

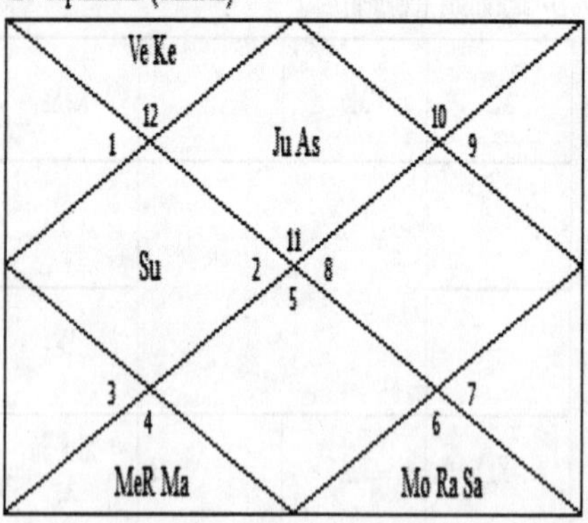

D7 Saptamsha (children)

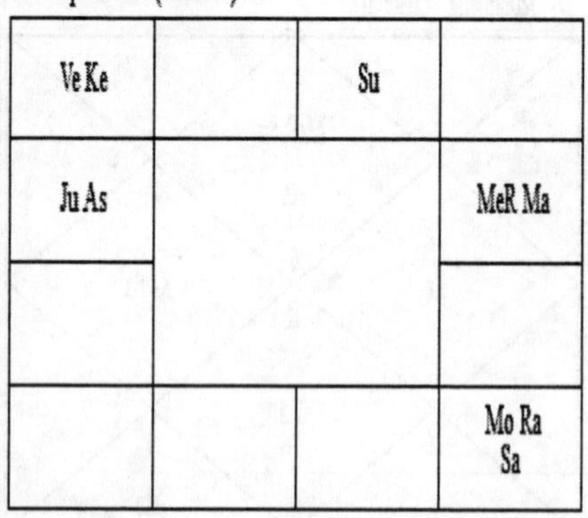

1. Shakat Yoga is present in Saptamsha.
2. Jupiter is Karaka of children and is in lagna.
3. Jupiter is aspected by Mars and have no other relation.
4. He is not married and have no children.

Example Amar Singh DOB 27 January 1956 TOB 6.40 POB Aligarh

Birth Chart

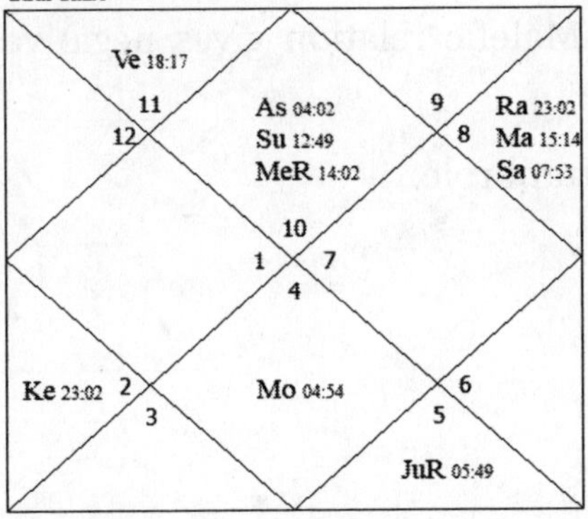

Birth Chart

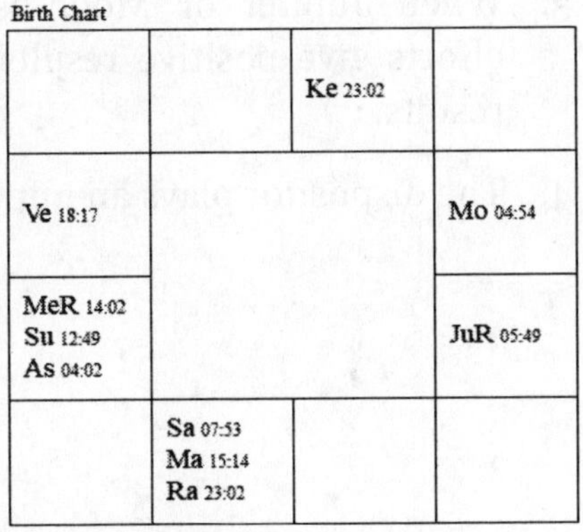

D6 Shashtamsha 1/6 Disease

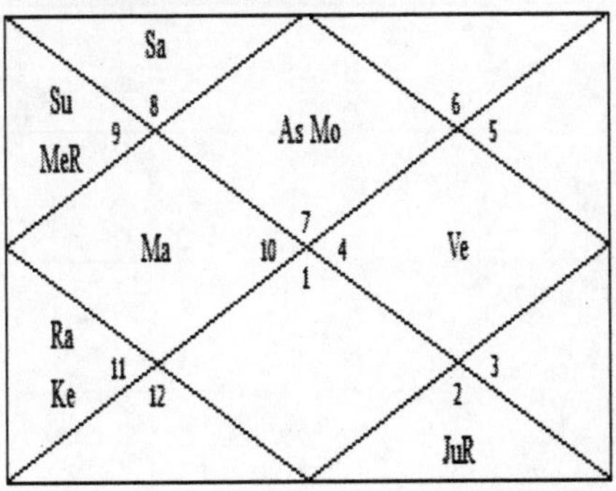

D6 Shashtamsha 1/6 Disease

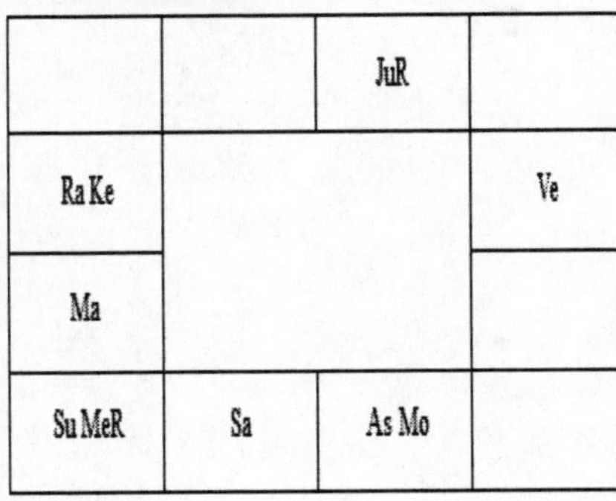

1. Shakat Yoga is present in Shashtamsha.
2. The sign lord of Jupiter and Moon is Venus.
3. Venus is afflicted by Mars.
4. He suffered from disease of Kidney.

Observation

1. Presence of Shakat Yoga in a divisional chart is important.

2. It indicates extra effort is required to handle the affairs of the concerned divisional chart.

3. When Jupiter or Moon is having benefic relations then efforts give positive results. Malefic relation gives negative results.

4. The dispositor plays an important role.

Chapter 4
Upchaya Houses

The literal meaning of Upchaya is to increase, nourish, improve and assimilate. These are houses of growth. The growth can be in good or bad direction. Some authors say that they are not always improving.

Brihat Jatak, Chapter 1

1. The sixth, tenth, eleventh and third houses are called Upchaya houses. If all the benefic planets Mercury, Jupiter and Venus occupy the Upchaya houses from ascendant at the time of birth, a person will become exceedingly wealthy; if the benefic planets will be found in the Upchaya houses from Moon, then the person becomes wealthy; if two benefic in these houses, less wealthy; if one then little wealthy. The effects take place in the face of other inauspicious results brought by other combinations. As such, the results in these houses are very strong.

Uttar Kalamrita (chapter 4)

1. Houses 3, 6, 10 and 11 from lagan are known as Upchaya houses. The sign where Moon is placed is the birth Rashi or Moon lagan. Note: It conveys the message to see the Upchaya houses from Moon also.

Phal Deepika

1. When all benefic planets are in third, sixth, tenth and eleventh house, which are Upchaya houses, then Vasuman Yoga is caused.

2. When all benefic planets are in third, sixth, tenth and eleventh house from Moon even then Vasuman Yoga is caused.

3. One who is born in Vasuman Yoga will stay at home and will be very wealthy.

Jatak Parijatham

1. Eminent astrologers say that third, sixth, tenth and eleventh houses are Upchaya houses. These houses if occupied or aspected by their lords or by Mercury, Jupiter or Venus, **but not occupied or aspected by others,** produce auspicious effects in birth horoscope.

2. If all the benefic planets be in Upchaya places and malefic in first or the tenth house, the person will be king quelling his numerous foes.

3. When lord of seventh house and Karaka of seventh house are in Upchaya houses then the person will be happy after marriage. Note; We can extend this principle to other lords and Karaka.

Summary

1. Third, sixth, tenth and eleventh houses from lagna or from Moon are Upchaya houses.

2. Third, sixth and eleventh houses are trishadaya houses. Their lords are malefic. Their placement in Upchaya houses will give good results.

3. Third house is the house of efforts. Sixth house is the house of determination, and eleventh house is of gains.

4. Tenth house is the house of Karma. When karma house is activated along with the houses of effort, determination and gains then the fruits of efforts are realized. **Without**

inclusion of tenth house these are not Upchaya houses.

5. Importance is given to the placement of planets in Upchaya house. We include Rahu and Ketu also in this consideration.
6. The lords of trishadaya are still malefic.
7. Even when malefic are placed in eleventh house then they also give growth.
8. Benefic give result with least effort and malefic need hard work.
9. Tenth house must have at least one planet. Other Upchaya houses are next.
10. More number of planets in Upchaya gives more wealth.
11. Upchaya indicates growth. The growth is relative to the birth circumstances.
12. Lord of a house and karaka of the house in Upchaya will promote a house.
13. Aspect of an Upchaya House lord on an Upchaya House promotes the house aspected.
14. Lord of one Upchaya House when related to other Upchaya house/ lord is good for growth of the house. This means that interconnection of Upchaya houses will promote the house.
15. The quality of Upchaya House increases if they are occupied or aspected by its lord, Venus, Mercury or Jupiter.
16. **According to Jatak Parijatham, these houses if occupied or aspected by their lords or by Mercury, Jupiter or Venus but not occupied or aspected by others produce auspicious effects in birth horoscope. When these are occupied or aspected by**

others then it will produce inauspicious results. This is an important factor to gauge the potency of results of Upchaya houses.

17. The concept of Upchaya can be applied in Divisional charts with success.

18. We can check Upchaya houses from Moon.

19. When the Ascendant lord is in Upchaya House from Moon and the Moon sign lord is in Upchaya House from Ascendant then the promise of horoscope increases manifold.

Example – DOB 30 April 1945, TOB 9.27 IST (10.27 war time), POB Delhi

Birth Chart

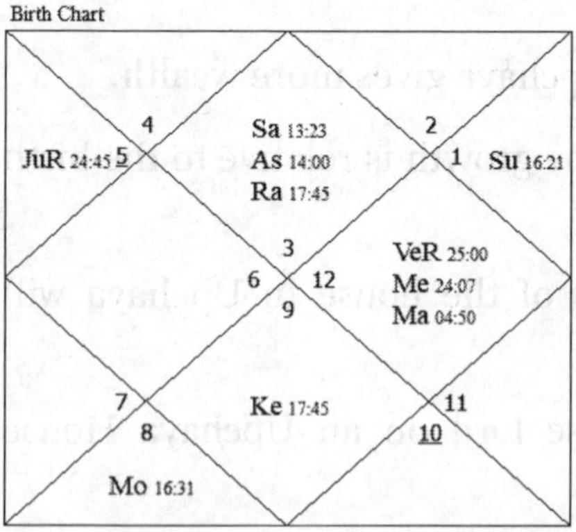

Birth Chart

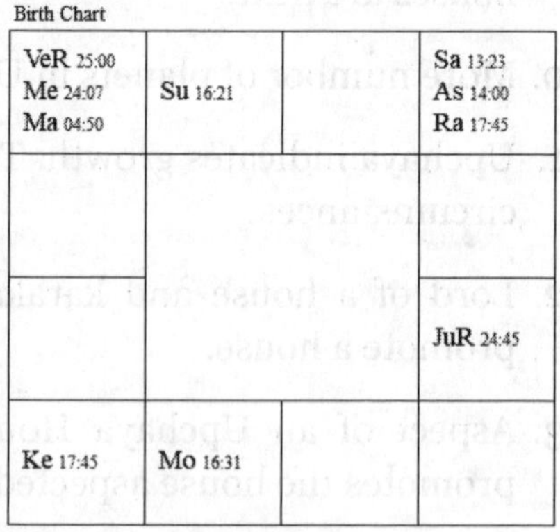

1. All four Upchaya houses from lagan are occupied.
2. Third lord is in eleventh house.
3. Sixth and eleventh lord is in tenth house.
4. Tenth lord is in third house.
5. All Upchaya houses are interconnected. There are five planets in Upchaya houses

6. Ascendant has malefic and all Upchaya houses are occupied. He will win over his enemies.

7. Sixth house is aspected by its lord Mars.

8. Jupiter is the lord of seventh house and Venus is the Karaka of marriage. Both are placed in Upchaya houses.

9. Jupiter and Mercury are in Upchaya houses. Jupiter is lord of tenth house and Mercury is karaka of business. He had a successful business.

10. Jupiter and Mercury are karaka of Astrology. They are in Upchaya house.

11. Mars is lord of sixth house and a karaka of disease. He suffered from various disease.

12. The drawback is the aspect of Saturn on tenth and third house. Saturn is not a lord of a Upchaya house.

13. Tenth and sixth houses are strongest of the Upchaya houses. Sixth house give success after hard work when related to malefic.

14. He was born in a middle-class family. By his hard work and blessings of God he is now a rich person and has a good status in life.

D10 Dashamsha (great successes)

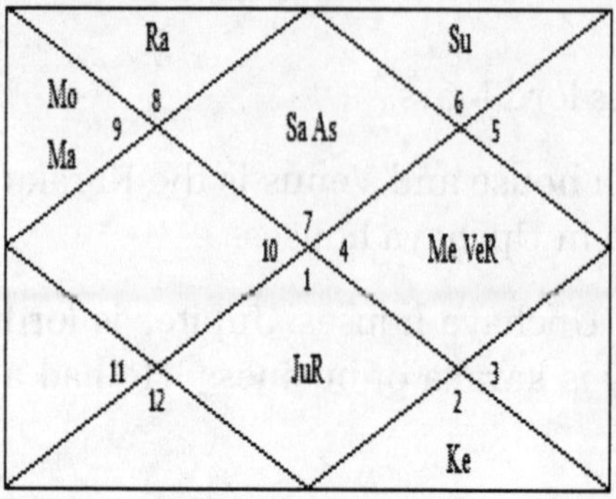

D10 Dashamsha (great successes)

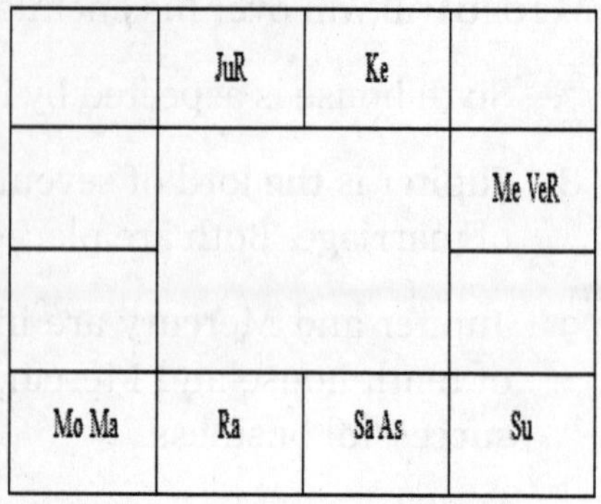

1. In Dashamsha chart Venus and Mercury are in tenth house. Third house has Moon and Mars.

2. Moon is an Upchaya House lord. Mars is not an Upchaya lord but has improved because of relation with Upchaya lord Moon.

3. He retired in Mars Maha Dasha. Mars is in third house and aspected by third lord Jupiter.

4. He joined Government as class 1 officer in Venus/ Venus. Resigned his job in Venus / Rahu. Mercury is twelfth and ninth lord.

5. He started his business in Venus/ Mercury.

6. The best periods of earning were Moon and Mars.

Example – DOB 21 November 1951, TOB 8.0, POB Meerut

Birth Chart

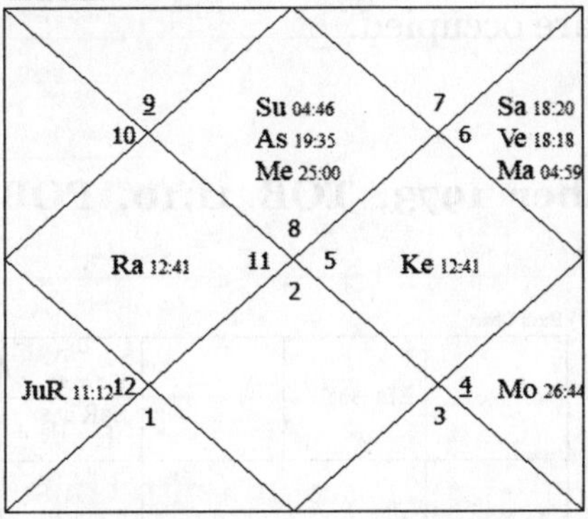

Birth Chart

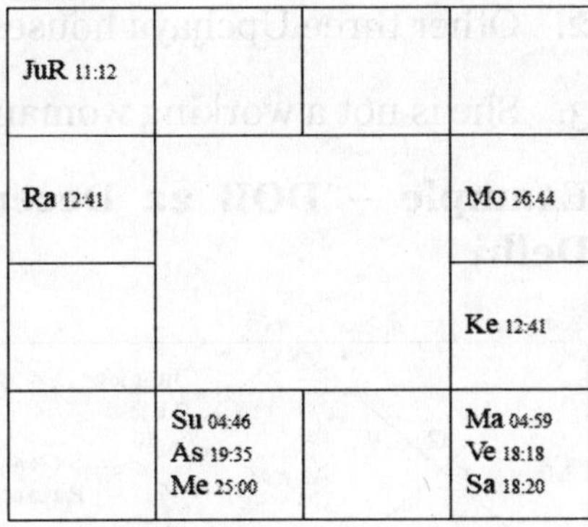

1. Tenth house has Ketu.
2. Eleventh house has three planets. Only two Upchaya houses are occupied. Mars is lord of non Upchaya house.
3. Sixth house is aspected by sixth lord.
4. Third and sixth lords are placed in eleventh house. This gives growth to eleventh house.
5. Eleventh house is strong, and she has good amount of wealth.

D10 Dashamsha (great successes)

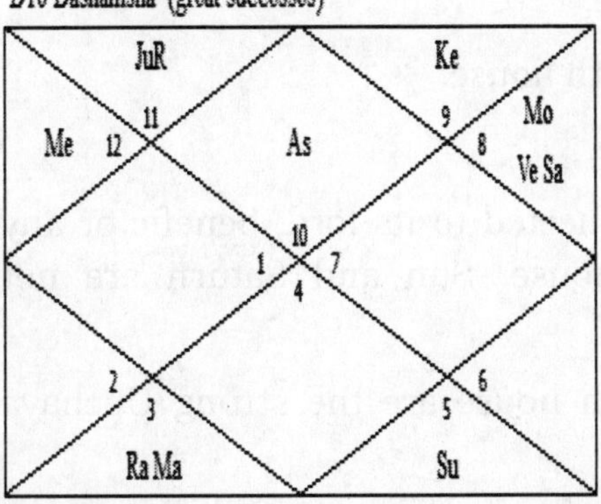

D10 Dashamsha (great successes)

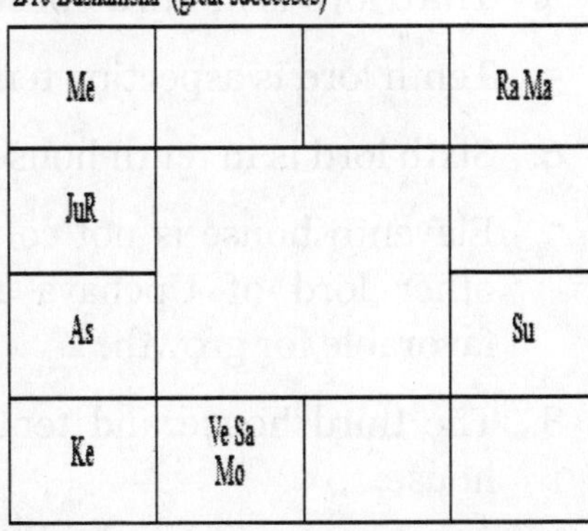

1. Tenth house has no planet. It is important to have a planet in tenth to qualify other Upchaya houses.
2. Other three Upchaya houses are occupied.
3. She is not a working woman.

Example – DOB 22 December 1973, TOB 11.10, POB Delhi

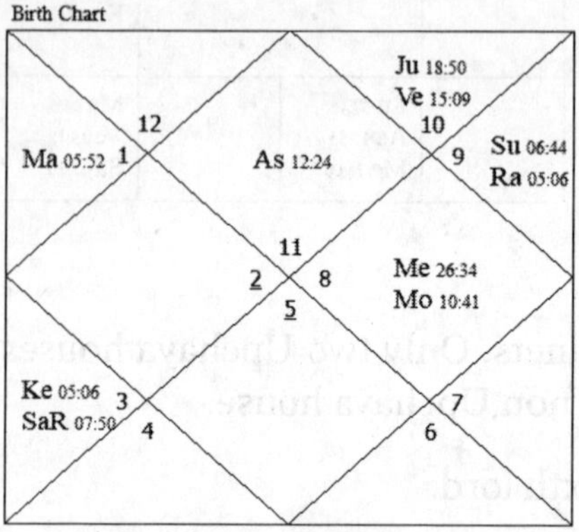

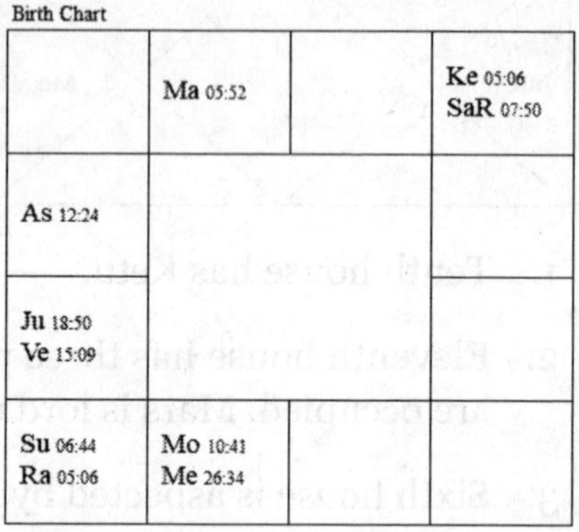

1. Tenth house has two planets. Both are conducive to growth. Moon is sixth lord.
2. Other two Upchaya houses are occupied.
3. There are five planets in Upchaya houses.
4. Third lord is in third house.
5. Tenth lord is aspecting tenth house.
6. Sixth lord is in tenth house.
7. Eleventh house is not connected to its lord, benefic or any other lord of Upchaya house. Sun and Saturn are not favorable for growth.
8. The third house and tenth house are the strong Upchaya house.
9. Efforts and determination are required for getting wealth.

10. She is running her well-established export business. Mars is the lord of tenth house and Mercury is the karaka of business.

D10 Dashamsha (great successes)

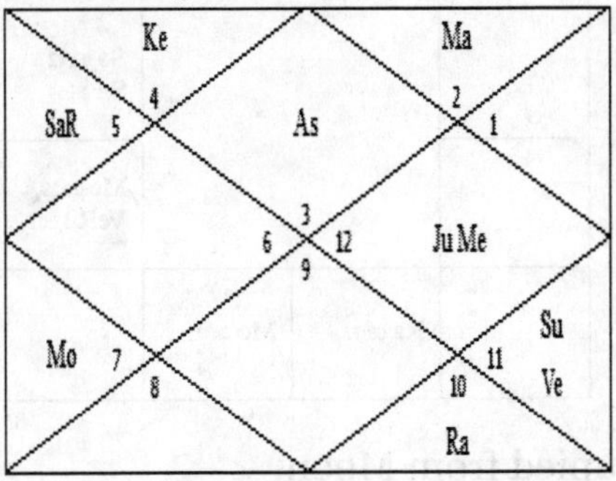

D10 Dashamsha (great successes)

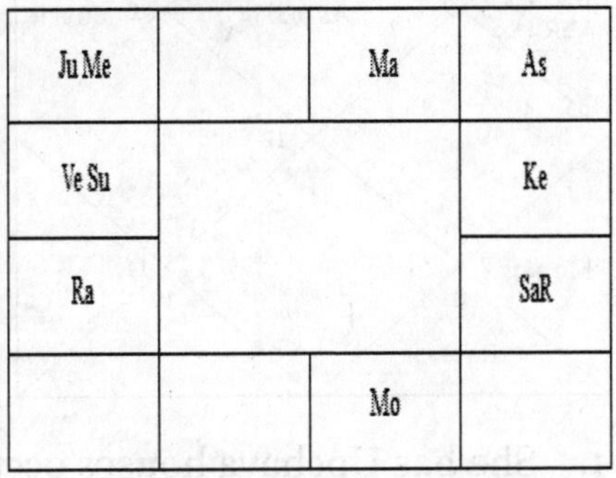

1. Jupiter and Mercury are in tenth house. Jupiter is the lord of tenth house also.

2. Saturn is in third house. Saturn is not a lord of an Upchaya house.

3. Saturn is aspecting Sun, Mars, Moon and Venus.

4. She started her business in Venus Dasha. Jupiter is tenth lord and Mercury is karaka of business.

5. The Dasha periods related to planets in Upchaya House are the periods of gain.

Example – DOB 14 August 1975, TOB 03.01.40, POB Agra

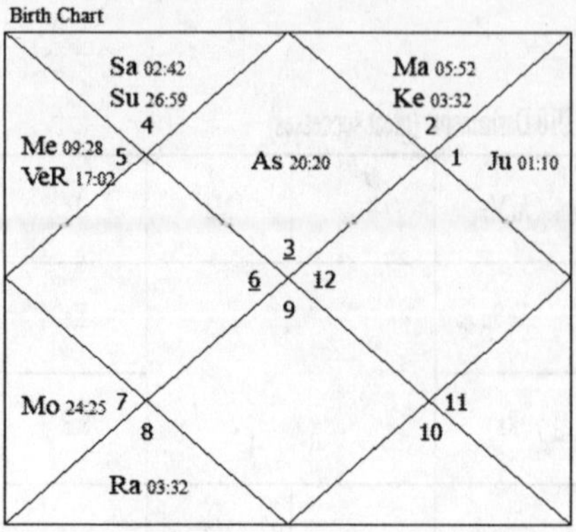

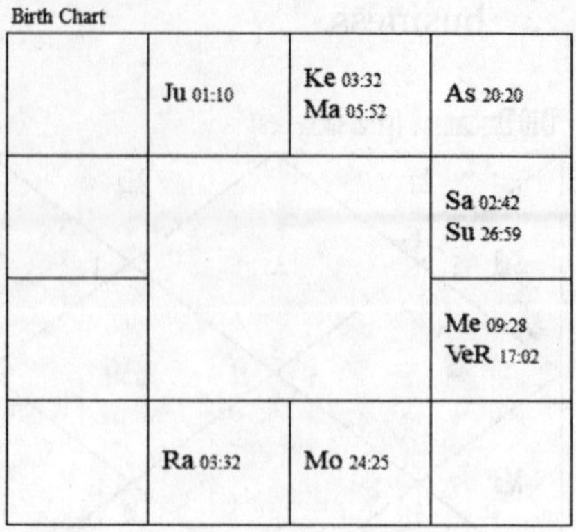

1. She has Upchaya houses occupied from Moon.
2. Tenth house has Saturn and Sun. Saturn is not a lord of any Upchaya house. Tenth house has malefic in it. This gives success after hard work.
3. Eleventh house has Mercury and Venus. They are aspected by sixth lord Jupiter.
4. Eleventh lord is in tenth house.
5. She is a director in a large foreign multinational company.
6. Her career has been growing. She started as a sales representative and has reached the level of a director in a 10,000 crores company in dasha of Mercury.

D10 Dashamsha (great successes)

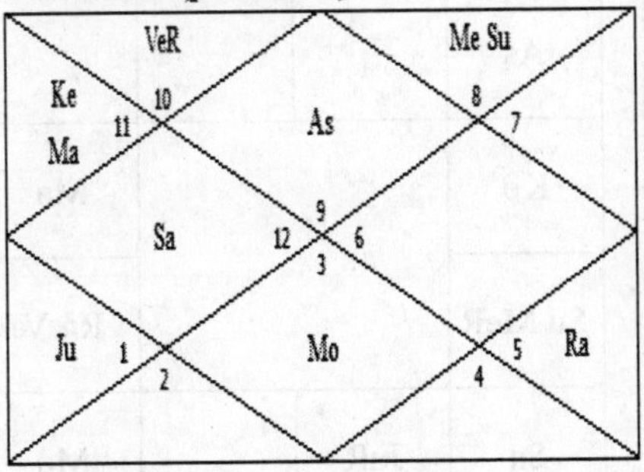

D10 Dashamsha (great successes)

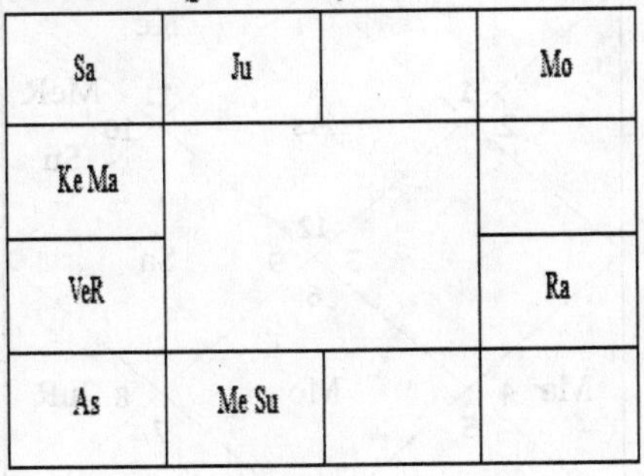

1. All Upchaya houses from Moon are occupied.

2. Lord of third is in sixth house.

3. Lord of tenth is in eleventh.

4. She started working in Saturn Maha Dasha. Saturn is not a lord of any Upchaya House from Moon. Growth in Saturn Dasha was not good.

5. The best Dasha period of rise have been of Mercury.

Example DOB 17 September 1950 TOB 10.10 POB Vadnagar

Birth Chart

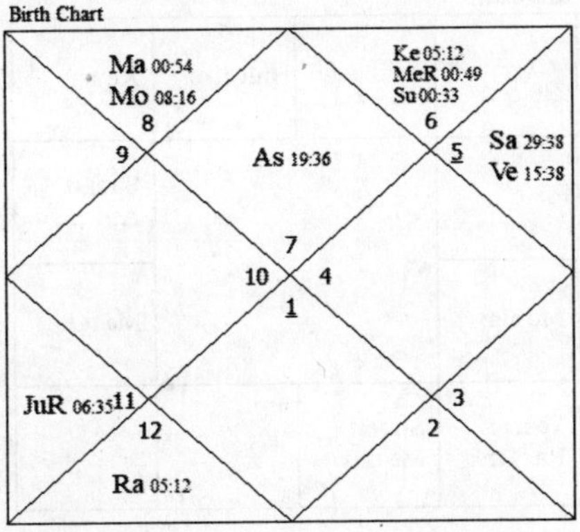

Birth Chart

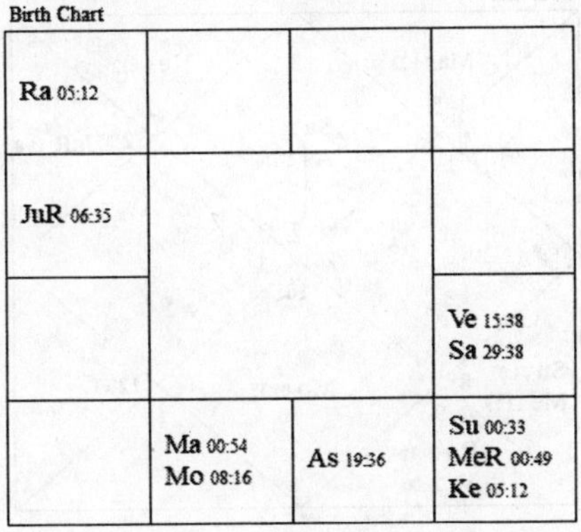

Tenth house is not occupied.

D9 Navamsha (spouse)

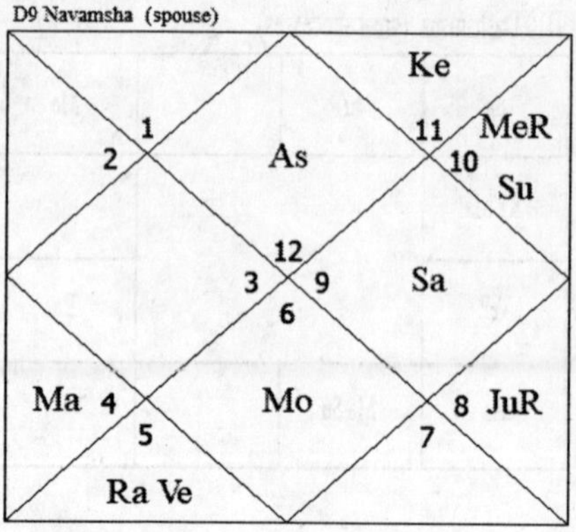

D9 Navamsha (spouse)

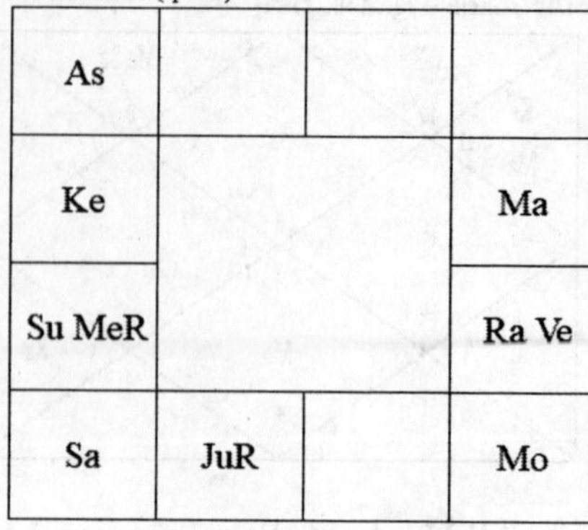

1. Five planets are placed in Upchaya houses.
2. Saturn is in tenth house.
3. Sun is sixth lord and is placed in eleventh house.
4. The Upchaya is strong.
5. He was married but did not stay in the marriage home.

Example DOB 19 November 1917 TOB 23.11.20 POB Allahabad

Birth Chart

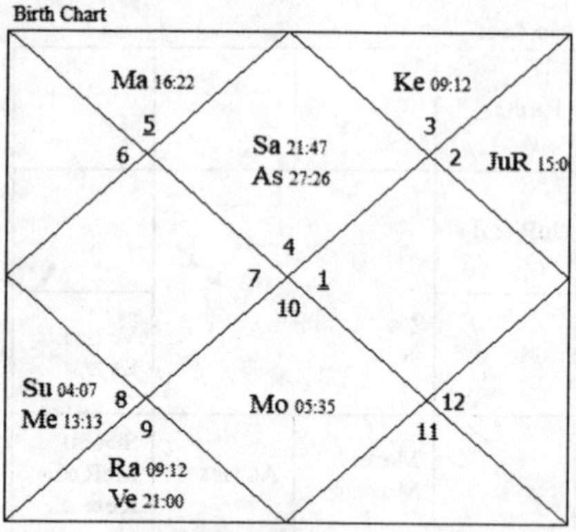

Birth Chart

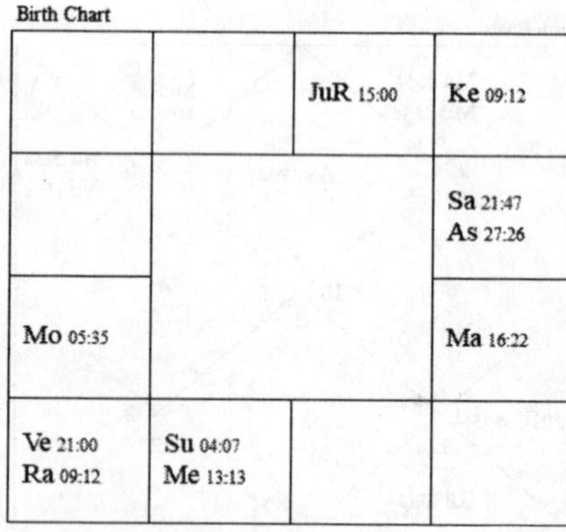

Tenth house is not occupied.

D9 Navamsha (spouse)

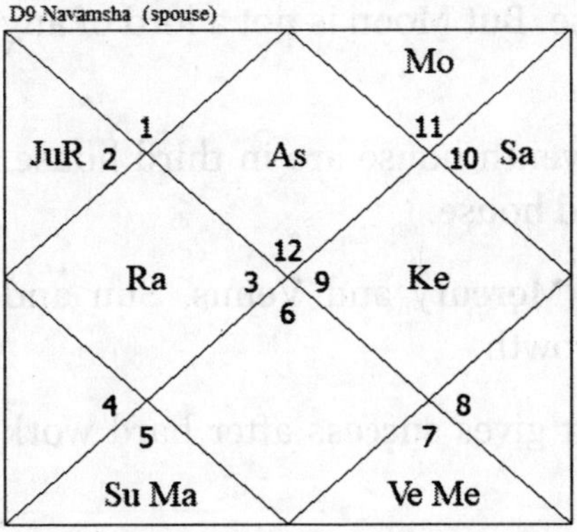

D9 Navamsha (spouse)

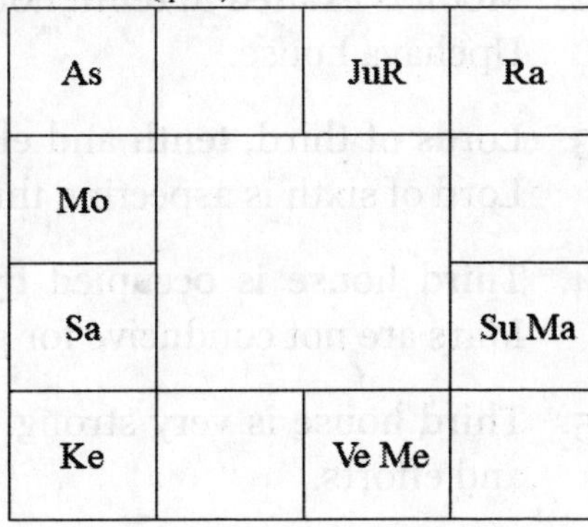

1. Ketu is in tenth house.
2. Jupiter is tenth lord and is placed in third house.
3. Saturn is eleventh lord and is in eleventh house.
4. Sun and Mars are in sixth house. Sun is sixth lord.
5. This is a better Upchaya combination than the previous case.
6. She was married which lasted for 20 years.

Example – DOB 20 October 1978, TOB 02.45, POB Delhi

Birth Chart

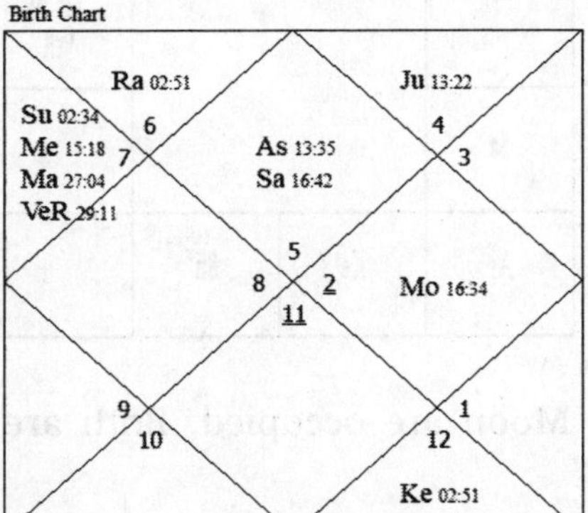

Birth Chart

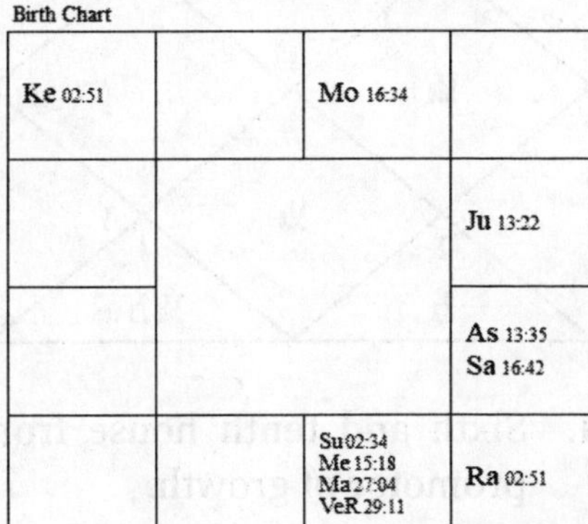

1. Only two Upchaya houses are occupied. There are five planets in Upchaya houses.

2. Moon is exalted in tenth house. But Moon is not a lord of any Upchaya house.

3. Lords of third, tenth and eleventh house are in third house. Lord of sixth is aspecting third house.

4. Third house is occupied by Mercury and Venus. Sun and Mars are not conducive for growth.

5. Third house is very strong. It gives success after hard work and efforts.

6. A malefic is in Ascendant.

7. Lord of third house and Karaka of sports, Mars, are in Upchaya house.

8. The tenth house from Moon is not occupied.

9. This chart is of Virendra Sehwag.

D10 Dashamsha (great successes)

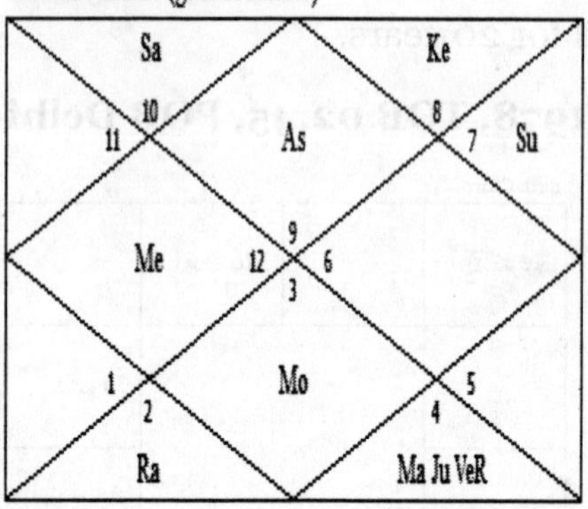

D10 Dashamsha (great successes)

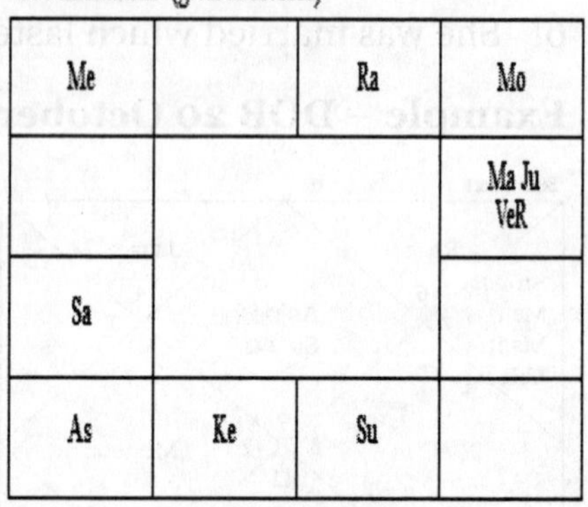

1. Sixth and tenth house from Moon are occupied. Both are promotor of growth.

2. From Ascendant tenth house is not occupied.

3. The active professional career of a sports person is normally short. This is confirmed by D 10.

Example – DOB 16 May 1929, TOB 16.00, POB Bharatpur

Birth Chart

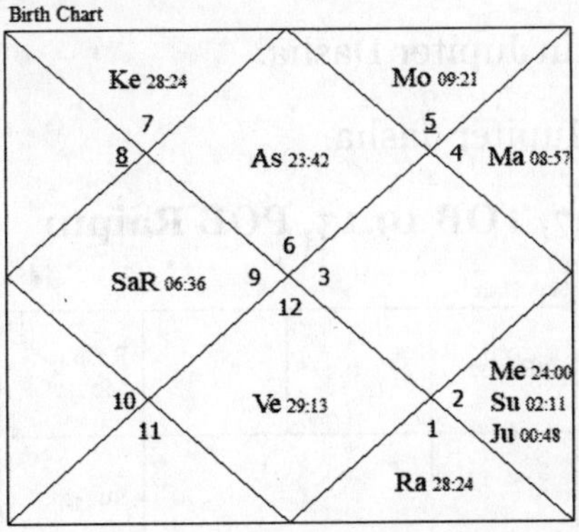

Birth Chart

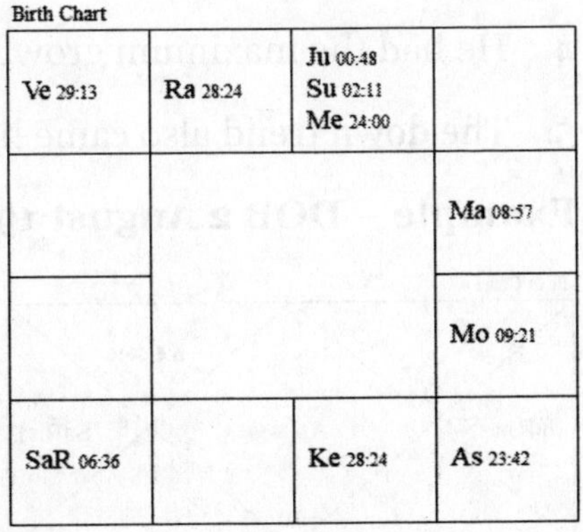

1. There is no planet in tenth house.
2. Mars is third lord and is placed in eleventh house. No other Upchaya lord is in Upchaya house.
3. Such situation does not give continuous growth.
4. He faced problems due to corruption case and further growth was denied.

D10 Dashamsha (great successes)

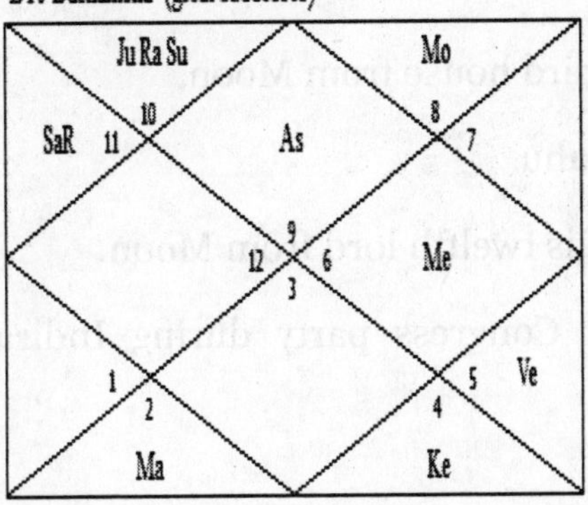

D10 Dashamsha (great successes)

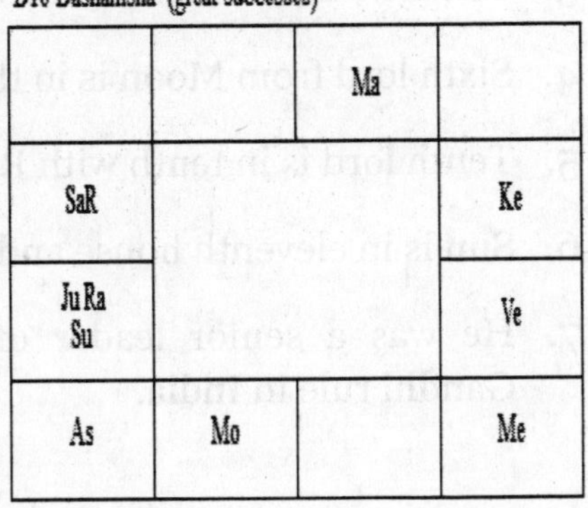

1. Exalted Mercury is in tenth house.
2. Saturn is placed in third house. Jupiter is not a lord of any Upchaya house.
3. No planet is in eleventh house.
4. He had the maximum growth in Jupiter Dasha.
5. The down trend also came in Jupiter dasha.

Example – DOB 2 August 1927, TOB 19.15, POB Raipur

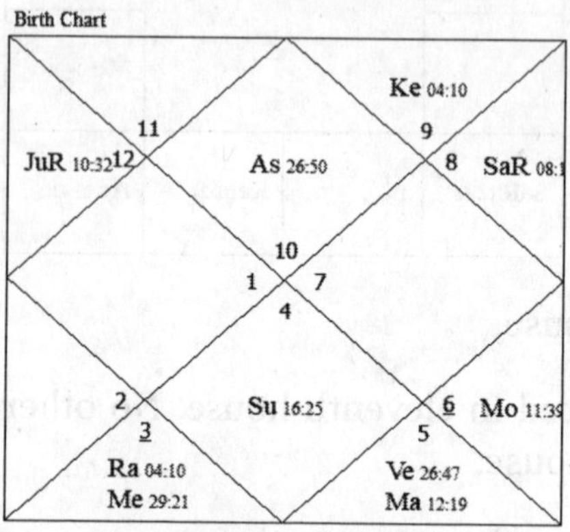

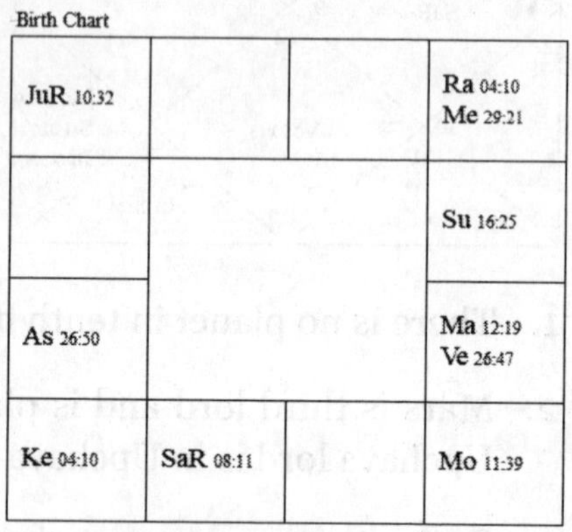

1. Tenth house from lagan is not occupied.
2. From Moon three Upchaya House are occupied.
3. Tenth house from Moon has a benefic and malefic.
4. Sixth lord from Moon is in third house from Moon.
5. Tenth lord is in tenth with Rahu.
6. Sun is in eleventh house and is twelfth lord from Moon.
7. He was a senior leader of Congress party during Indira Gandhi rule in India.

D10 Dashamsha (great successes)

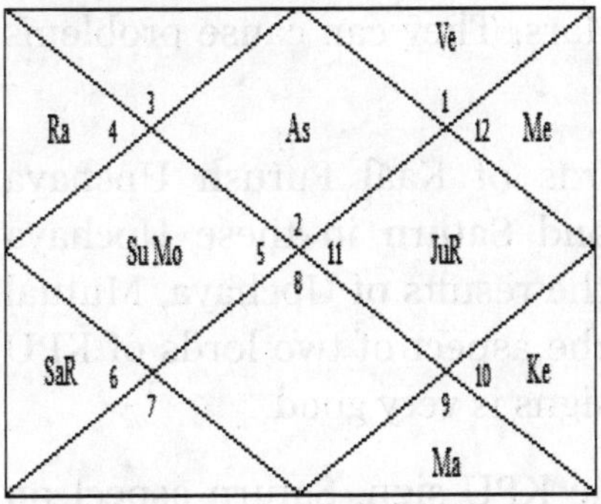

D10 Dashamsha (great successes)

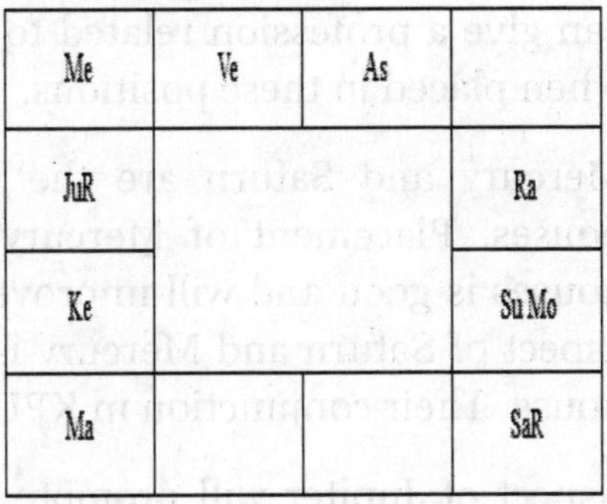

1. Jupiter is in tenth house. Jupiter is eleventh lord.
2. Mercury is in eleventh house and Rahu is in third house.
3. Dashamsha is strong.
4. He remained in good position till his death.

Kaal Purush Upchaya (KPU)

The kaal Purush horoscope is casted with Aries as Ascendant. The Upchaya houses in Kaal Purush horoscope are Gemini, Virgo, Capricorn and Aquarius. When these houses are occupied by planets, we can consider it as an Upchaya House Yoga. In this scheme, Capricorn must be occupied. This also gives the results of Upchaya in the horoscope.

Capricorn is the tenth house of Kaal Purush Horoscope. Tenth house is a very important house as the era we are living is the Karma era.

The planets placed in these four houses have an important role to play. Jupiter placed in Gemini will influence Aquarius. Jupiter placed in Virgo will influence Capricorn. The placement of Jupiter in signs of Mercury is not welcome as Mercury is not a friend of Jupiter. Similarly, placement of Mars in sign of

Mercury is not good. From Gemini it will aspect Capricorn and can give a profession related to Mars. They can cause problems when placed in these positions.

Mercury and Saturn are the lords of Kaal Purush Upchaya houses. Placement of Mercury and Saturn in these Upchaya houses is good and will improve the results of Upchaya. Mutual aspect of Saturn and Mercury is the aspect of two lords of KPU house. Their conjunction in KPU signs is very good.

Aspect of Jupiter will promote the KPU sign. Saturn aspect on KPU sign gives concentration and dedication to the sign.

More than four planets in KPU signs will make it strong to give good results. More number of planets better it is.

Dasha of planets related to KPU signs are important Dasha.

Occupation of Upchaya signs/ houses is like a booster to the Yoga present in the horoscope.

These rules are applied on few charts.

Example Sofia Loren DOB 20 September 1934 TOB 14.10 POB Rome

Birth Chart

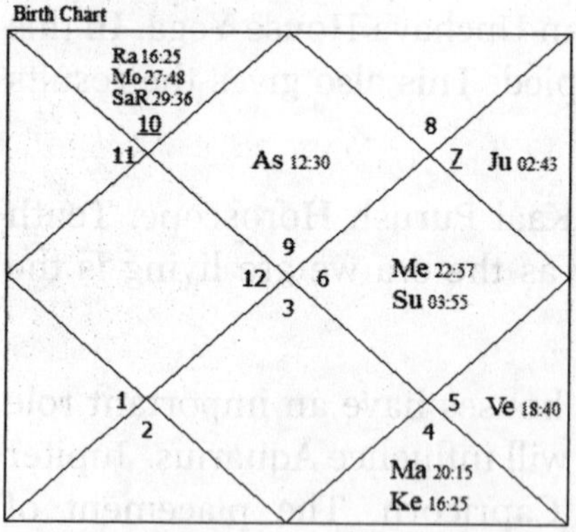

Birth Chart

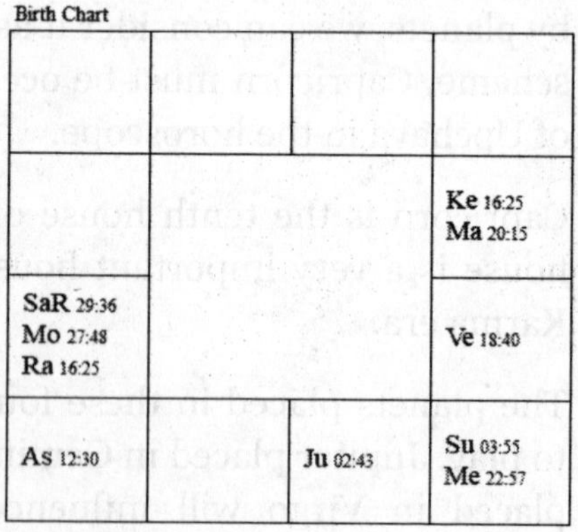

1. Capricorn and Virgo are occupied by planets.

2. Jupiter or Mars are not in Virgo or Gemini.
3. Saturn and Mercury are in in their own sign.
4. It is a good position.
5. She is one of the greatest stars of Hollywood. She has won many awards. These include five Grammy, six best actress, five golden globe and lifetime achievement award besides many other awards.
6. She married twice and have two children.
7. There are other Yoga present in the horoscope and their impact is increased with the presence of KPU.

Example C S Patel DOB 31 December 1915 TOB 7.44 POB Ahmedabad

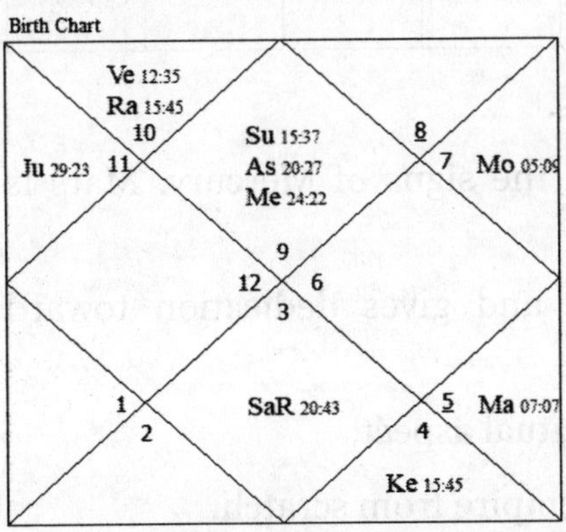

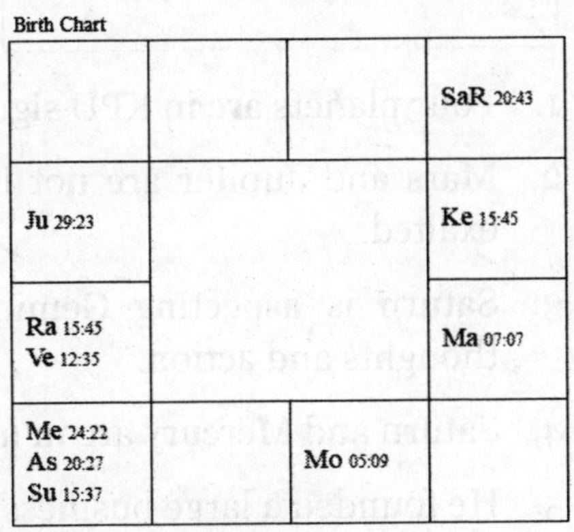

1. Capricorn, Aquarius and Gemini are occupied.
2. Jupiter and Mars are not in the sign of Mercury.
3. Mercury and Saturn are in mutual aspect.
4. There are four planets in KPU.
5. He was a great astrologer and wrote many books.

6. Jupiter in Aquarius will aspect Gemini and promotes the significations of Gemini. Jupiter is lord of lagna and its aspect is very good.

Example G D Birla DOB 14 April 1894 TOB 2.54 POB Pilani

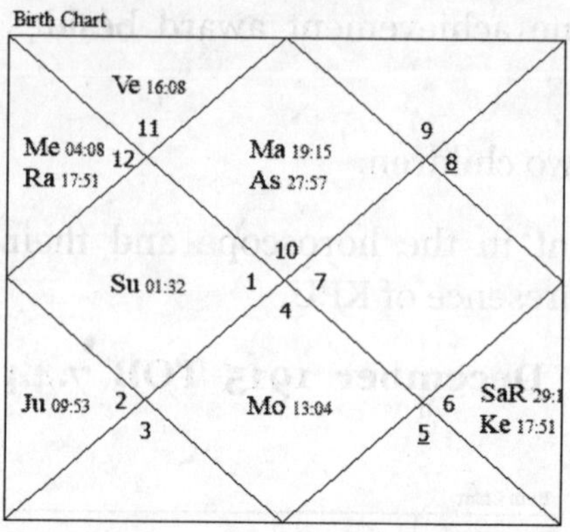

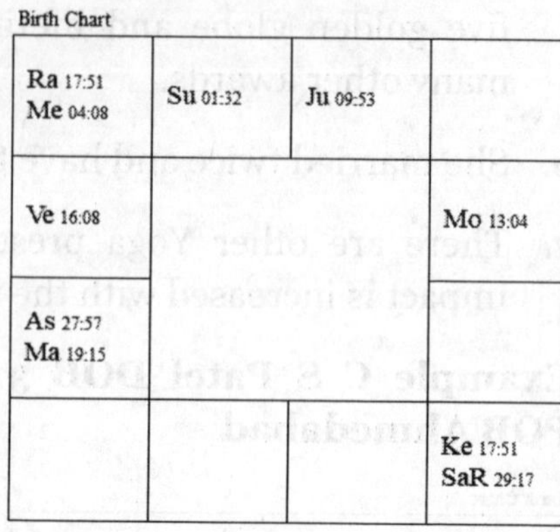

1. Four planets are in KPU signs.
2. Mars and Jupiter are not in the signs of Mercury. Mars is exalted.
3. Saturn is aspecting Gemini and gives dedication toward thoughts and action.
4. Saturn and Mercury are in mutual aspect.
5. He founded a large business empire from scratch.

Example Barack Obama DOB 4 August 1961 TOB 19.24 POB Honolulu

Birth Chart

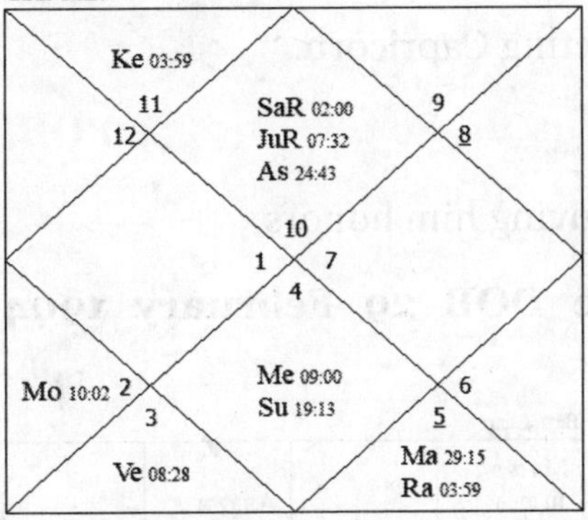

Birth Chart

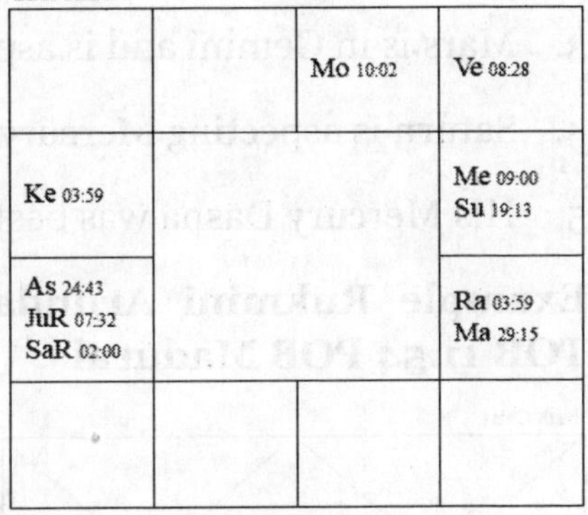

1. Four planets are in KPU signs.
2. Saturn and Mercury are in mutual aspect.
3. Mars and Jupiter are not placed in the signs of Mercury.
4. Capricorn is very strong. Debilitated Jupiter is placed in lagna.
5. He became President of USA in MD of Jupiter.

Example Manekshaw DOB 3 April 1914 TOB 16.30 POB Amritsar

Birth Chart

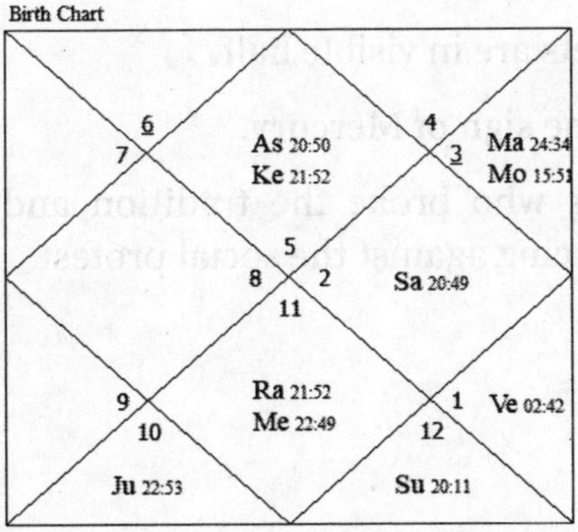

Birth Chart

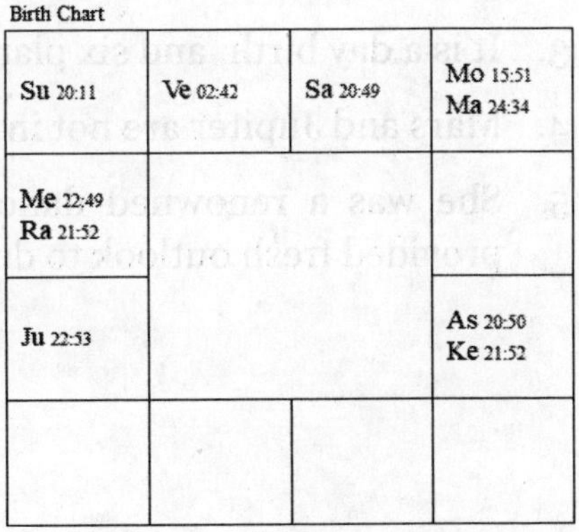

1. He is the second Field Marshal of India.
2. **Five** planets are placed in KPU signs.
3. Mars is in Gemini and is aspecting Capricorn.
4. Saturn is aspecting Mercury.
5. His Mercury Dasha was best giving him honors.

Example Rukmini Arundale DOB 29 February 1904 TOB 11.54 POB Madurai

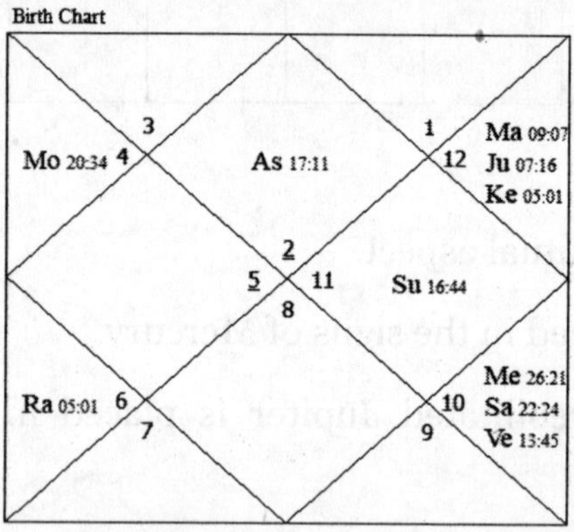

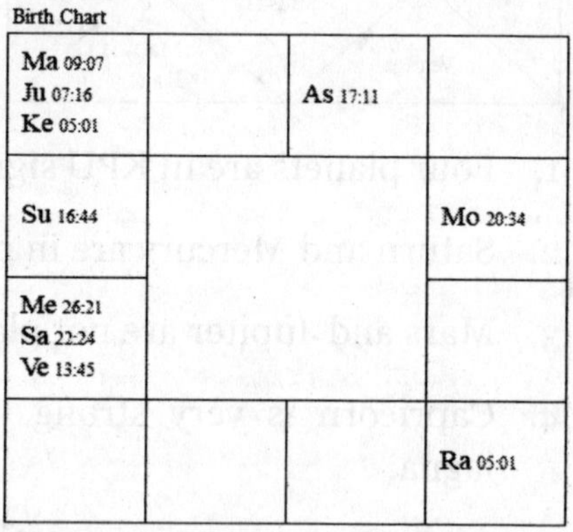

1. **Five** planets are in KPU signs.
2. Saturn and Mercury are conjunct are causing a raj Yoga. This improves the results of KPU Yoga.
3. It is a day birth, and six planets are in visible half.
4. Mars and Jupiter are not in the sign of Mercury.
5. She was a renowned dancer who broke the tradition and provided fresh outlook to dancing against the social protest.

Example B K Nehru DOB 7 March 1907 TOB 0.22 POB Allahabad

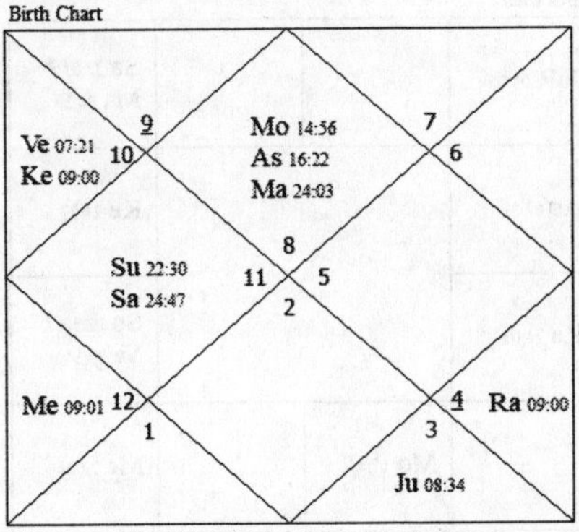

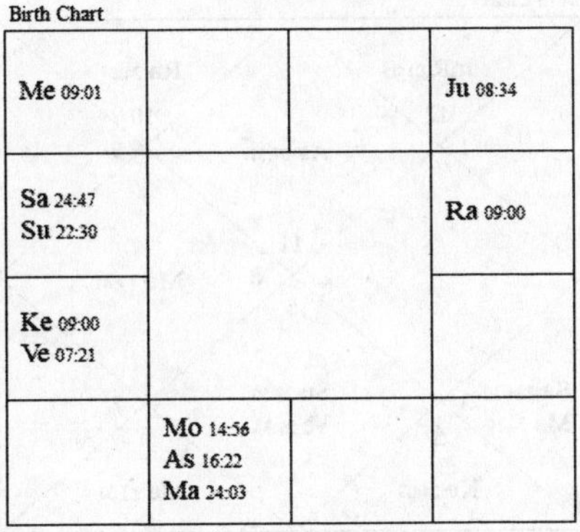

1. Five planets are in KPU sign.
2. Jupiter is in Gemini.
3. Saturn and Mercury are not in relation.
4. He was a diplomat and was Indian ambassador to USA.
5. Mercury is debilitated and lagna lord Mars is in lagna is a Yoga.

Example Untawalia DOB 15 September 1915 TOB 17.00 POB Sitamarhi Bihar

Birth Chart

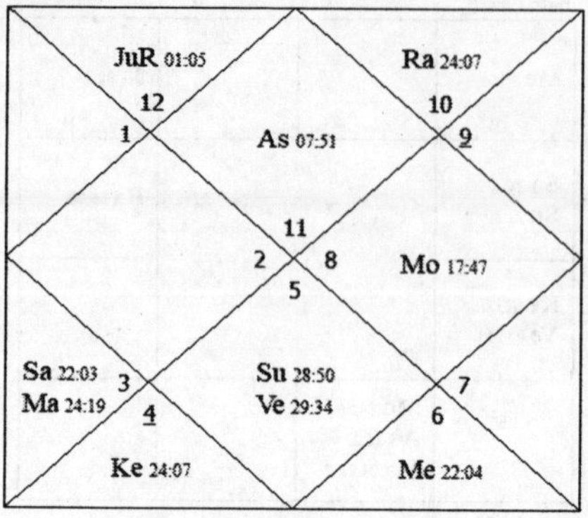

Birth Chart

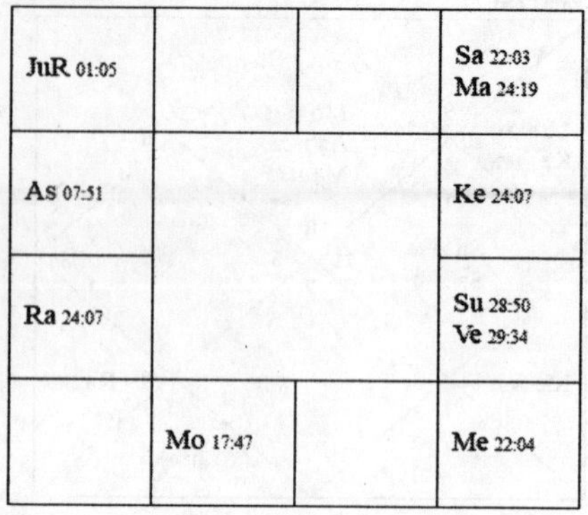

1. Conjunction of Sun and Venus is a raj Yoga.
2. Four planets are in KPU signs.
3. Mars is in Gemini.
4. Mercury and Saturn are not related. Saturn is in the sign of Mercury and Mercury is exalted.
5. He was a Justice of Supreme Court of India. He had obstacles in his elevation to Supreme Court.

Example J R D Tata DOB 29 July 1904 TOB 12.39 POB Paris

Birth Chart

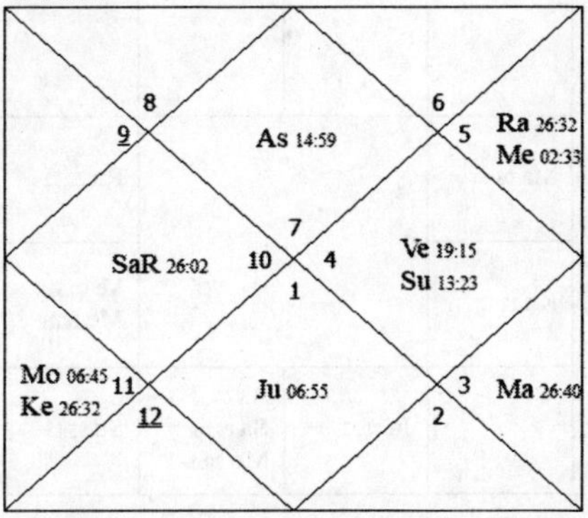

Birth Chart

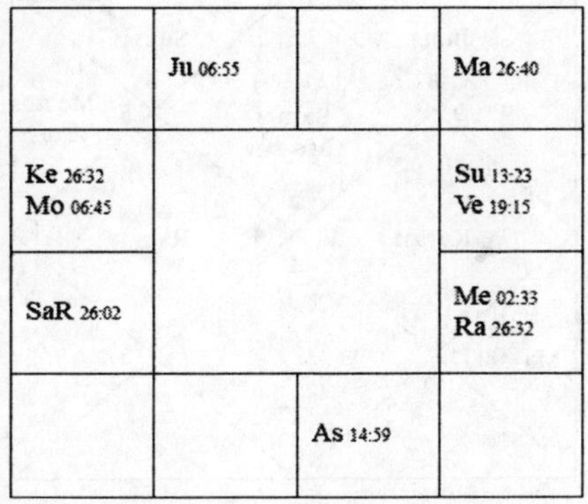

1. This chart has good Dhana Yoga, and they are boosted by presence of KPU Yoga.
2. Four planets are in KPU signs.
3. Mars in Gemini and Saturn in Capricorn gave hard life and he worked like a soldier.
4. Saturn and Mercury are not related.
5. Upchaya from lagna are also occupied.

Example Jimmy Carter DOB 1 October 1924 TOB 7.0 POB Plains Georgia

Birth Chart

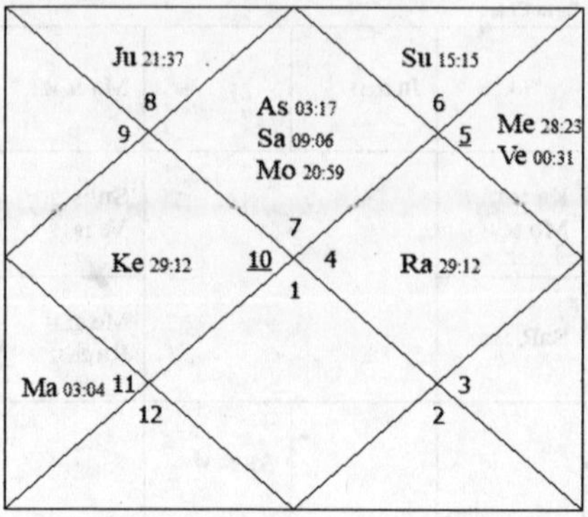

Birth Chart

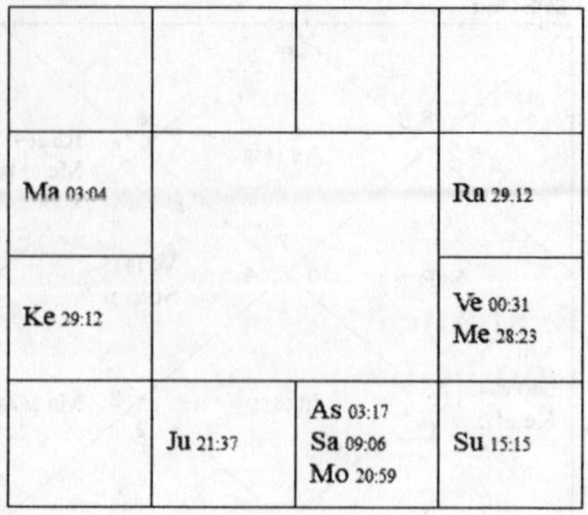

1. There are raj Yoga present in the horoscope.
2. Three planets are in KPU signs.
3. Saturn and Mercury are not related.
4. He was 39th President of USA and served for full term.

Example K R Narayanan DOB 4 February 1921 TOB 17.00 POB Cochin

Birth Chart

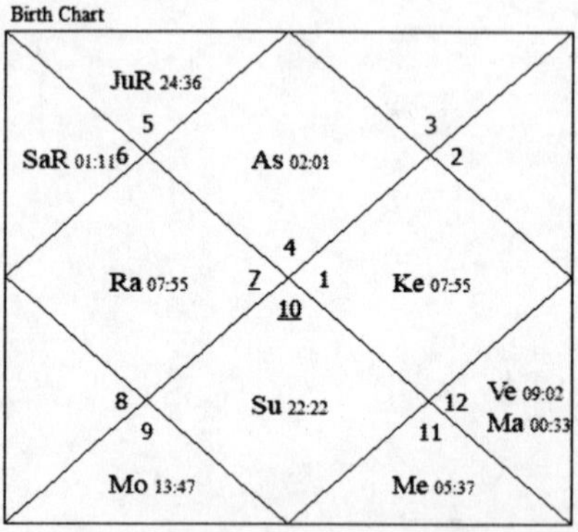

Birth Chart

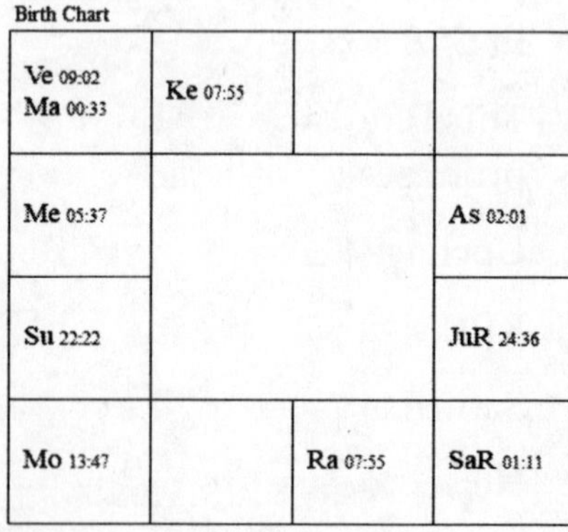

1. Three planets are in KPU signs.
2. Venus, Mars and Saturn are in raj Yoga.

3. Mercury and Saturn have exchanged sign. This improves the KPU results. This is Khala Yoga also.
4. Mars and Jupiter are not in the sign of Mercury.
5. He was President of India from 1992 to 1997.
6. The horoscope has normal Upchaya House occupied.

Example Madhavrao Scindhia DOB 10 March 1945 TOB 1.00 POB Gwalior

Birth Chart

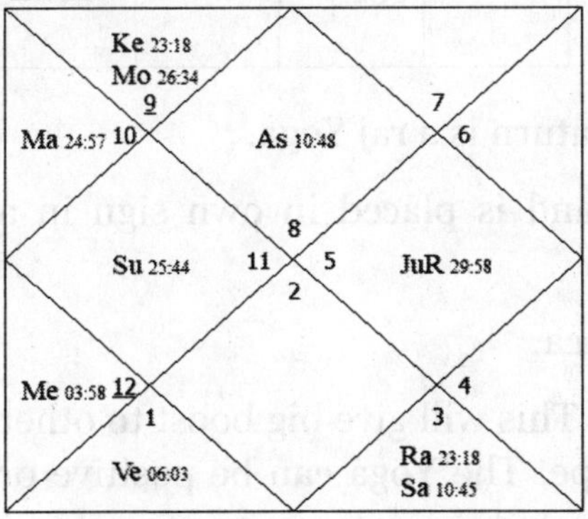

Birth Chart

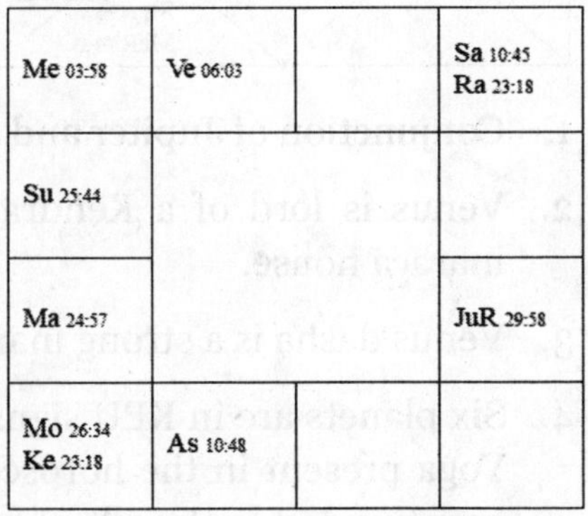

1. Saturn and Moon are in raj Yoga. This Yoga is in RKA and is in 2/ 8 axis.
2. Third lord in eighth house is a strong Vipreet Raj Yoga. It promises wealth and fame.
3. Upchaya houses from Ascendant are occupied.
4. KPU signs are occupied. Mars is exalted.
5. Saturn is aspecting Mercury.
6. He was a very promising politician but had a short life.

Example Princess Diana DOB 1 July 1961 TOB 19.45 POB Sandringham UK

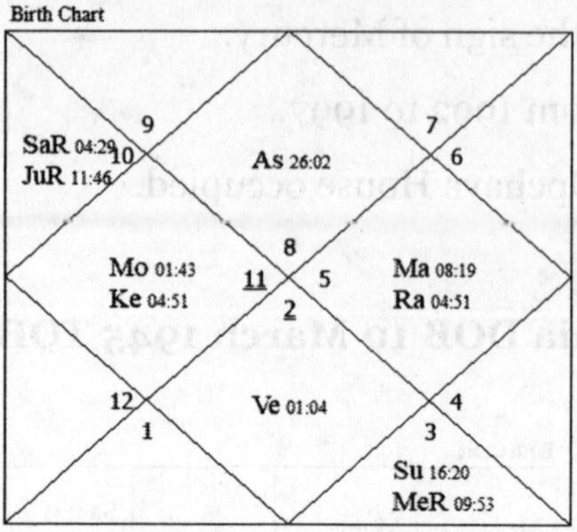

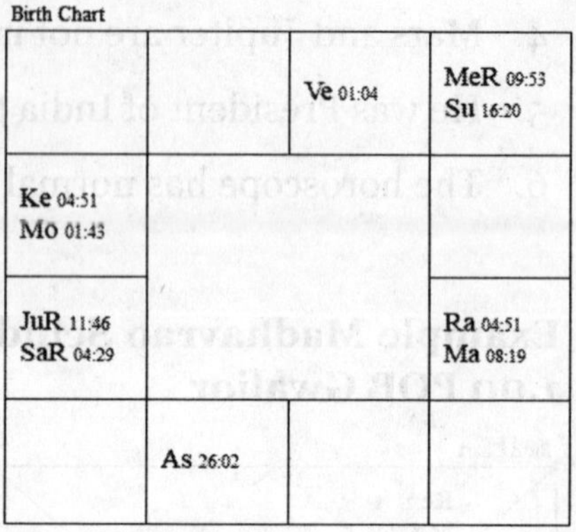

1. Conjunction of Jupiter and Saturn is a raj Yoga.
2. Venus is lord of a Kendra and is placed in own sign in a maraca house.
3. Venus dasha is a strong maraca.
4. Six planets are in KPU signs. This will give big boost to other Yoga present in the horoscope. The Yoga can be positive or negative, but both will get boosted.
5. She died in a road accident.

Example Queen Elizabeth II DOB 21 April 1926 TOB 02.48 POB London Conley

Birth Chart

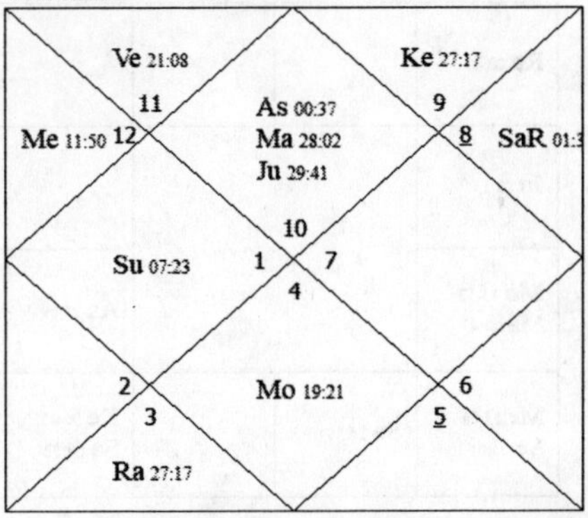

Birth Chart

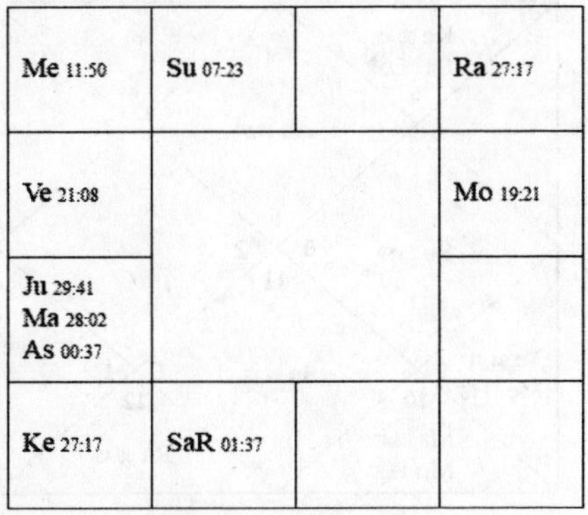

1. Debilitated Jupiter is in Ascendant and is aspected by lord Saturn. Jupiter is lord of third and twelfth house.
2. This constitutes a strong raj Yoga.
3. The tenth house from lagna is not occupied and the Upchaya Yoga from Ascendant is not present.
4. The KPU signs are occupied by four planets. Mars is exalted.
5. Value of the raj Yoga is increased manifold.

Example Rajnikant DOB 12 December 1950 TOB 23.50 POB Madras

Birth Chart

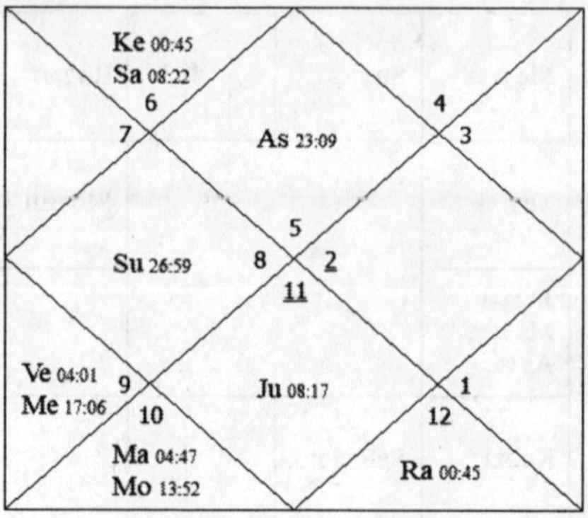

Birth Chart

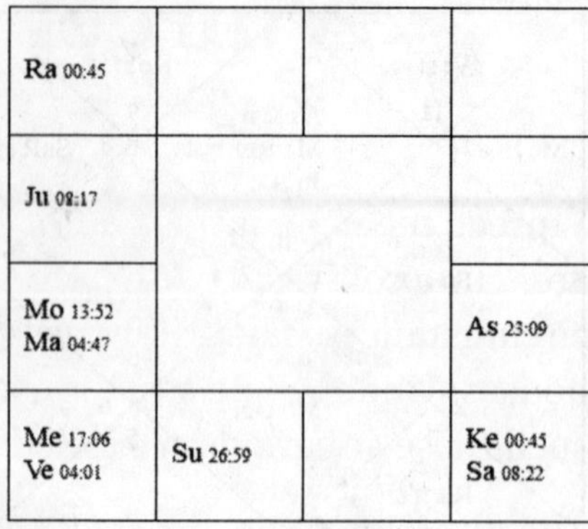

1. Good Dhana Yoga is present.
2. The KPU signs are occupied by five planets. Mars is exalted.
3. He is a well-known movie actor of South India.
4. His Dhana Yoga is getting a better due to the formation of KPU.

Chapter 5
Vipreet Raj Yoga

Vipreet means contrasting or reverse. The results experienced are in contrast with the results expected in normal circumstances. The trik houses are generally considered adverse houses. Under some situations they give favorable results and as such these situations are called Vipreet.

The directions given by classics are detailed.

Uttar Kalamrita (Chapter 4, Shloka 22)

1. There are three Yoga.

   a. The lord of sixth house is in eighth or twelfth house.

   b. The lord of eighth house is in sixth or twelfth house.

   c. The lord of twelfth house is in sixth or eighth house.

   These three are Vipreet Raj Yoga - extra ordinary Raj Yoga. These lords must be mutually related. They should not have any relation with any other planets. Then the person becomes a famous, prosperous and powerful king.

Phaldeepika (Yoga chapter)

1. When lord of sixth house is conjunct with malefic planet or aspected by malefic and is placed in bad house then **Harsh Yoga** is caused. The person will be blessed with Happiness, good fortune and a strong constitution. He will conquer his enemies and will hesitate in indulging in sinful deeds. He

will become a friend of illustrious People with class. He will be wealthy, splendorous and famous and will have Friends and sons. (In this and in Vimal Yoga the conjunction or aspect of malefic is mentioned).

2. When lord of eighth house is placed in sixth or twelfth house then **Saral Yoga** is caused. This Yoga gives excellent results. This Yoga enables the native to be long lived, resolute, fearless, prosperous, learned and blessed with children and wealth. The person with this Yoga will achieve success in all his ventures and will be victorious.

3. When lord of twelfth house is conjunct with malefic planet or aspected by malefic and is placed in bad house then **Vimal Yoga** is caused. The person with his birth in Vimal Yoga will be frugal in his expenses and clever in saving money. He will be equipped with good behavior towards others, will enjoy happiness, will be independent, will follow a respectable profession or conduct and will be well known for his good qualities.

BPHS (Effects of house)

1. When sixth lord is in own house, in lagan or in eighth house then he will have ulcer in the limb of the body represented by the sign in sixth house.

2. The eighth lord is with a malefic and is placed in eighth house along with lagan lord then the person is short lived.

3. When sixth lord or twelfth lord are placed in sixth or twelfth or eighth house then the person is long lived.

4. If twelfth lord is conjunct a benefic, own sign or is exalted then the expenses are made on good account.

BPHS (Effects of house lords)

1. If the sixth lord is in sixth house the person will have enmity with his own kinsmen and friendship with others and will have mediocre happiness in matters like wealth.

2. If sixth lord is in eighth house the person will be sickly, inimical to the learned and the wise. He will desire others wealth and will be interested in other's wives and be impure.

3. When sixth lord is in twelfth house then he will spend on vices. He is inimical to learned and does violence on animals.

4. If eighth lord is in sixth house, the person will win over his enemy. He will have a diseased body in childhood and be afraid from snake and water.

5. The eighth lord in eighth house make a person long lived. When eighth lord is weak then the longevity will be medium, and the person will be a thief. He will be blame worthy himself and will blame others.

6. If eighth lord is in twelfth house, he will squander his wealth on evil deeds and will be short lived. The effect will be more if it is in conjunction with a malefic.

7. When twelfth lord is in sixth house then the person will incur enmity with his own men, will be given to anger, be sinful, miserable and will traverse other's wives.

8. The placement of twelfth lord in eighth house will make a person to be a gainer always, will speak softly, will have medium span of life and will be endowed with good qualities.

9. Twelfth lord in twelfth house will make a person to spend heavily. He will not have physical felicity. He will be irritable and spiteful.

Mansagari (House lords)

1. When the sixth lord is placed in sixth house then the person will be free from sickness. He will have enmity with others. He will be happy, stingy and will never get into distress but will live in dirty place.
2. When the lord of sixth house is in eighth house then it will cause disease according to the nature of sixth lord.
3. When sixth lord is placed in twelfth house then person will incur loss in trade of animals. He will incur unnecessary expenditure in travelling and have great faith in destiny.
4. The placement of eighth lord in sixth will cause problems according to the nature of eighth lord.
5. When eighth lord is in eighth house then the person will be hard working, without any disease and is born in a disrepute family. He will become famous and a deceitful person.
6. When eighth lord is in twelfth house then the person will be a rude talker, thief, wicked, merciless, and straightforward and have physical deformity. His dead body will be eaten away by crows and dogs.
7. When twelfth lord is in sixth house then the person will be miser, suffer eye disease and meet a sudden death.
8. When twelfth lord is benefic and is placed in eighth house then he will be wealthy. When the twelfth lord is malefic then he will be lethargic and revolt against people.
9. When twelfth lord is in twelfth house then the person will be a landlord and stays in his birthplace. He will be a miser and raise cattle. He will become village head if he lives long.

Laghu Parasari

1. Trik house are evil houses.
2. Trishadaya lords are papa planets.

Prashan Marg (Chapter 1 Shloka 97)

1. The third, sixth and twelfth houses are as evil as the eighth house.

Summary of rules

We can now summarize the directions given by classics.

1. Third, sixth, eighth and twelfth house are Vipreet houses.
2. These are Vipreet houses from lagan.
3. Phaldeepika stresses the association of malefic planet with Vipreet house lord to cause Vipreet Raj Yoga.
4. Three Vipreet Raj Yoga are given in classics and these are Harsha, Saral and Vimal.

Two examples of each of the three classic Yoga are given.

Example 1 Harsha Yoga 1 – DOB 11 December 1931, TOB 17.23, POB Kuchwada

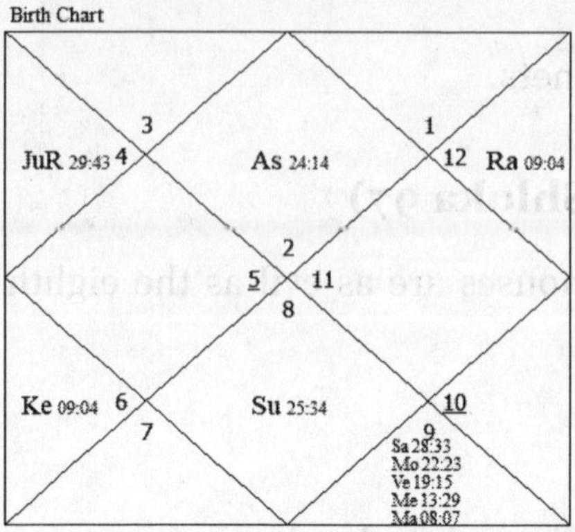

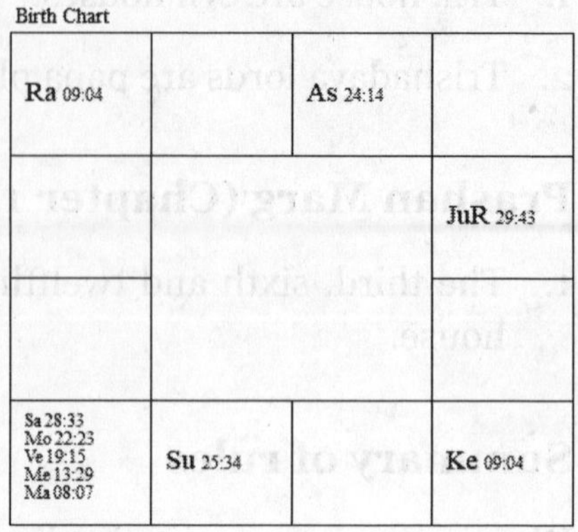

1. Lord of sixth house is Venus and is placed in eighth house.
2. Lord of twelfth house is in eighth house.
3. It is in conjunction with malefic and benefic.
4. Venus is in kartari of Moon and Mercury.
5. Phaldeepika says that for Harsha Yoga only malefic should relate to sixth lord.
6. BPHS gives disease of the nature of lord of sixth house. Twelfth lord gives expenses for good cause.

Example 2 Harsha Yoga 2 – DOB 17 March 1920, TOB 22.38, POB Bangladesh

Birth Chart

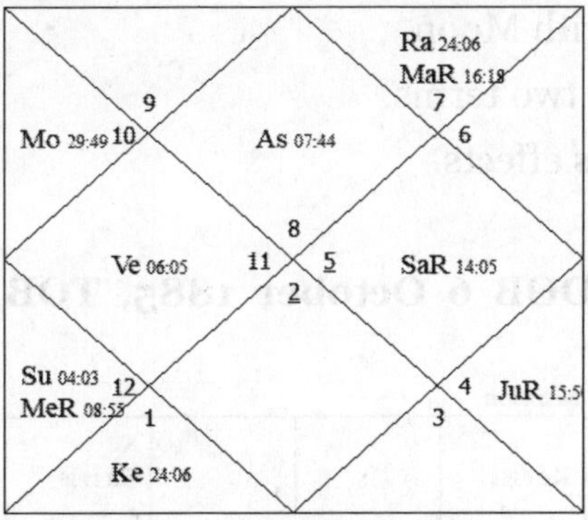

Birth Chart

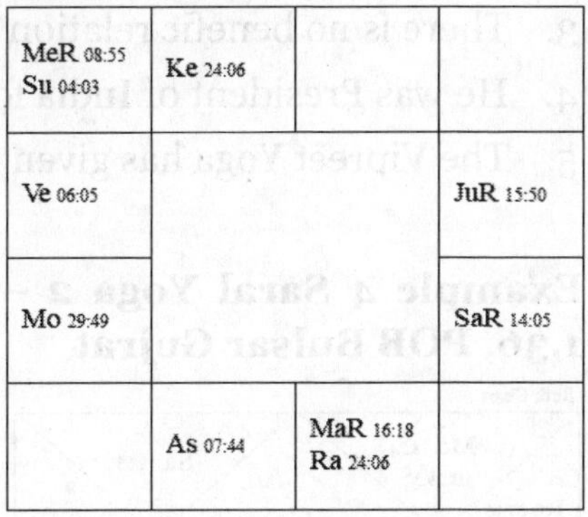

1. Sixth lord Mars is placed in twelfth house.
2. Mars is with a malefic and aspected by another malefic Saturn.
3. This meets the conditions of Harsha Yoga of Phaldeepika.
4. The sixth lord in twelfth house gives expenditure, trade of animals and spends money on vices.

Example 3 Saral Yoga 1 – DOB 3 December 1884, TOB 8.18, POB Chapra

Birth Chart

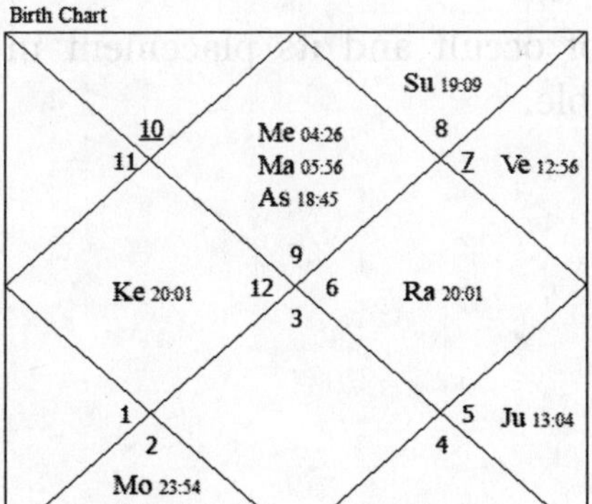

Birth Chart

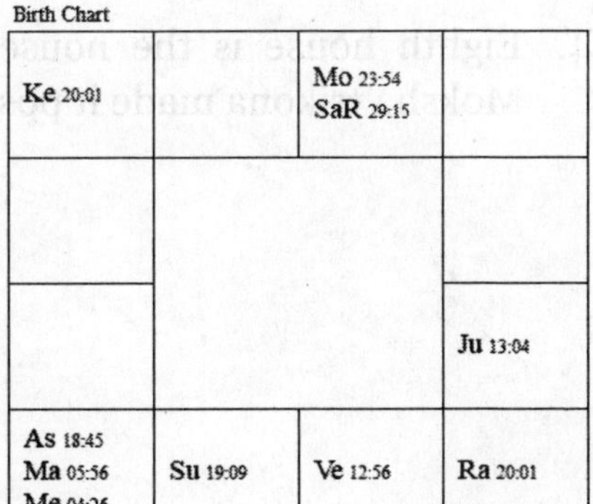

1. Eighth lord Moon is placed in sixth house.
2. Moon is with Saturn and is aspected by Sun.
3. There is no benefic relation with Moon.
4. He was President of India for two terms.
5. The Vipreet Yoga has given its effects.

Example 4 Saral Yoga 2 – DOB 6 October 1885, TOB 1.36, POB Bulsar Gujrat

Birth Chart

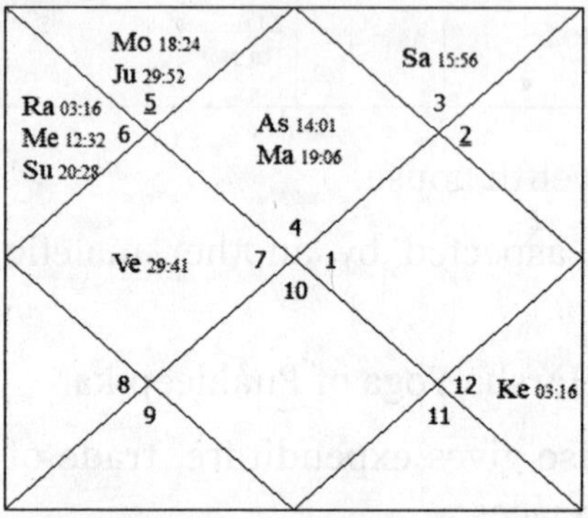

Birth Chart

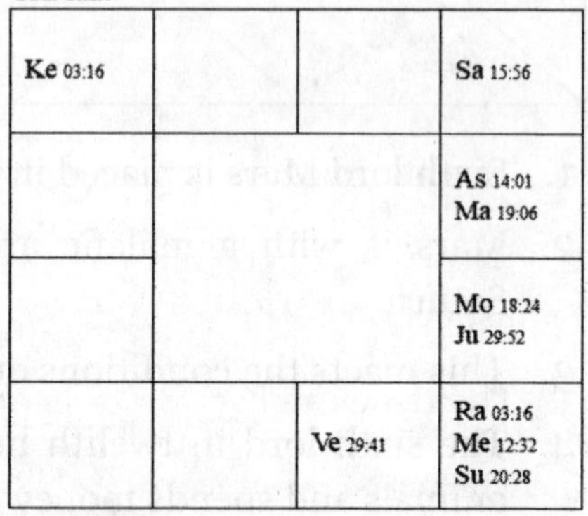

1. Eighth lord Saturn is in twelfth house.
2. Saturn is not associated or aspected by any planet.
3. He was a Tantric and practiced it.
4. Eighth house is the house of occult and its placement in Moksha trikona made it possible.

Example 5 Vimal Yoga 1 – DOB 1 May 1896, TOB 3.02, POB Kheora

Birth Chart

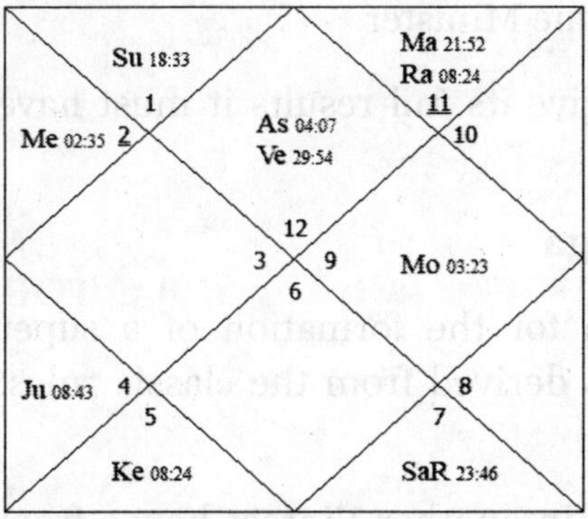

Birth Chart

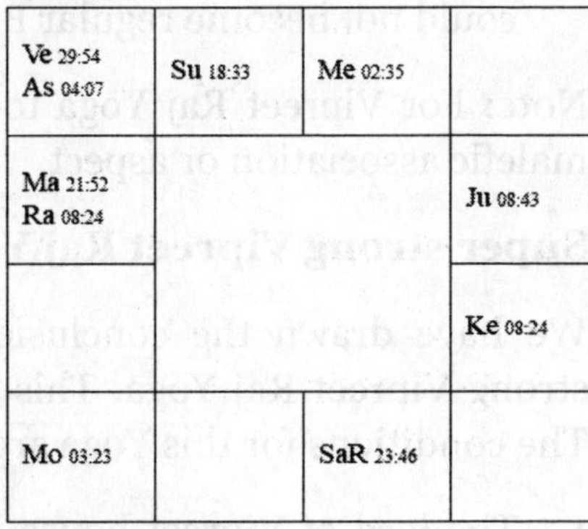

1. Twelfth lord is exalted in eighth house.
2. Saturn is aspected by Sun. There is no benefic association or aspect on Saturn.
3. The trine involved is Moksha trine.
4. She was a great saint.

Example 6 Vimal Yoga 2 – DOB 4 July 1898, TOB 0.53.20, POB Sialkot

Birth Chart

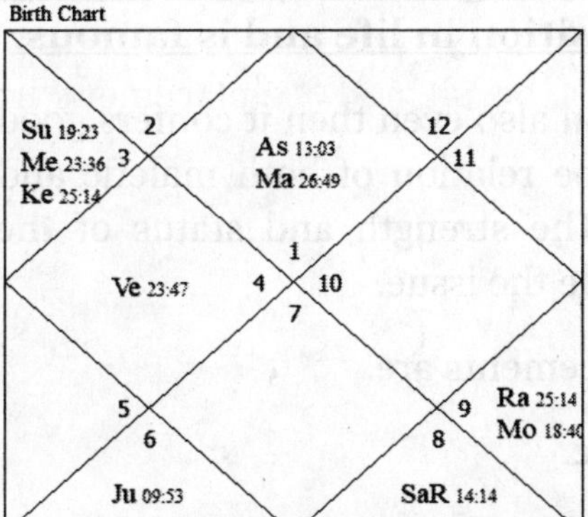

Birth Chart

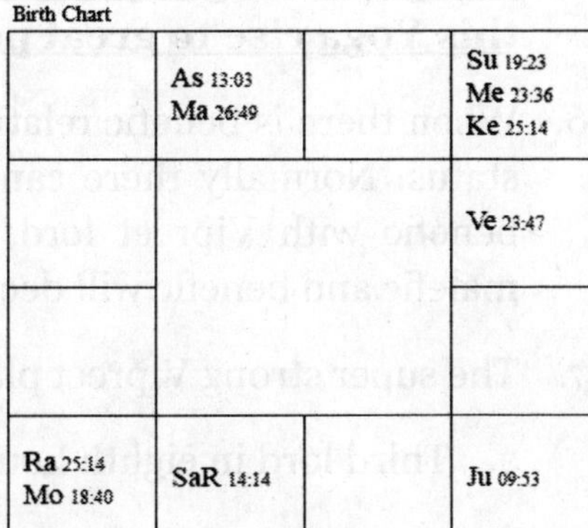

1. Twelfth lord Jupiter is placed in sixth house.

2. Jupiter is not associated or aspected by any planet.
3. He became caretaker Prime Minister for three times. He could not become regular Prime Minister.

Note: For Vipreet Raj Yoga to give its full results it must have malefic association or aspect.

Super strong Vipreet Raj Yoga

We have drawn the conclusion for the formation of a super strong Vipreet Raj Yoga. This is derived from the classic rules. The conditions for this Yoga are:

1. The lord of Vipreet house is in another Vipreet house from lagan.
2. The lord of any Vipreet house is` also in a Vipreet house from it. For example, third lord in eighth is in Vipreet house from lagan and third house.
3. The sign of its placement is an inimical or debilitation sign.
4. They have only malefic relation.
5. **When the above four conditions are met then this is a super strong Vipreet Raj Yoga and the person with this Yoga rise to great position in life and is famous.**
6. When there is benefic relation also even then it confers good status. Normally there can be relation of both malefic and benefic with Vipreet lord. The strength and status of the malefic and benefic will decide the issue.
7. The super strong Vipreet placements are.
    a. Third lord in eighth house.
    b. Sixth lord in eighth house.
    c. Eighth lord in third house.

8. The placements for a normal Vipreet Raj Yoga are.
    a. Third lord in sixth, eighth or twelfth house.
    b. Sixth lord in third, eighth or twelfth house.
    c. Eighth lord in third, sixth or twelfth house.
    d. Twelfth lord in third or eighth or in sixth house.
9. The effects of Vipreet Raj Yoga are experienced in its Dasha.
10. **The Vipreet Raj Yoga does not promote the Jeeva Tatva.**
11. *When the lord of Vipreet house is exalted and is in Super strong Vipreet Yoga then it can promote the evil effects of the house.*
12. *If Vipreet lord is a dispositor of Rahu/ Ketu or Gulika and is placed in Vipreet house and the lord have benefic relation, then it gives problems of the house.*
13. *In rule 11, if Vipreet lord is a dispositor of a benefic then it gives good result of the house.*

Example 7 Albert Einstein – DOB 14 March 1879, TOB 11.28, POB ULM

Birth Chart

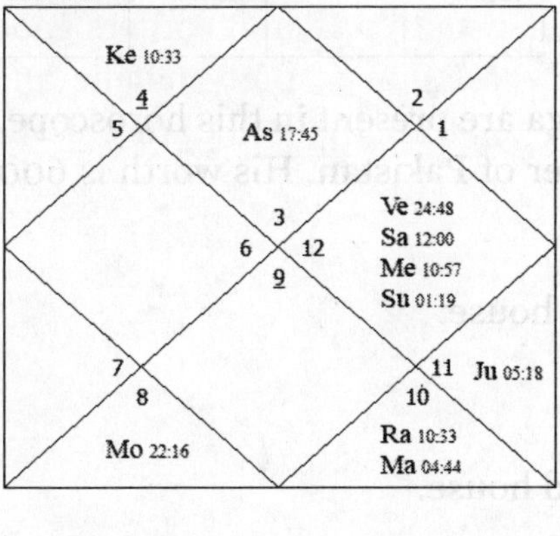

Birth Chart

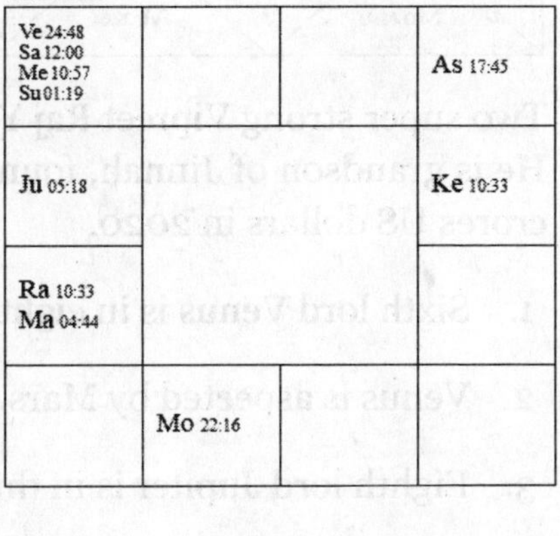

This example shows the super strong Vipreet Raj Yoga.

1. Mars is lord of sixth house and placed in eighth house.

2. Eighth house is Vipreet house from lagan and sixth house.

3. Mars is with Rahu and has no benefic relation.

4. Mars is exalted but there is no benefic relation. He faced problems of sixth house.

5. Mars Dasha operated from 1932 to 1939. He was at the peak of his career.

6. Rahu Dasha followed and lasted till his death.

Example 8 Nusli Wadia – DOB 15 February 1944, TOB 13.30, POB Mumbai

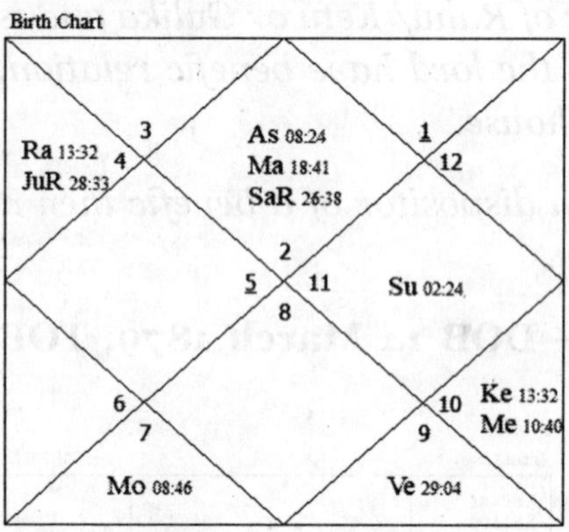

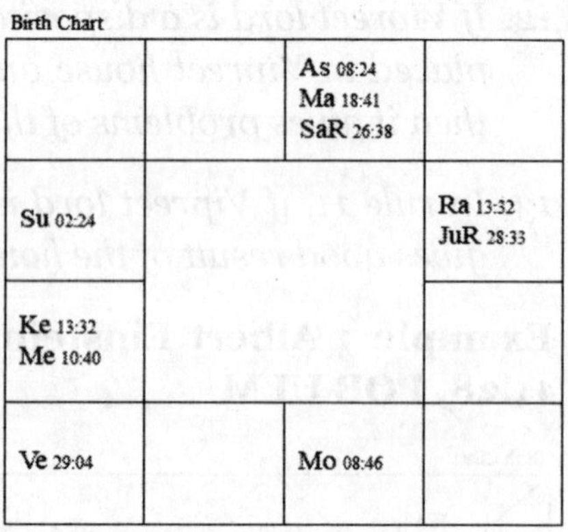

Two super strong Vipreet Raj Yoga are present in this horoscope. He is grandson of Jinnah, founder of Pakistan. His worth is 600 crores US dollars in 2020.

1. Sixth lord Venus is in eighth house.

2. Venus is aspected by Mars.

3. Eighth lord Jupiter is in third house.

4. Jupiter is with Ketu. Jupiter is exalted but did not give bad effect of eighth house because Venus is in eighth house. It gave good inheritance.

5. He was born in Dasha of Rahu. He had Dasha of Jupiter and Venus at the peak of life.

Example 9 Zia Ul Hague – DOB 11 August 1924, TOB 00.30, POB Jalandhar

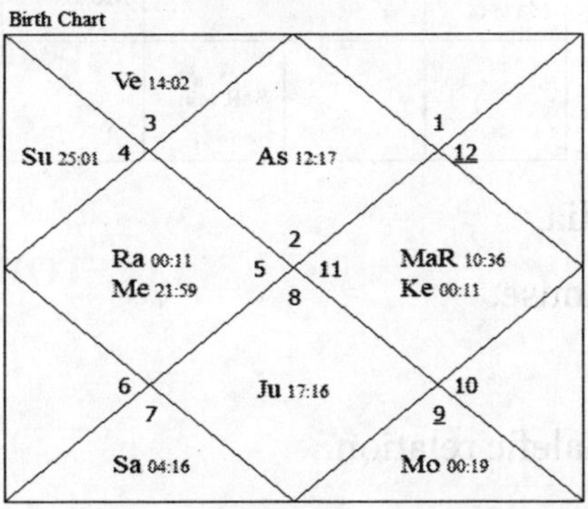

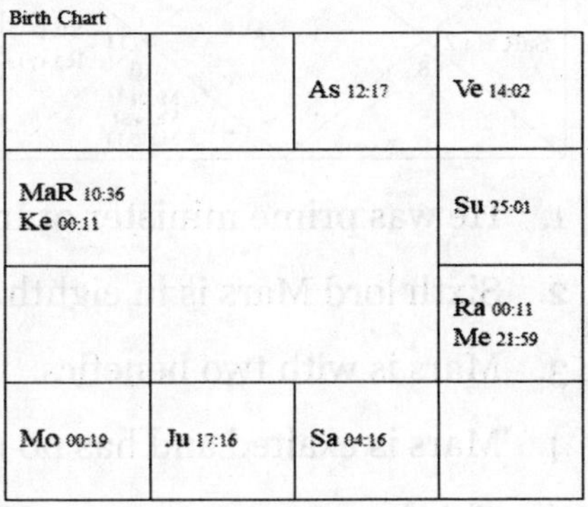

1. He was president of Pakistan.
2. Third lord Moon is placed in eighth house.
3. A malefic is in third house. It gave displacement from home.
4. Moon is aspected by Saturn and Venus.
5. Aspect of Venus is a benefic aspect.
6. He was president of Pakistan from 1978 till his death in a plane crash on 17 August 1988. The Dasha was of Rahu.

Example 10 Morarji Desai – DOB 29 February 1896, TOB 13.27, POB Billimora

Birth Chart

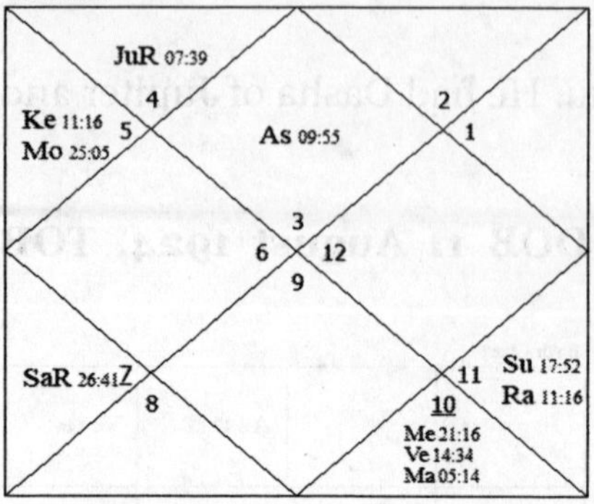

Birth Chart

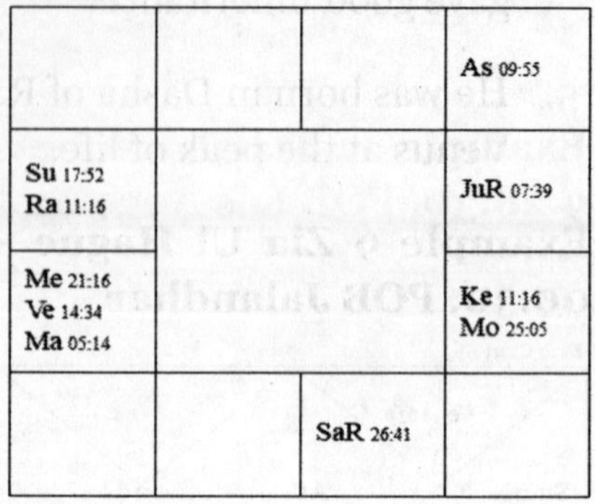

1. He was prime minister of India.
2. Sixth lord Mars is in eighth house.
3. Mars is with two benefics.
4. Mars is exalted and has no malefic relation.
5. This is not a super strong Vipreet Yoga.

Example 11 Amitabh Bachchan – DOB 11 October 1942, TOB 16.05, POB Allahabad

Birth Chart

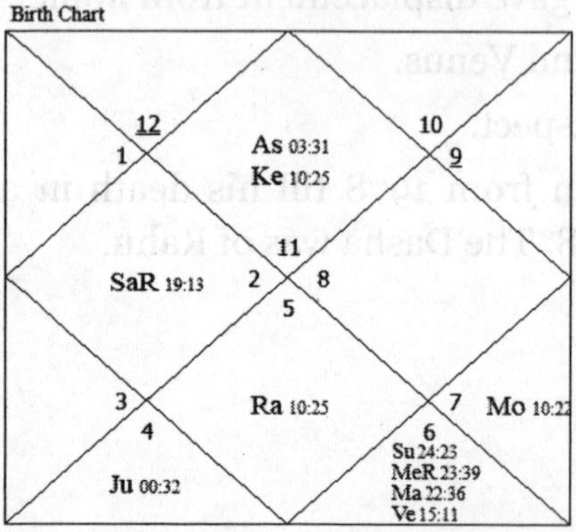

Birth Chart

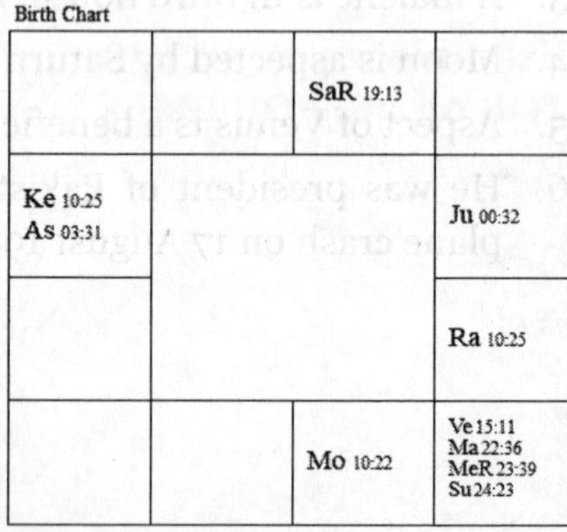

1. He is a super star of Indian Cinema.
2. Third lord Mars is in eighth house.

3. Mars has one malefic and two benefic conjunctions.
4. It is not meeting all conditions of a super strong Vipreet Yoga.

Example 12 Marilyn Monroe – DOB 1 June 1926, TOB 9.28.30, POB Los Angeles

Birth Chart

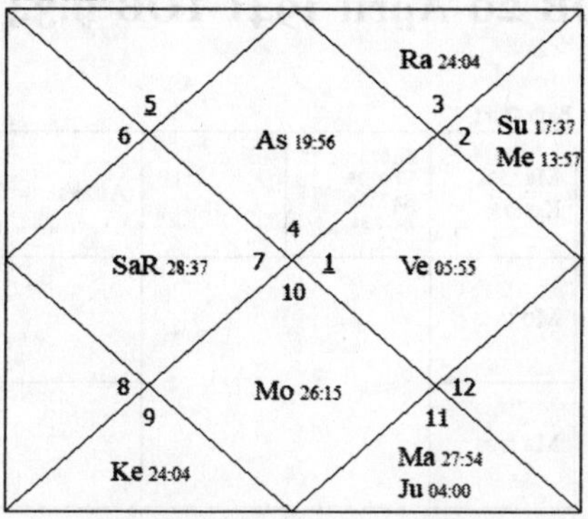

Birth Chart

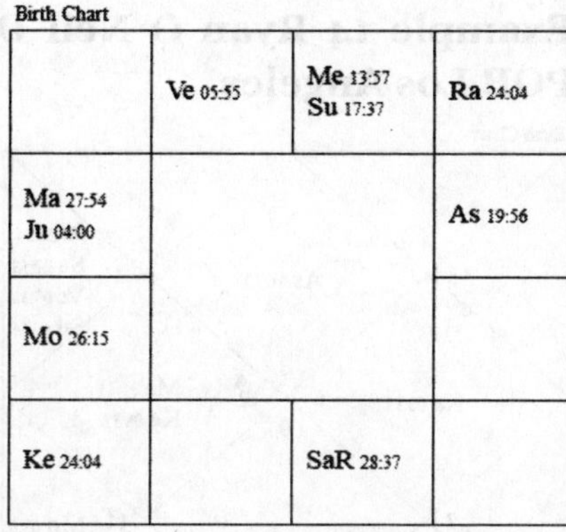

1. She was a very famous actor of Hollywood. She was not born with luxuries of life.
2. Sixth lord Jupiter is in eighth house.
3. Jupiter is with Mars and has no other association or aspect.

Example 13 Senior Judge – DOB 31 December 1961, TOB 02.26, POB Delhi

Birth Chart

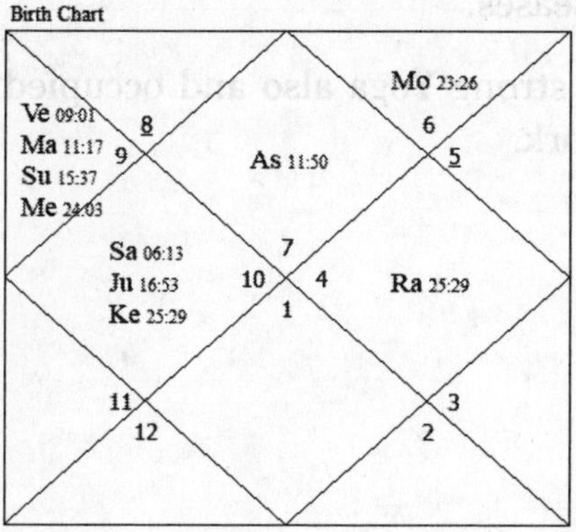

Birth Chart

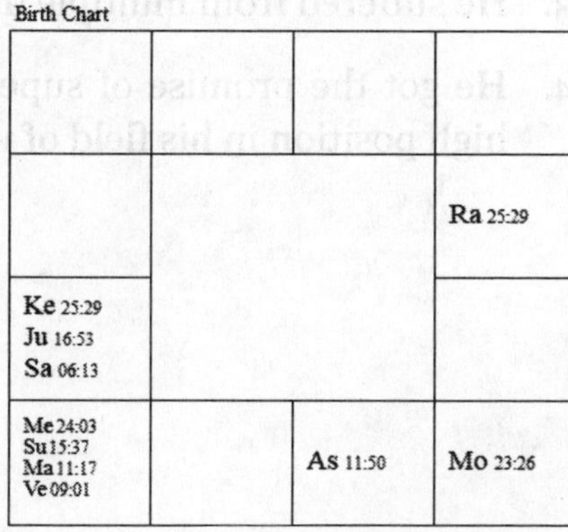

1. Eight lord Venus is in third house.
2. Venus is in enemy sign and with Mars and Sun. Mercury conjunction is a benefic conjunction.
3. Association of Mercury will not give full results of super strong Yoga.

Example 14 Ryan O Neil DOB 20 April 1941 TOB 9.34 POB Los Angeles

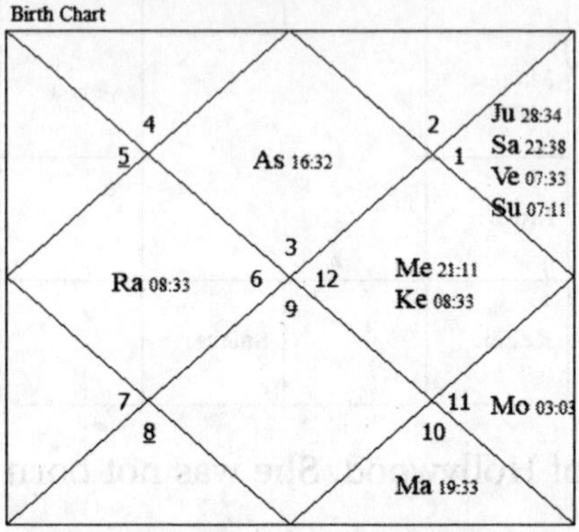

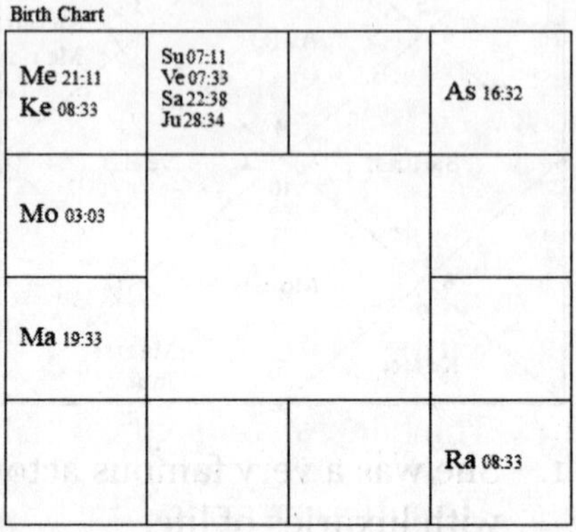

1. Sixth lord is exalted in eighth house.
2. Exalted lord of sixth house will give disease. For super strong Yoga the lord must be weak.
3. He suffered from multiple diseases.
4. He got the promise of super strong Yoga also and occupied high position in his field of work.

Example 15 Philip Berrigan DOB 5 October 1923 TOB 0.45 POB Two Harbors Minnesota

Birth Chart

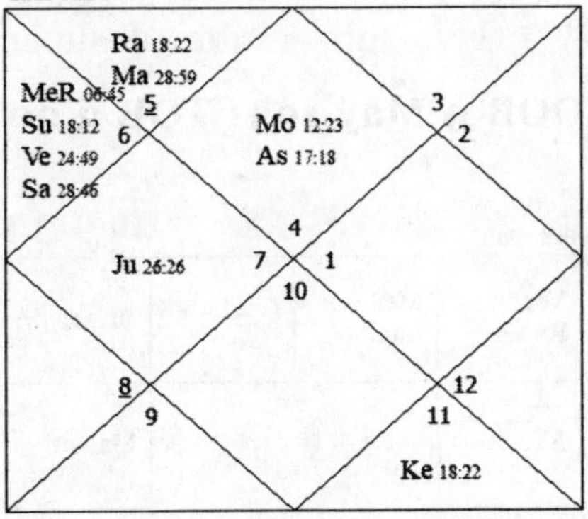

Birth Chart

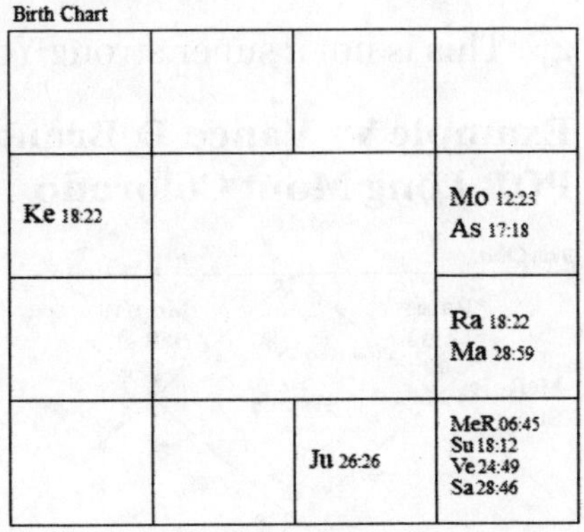

1. Ketu is in eighth house.
2. Saturn is in third house with two benefic and one malefic.
3. The benefic association is stronger than malefic association.
4. He suffered from Kidney cancer.

Example 16 Tim Robbins DOB 16 October 1958 TOB 2.12 POB West Covina CA

Birth Chart

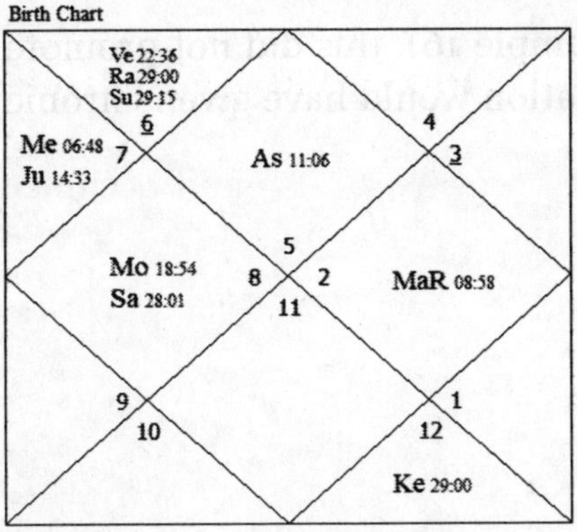

Birth Chart

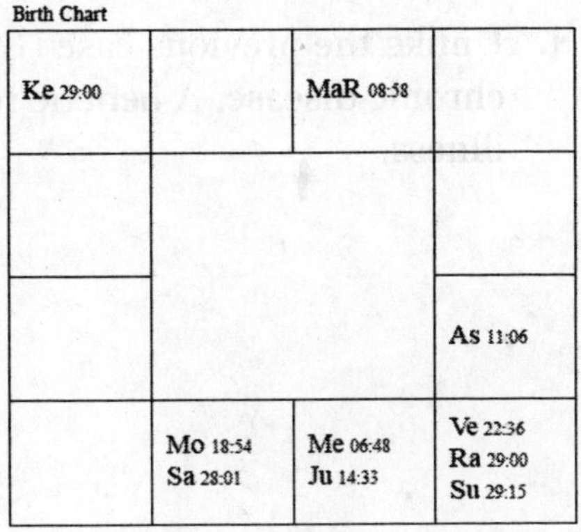

1. Ketu is in eighth house.

2. Jupiter is in third house with Mercury.

3. Jupiter is not having any malefic association or aspect.

4. This is not a super strong Yoga.

Example 17 Vance D Brand DOB 9 May 1931 TOB 2.20 POB Long Mont Colorado

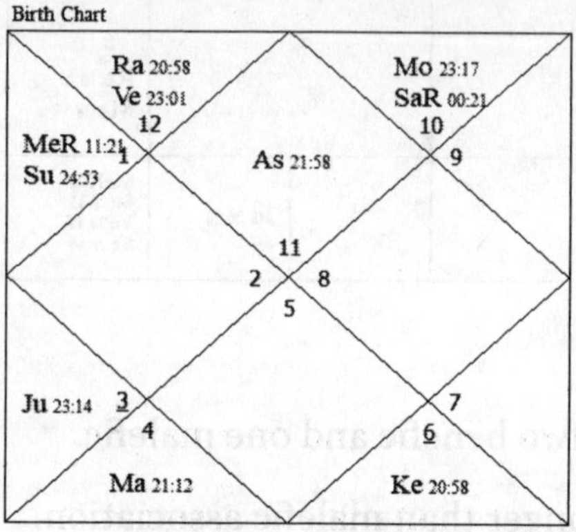

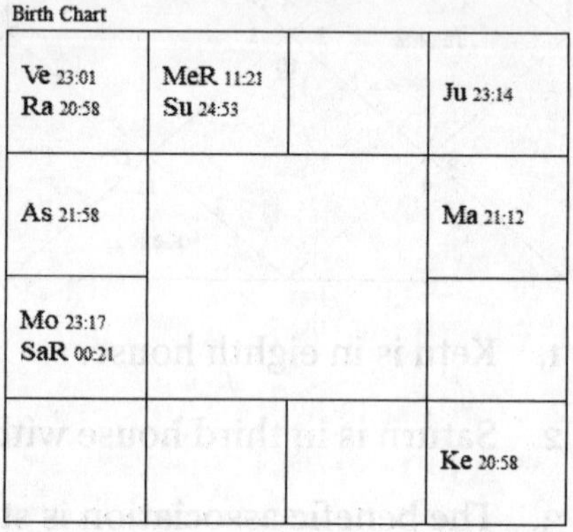

1. In this case also, Ketu is in eighth house.

2. Eighth lord is in third house with Sun.

3. There is no benefic relation with Mercury.

4. Unlike the previous case (Example 16), this did not promote chronic disease. A benefic relation would have given chronic illness.

Example 18 Jean Harlow DOB 3 March 1911 TOB 19.40 POB Kansas City Missouri

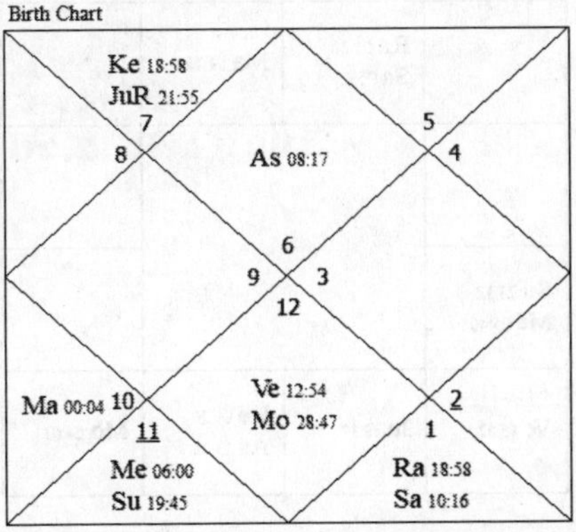

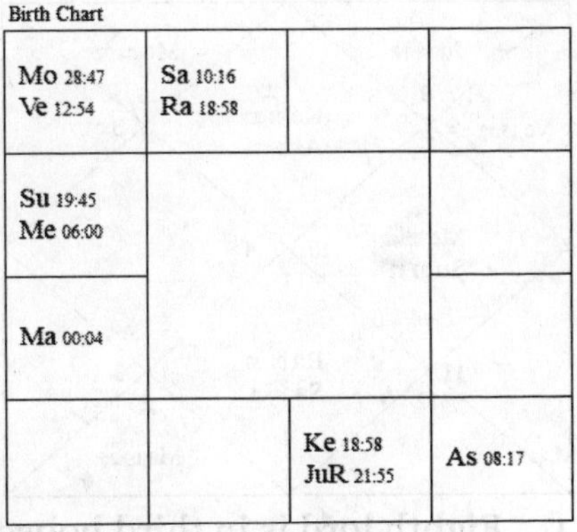

1. Sixth lord is in eighth house and is debilitated.
2. Saturn is with Rahu and is aspected by Mars and Jupiter. Jupiter aspect will promote the effects of Saturn as sixth. The aspect of Jupiter has lowered the potential of super strong Vipreet Yoga.
3. Mercury is placed in sixth house and will promote bad effect of sixth house.
4. Benefic aspect on sixth lord is promoting ill effect of sixth lord.
5. He died of Kidney failure on 7 June 1937.

Example 19 Eva Braun DOB 6 February 1912 TOB 0.30 POB Munich Germany

Birth Chart

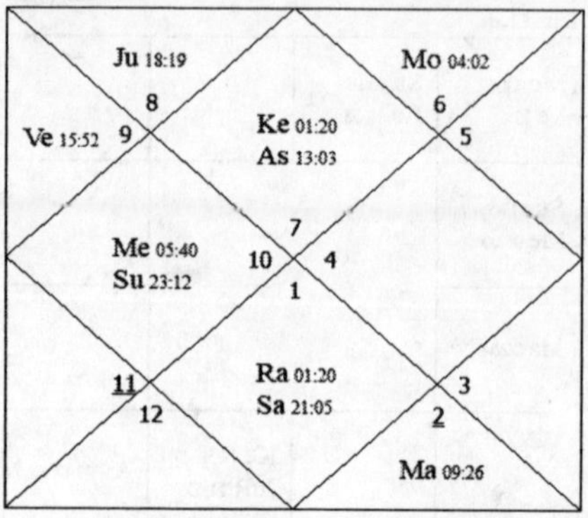

Birth Chart

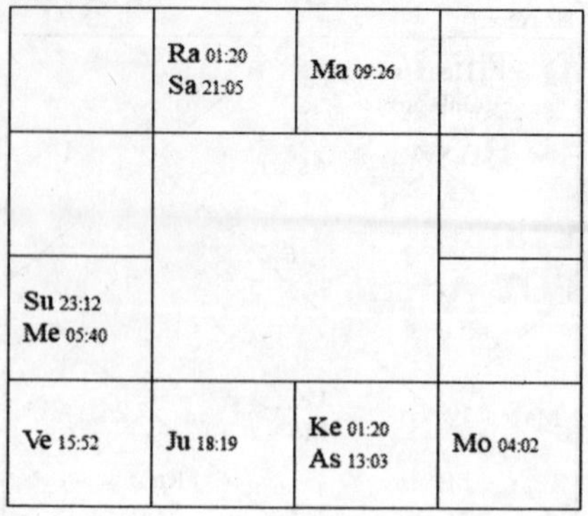

1. Eighth lord is in third house.
2. There is no malefic relation with Venus.
3. Venus is in Subh Kartari.
4. This is not a super strong Yoga.
5. She committed suicide with Hitler on 30 April 1945.

Example 20 Leonard Nathan DOB 8 November 1924 TOB 15.30 POB Los Angeles CA

Birth Chart

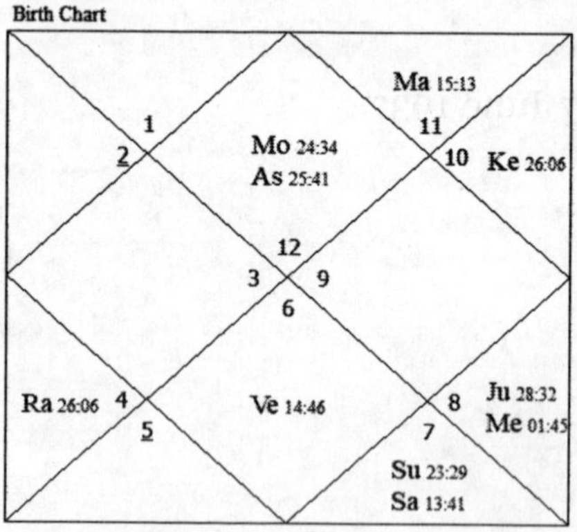

Birth Chart

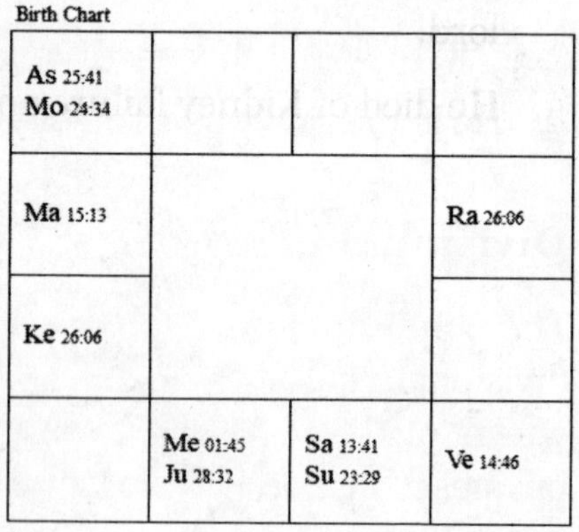

1. Sixth lord is in eighth house.

2. Sun is debilitated and is with Saturn.

3. Sun is not having any benefic relation.

4. This is a super strong Yoga.

5. He was a renowned professor.

Example Mukesh Ambani DOB 19 April 1954 TOB 7.13 POB Adena

Birth Chart

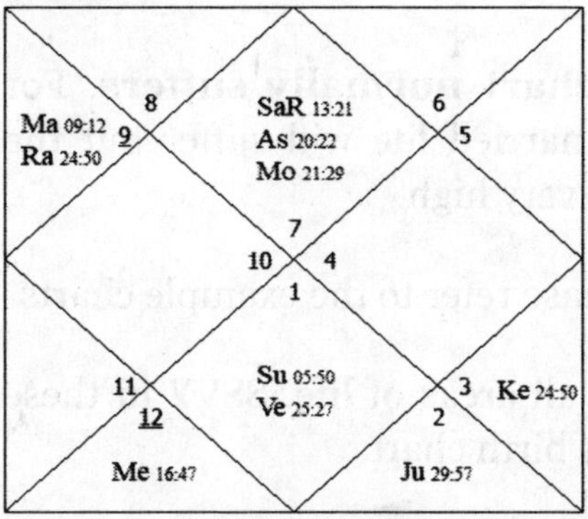

Birth Chart

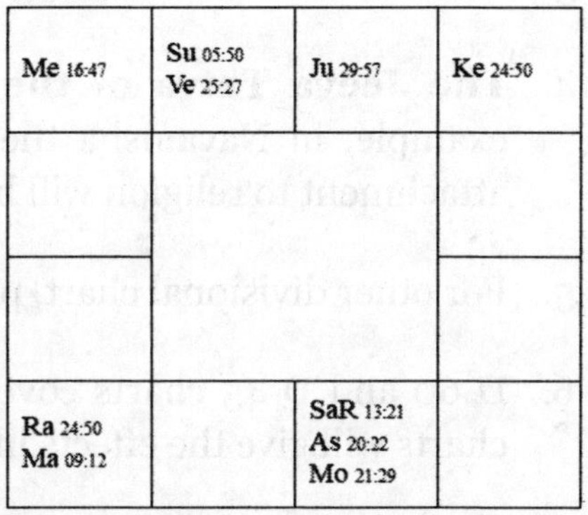

1. Third lord and sixth lord is Jupiter.

2. Jupiter is in eighth house causing SSVY.

3. Jupiter is not having any benefic or malefic relation.

4. He is the richest person of India.

Divisional Charts

The application of Super strong Vipreet Yoga is found on divisional charts also. The presence of this Yoga enhances the effects of the Varga. In D 10, it will promote the profession or business. In D 20 it will give spiritual highs. The presence of Super Strong Vipreet Yoga is one condition to check the result of a divisional chart. There are other combinations which can lift the result of a divisional chart.

Rules

1. A divisional chart indicates a specific area of life and the presence of SSVY will promote the significations of the chart.

2. This Yoga is a Vipreet Yoga, and the results are generally experienced after problems faced regarding the significations of the chart.

3. This will lift the Non Jeeva Tatva of the chart.

4. **The Jeeva Tatva of the chart normally suffers**. For example, in Navamsha the married life will suffer but the attachment to religion will be very high.

5. For other divisional chart, please refer to the example charts.

6. D 60 and D 45 charts cover all areas of life. SSVY in these charts will give the effects like birth chart.

We will examine this on few horoscopes.

Example Sage of Kochi DOB 20 May 1894 TOB 13.16 POB Villupuram

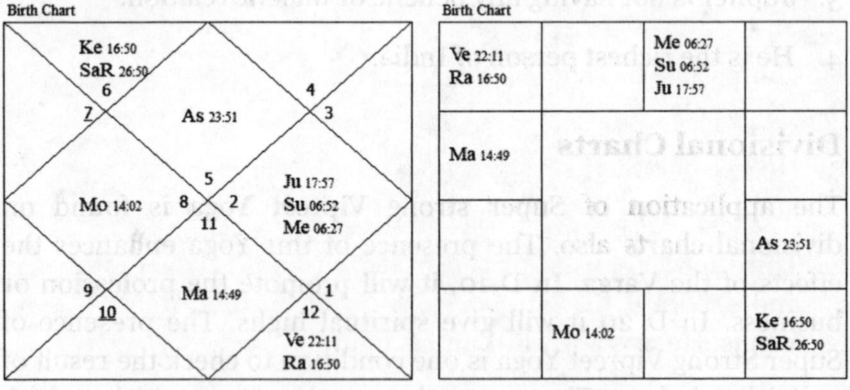

D20 Vimshamsha (spiritual progress)

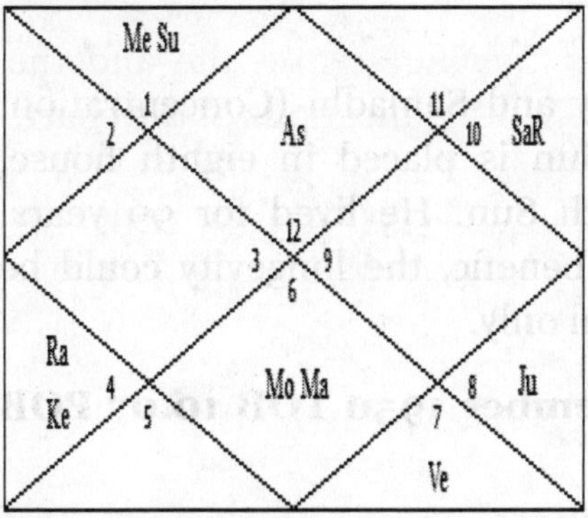

D20 Vimshamsha (spiritual progress)

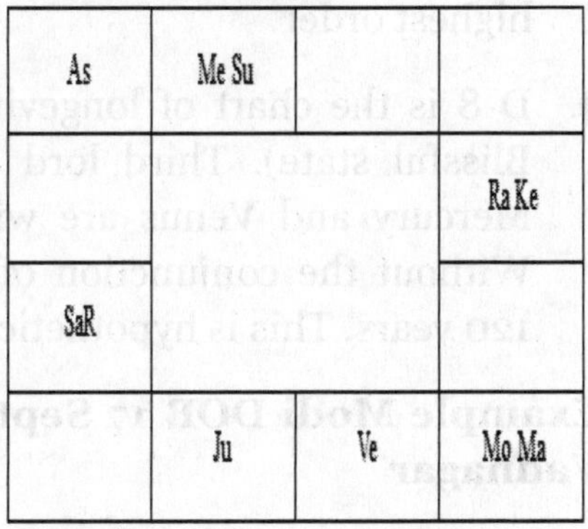

D8 Ashtamsha 1/8 Accidents

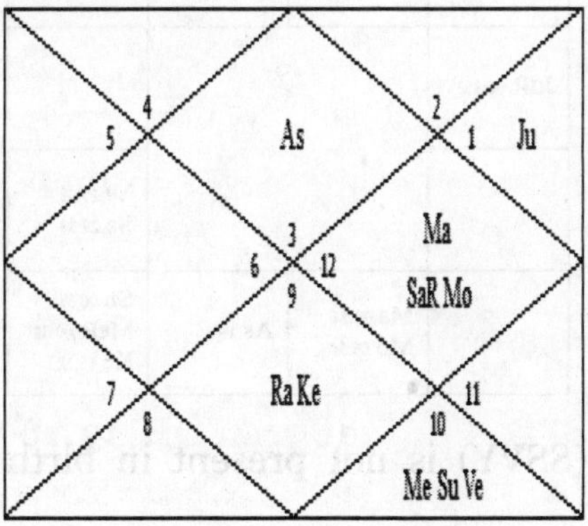

D8 Ashtamsha 1/8 Accidents

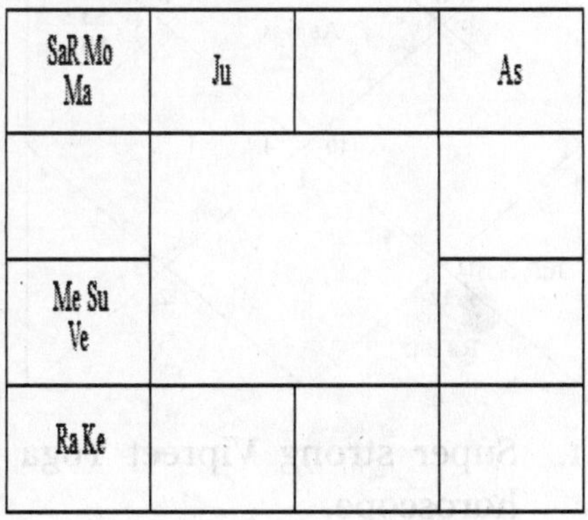

This horoscope has super strong Vipreet Yoga in D 1, D 20 and D 8.

1. He became Shankaracharya of Kochi at the age of 14 years and remained in this position till the age of 99 years.

2. Third lord Venus is placed in eighth house. It is with Rahu and aspected by Saturn. There is no benefic relation with Venus. He was a world-famous figure.

3. D 20 is the chart of spiritual attainments. In this chart, Venus is third lord and is placed in eighth house. Venus is

aspected by Mercury, Saturn and Sun. His spirituality is of highest order.

4. D 8 is the chart of longevity and Samadhi (Concentration, Blissful state). Third lord Sun is placed in eighth house. Mercury and Venus are with Sun. He lived for 99 years. Without the conjunction of benefic, the longevity could be 120 years. This is hypothetical only.

Example Modi DOB 17 September 1950 TOB 10.07 POB Vadnagar

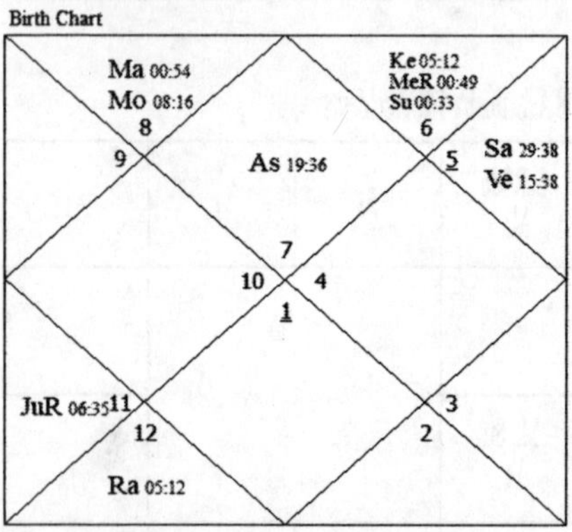

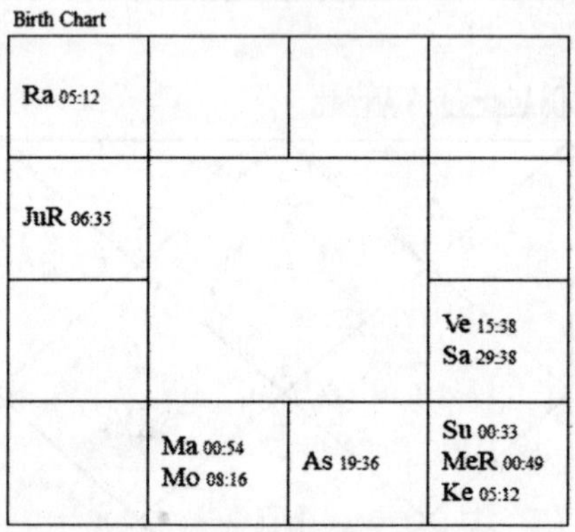

1. Super strong Vipreet Yoga (SSVY) is not present in birth horoscope.

D45 Akshavedamsha (All areas)

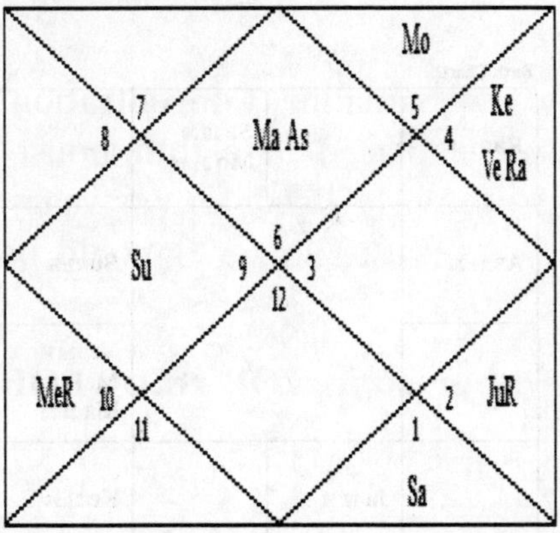

D45 Akshavedamsha (All areas)

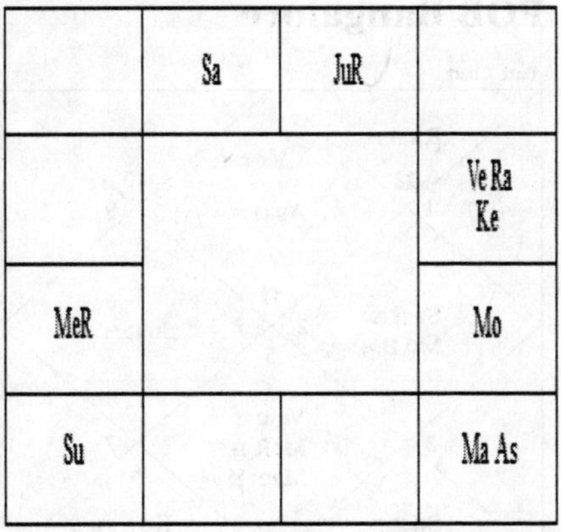

1. Saturn is the lord of sixth house and is placed in eighth house.
2. Saturn is causing SSVY.
3. Saturn is debilated and is aspected by Mars.
4. D 45 is seen for all areas of life. The important application is the conduct and character of the person.
5. It promotes the horoscope in all areas. Like birth chart, it gives fame.

Example B V Raman DOB 8 August 1912 TOB 19.52.30 POB Bangalore

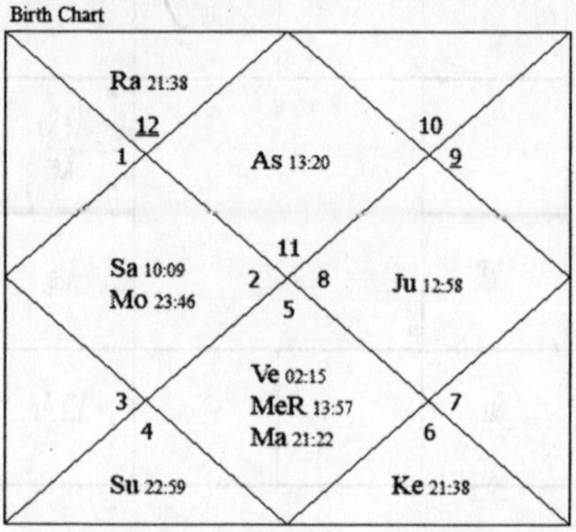

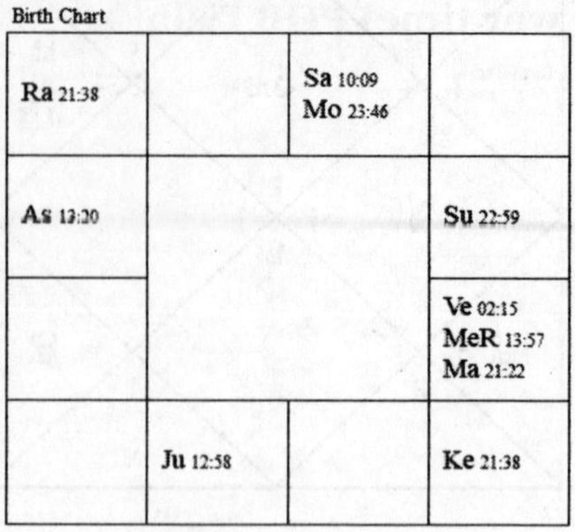

SSVY is not present in birth horoscope.

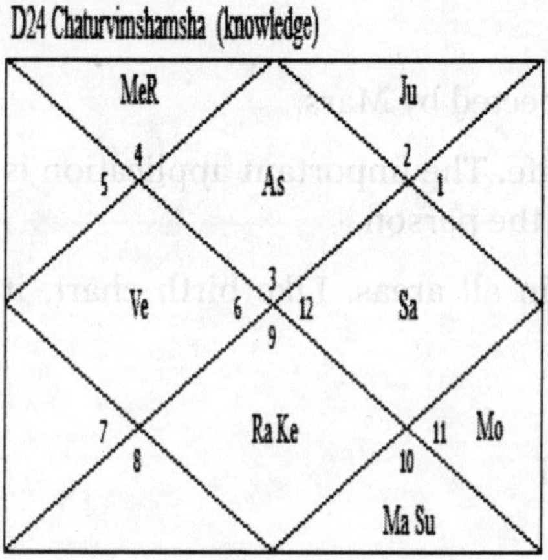

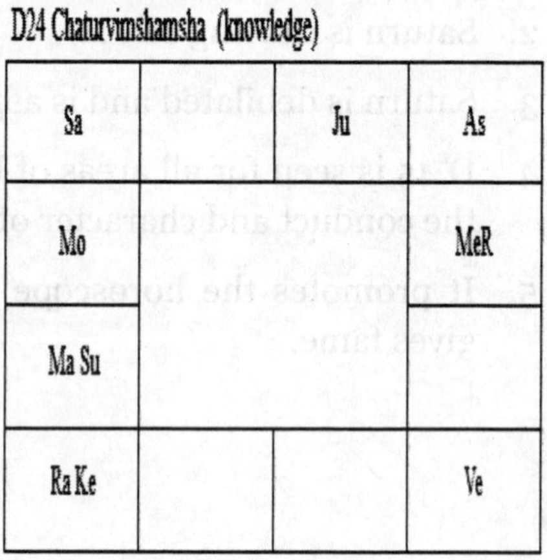

1. Mars is sixth lord and Sun is third lord.
2. Both are placed in eighth house.
3. They are aspected by Mercury and Jupiter.
4. Mars is with Sun and Sun is with Mars and as such there is a malefic connection.
5. There are two benefic aspects. The SSVY Yoga is present.
6. He was a renowned astrologer.

7. The learning and knowledge are promised.

Example V P Goel DOB 30 April 1945 TOB 9.27 (10.27 war time) POB Delhi

Birth Chart

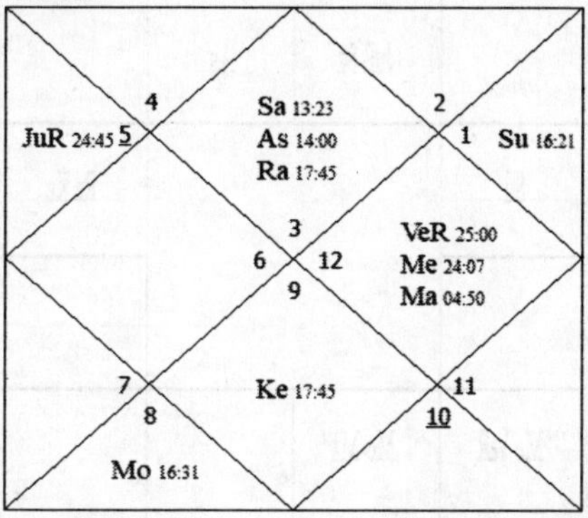

Birth Chart

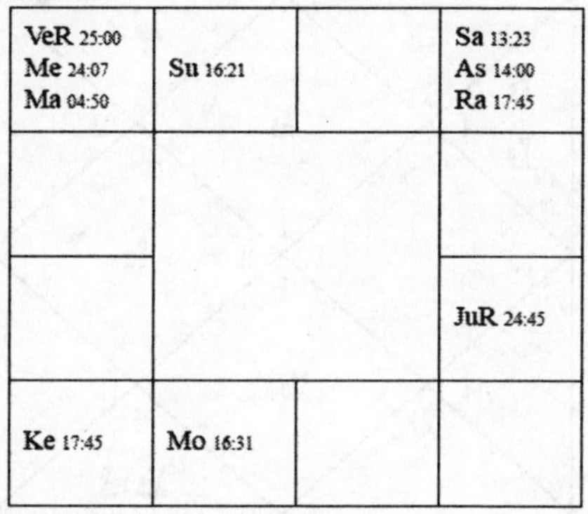

SSVY is not present in birth horoscope.

D24 Chaturvimshamsha (knowledge)

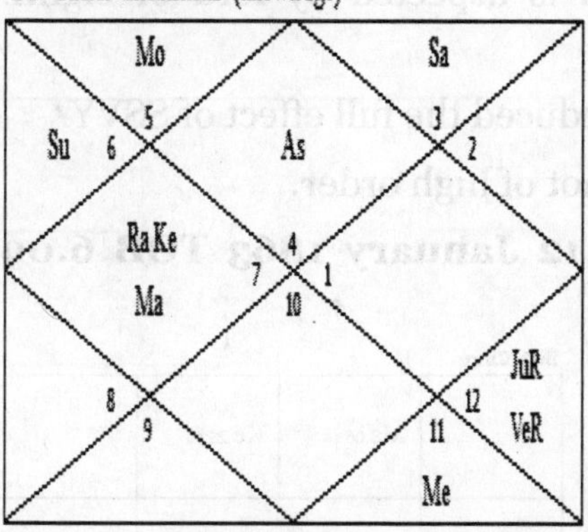

D24 Chaturvimshamsha (knowledge)

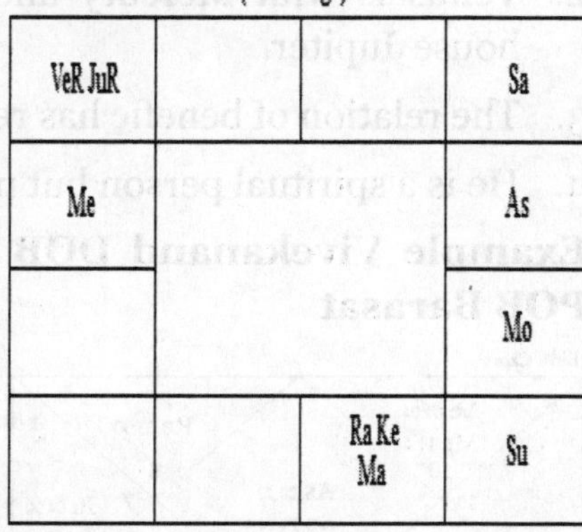

1. Mercury is third lord and is placed in eighth house.
2. Mercury is aspected by waning Moon and have no other relation.
3. He is an astrologer and has written 26 books on astrology till date. This is inherent knowledge granted by the grace of God.
4. He holds a post graduate degree in engineering and has served Government of India at a class 1 post.

5. He has been an adviser to Ministry of Defense.
6. D 24 shows this promise because of SSVY.

D20 Vimshamsha (spiritual progress)

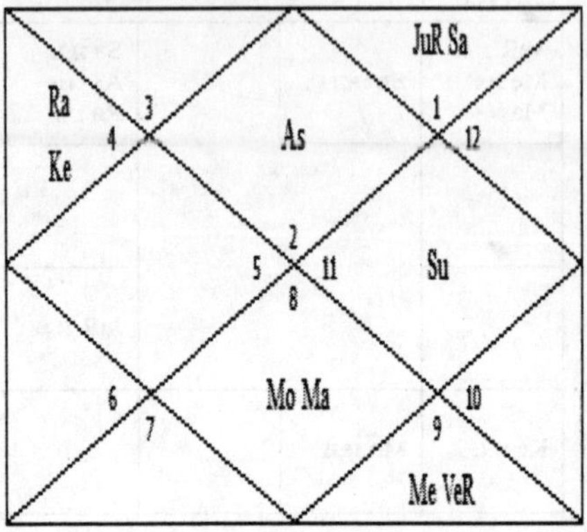

D20 Vimshamsha (spiritual progress)

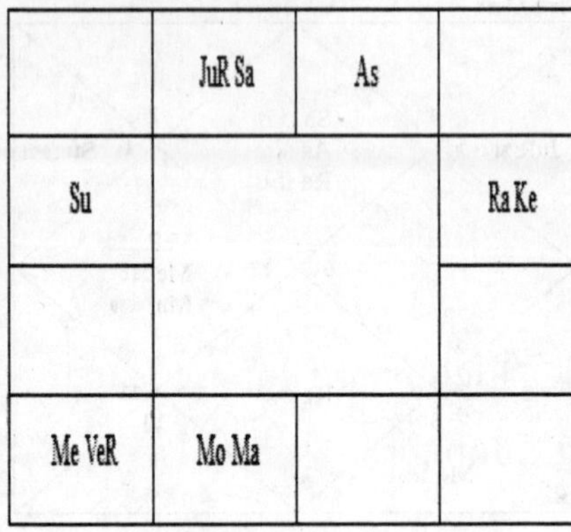

1. Venus is sixth lord and is placed in eighth house.
2. Venus is with Mercury and is aspected by lord of eighth house Jupiter.
3. The relation of benefic has reduced the full effect of SSVY.
4. He is a spiritual person but not of high order.

Example Vivekanand DOB 12 January 1863 TOB 6.09 POB Barasat

Birth Chart

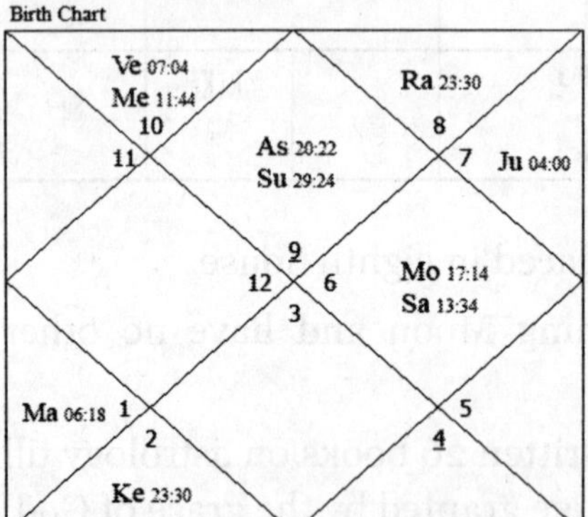

Birth Chart

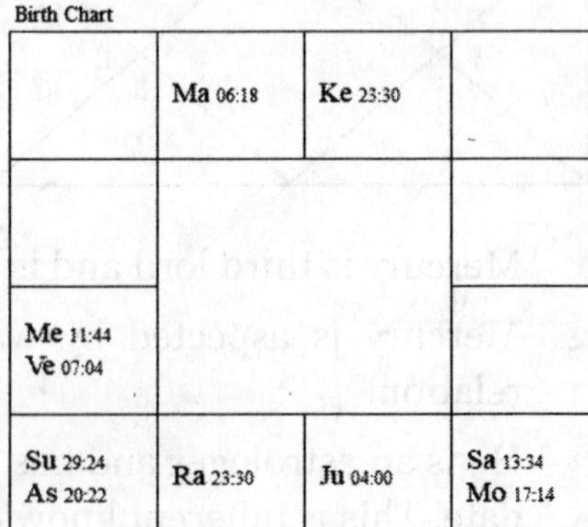

SSVY is not present in birth chart.

D3 Dreshkana (happiness siblings)

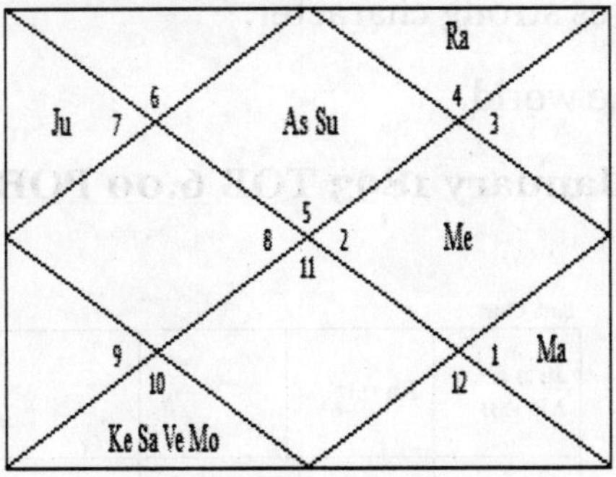

D3 Dreshkana (happiness siblings)

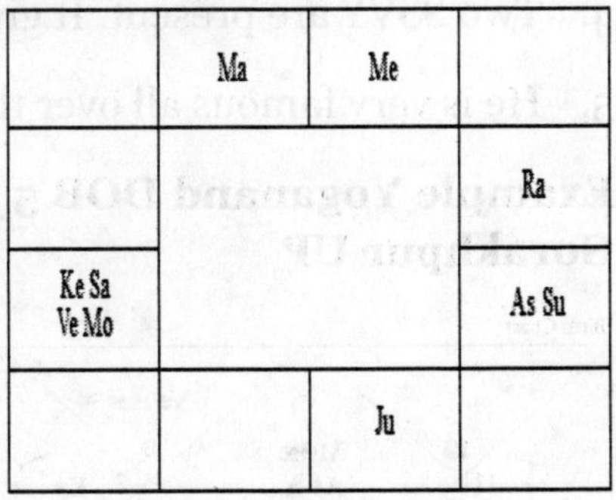

1. Eighth lord Jupiter is in third house.
2. Jupiter is aspected by Mars.

1. SSVY is present.
2. This makes him very courageous.
3. The Coborn will suffer.

D45 Akshavedamsha (All areas)

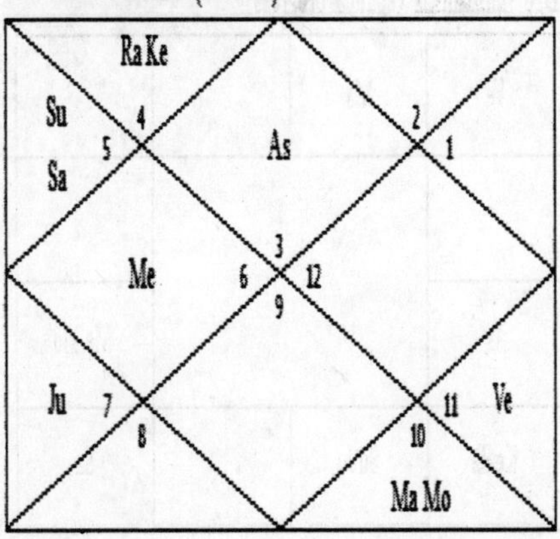

D45 Akshavedamsha (All areas)

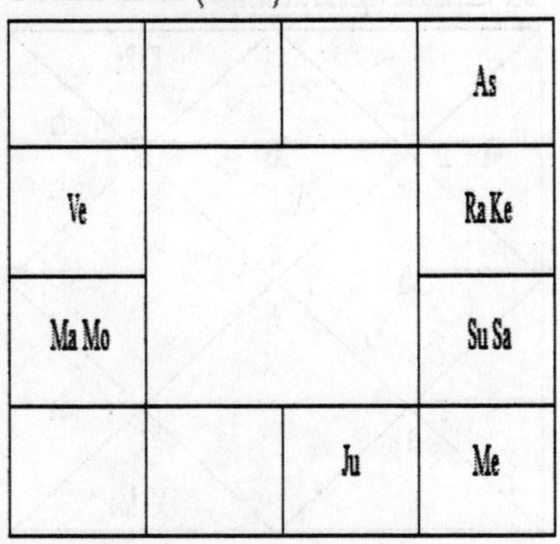

1. Eighth lord Saturn is placed in third house.
2. Saturn is with Sun and is aspected by Mars and Venus.
3. Sixth lord Mars is in eighth house in RKA.

4. Two SSVY are present. It gives strong character.

5. He is very famous all over the world.

Example Yoganand DOB 5 January 1893 TOB 6.00 POB Gorakhpur UP

Birth Chart

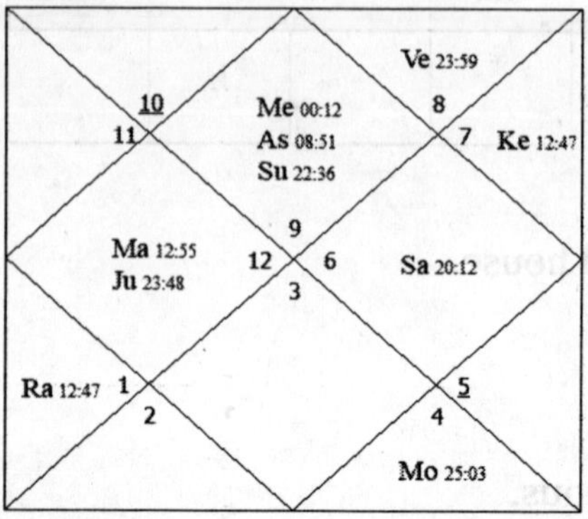

Birth Chart

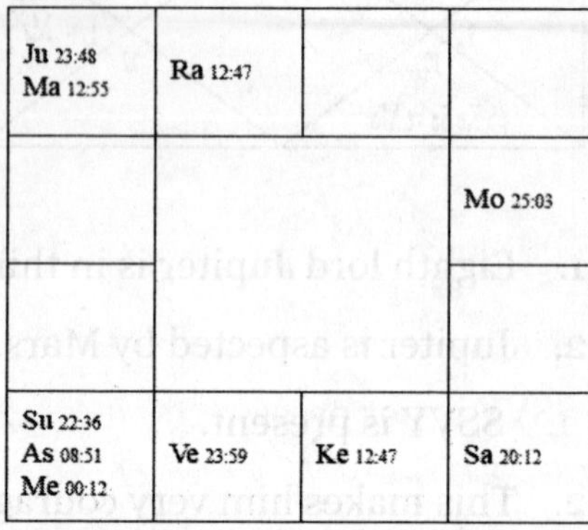

SSVY is not present in birth horoscope.

D20 Vimshamsha (spiritual progress)

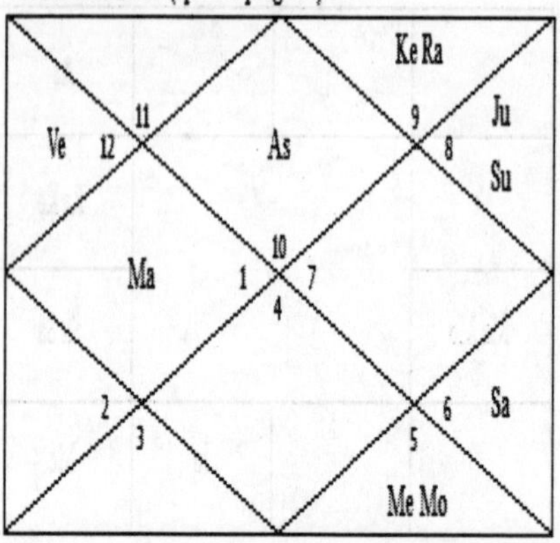

D20 Vimshamsha (spiritual progress)

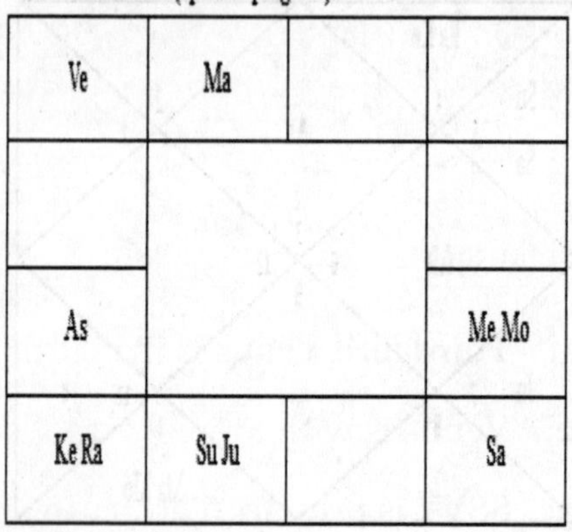

1. Sixth lord is Mercury.
2. Mercury is placed in eighth house with waning Moon.
3. There is no benefic relation.
4. He was a great saint and is famous worldwide.

Example Indira Gandhi DOB 19 November 1917 TOB 23.11.20 POB Allahabad

Birth Chart

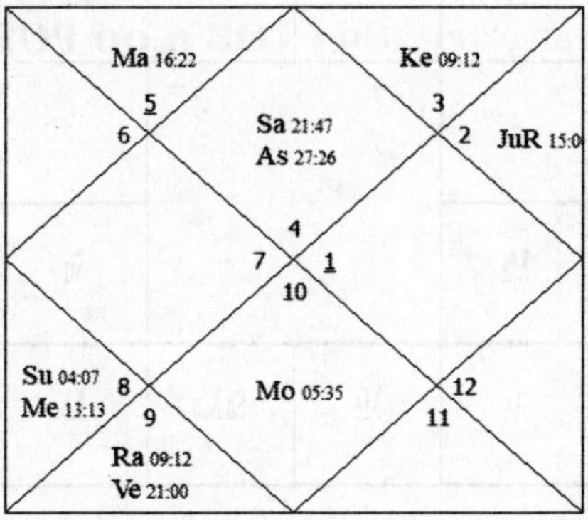

Birth Chart

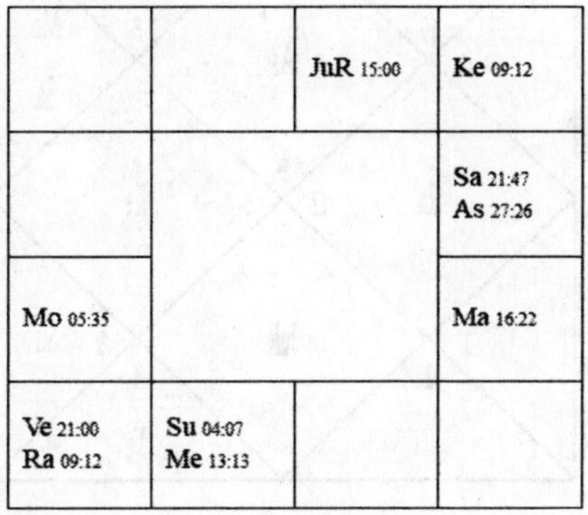

SSVY is not present in birth horoscope.

D9 Navamsha (spouse)

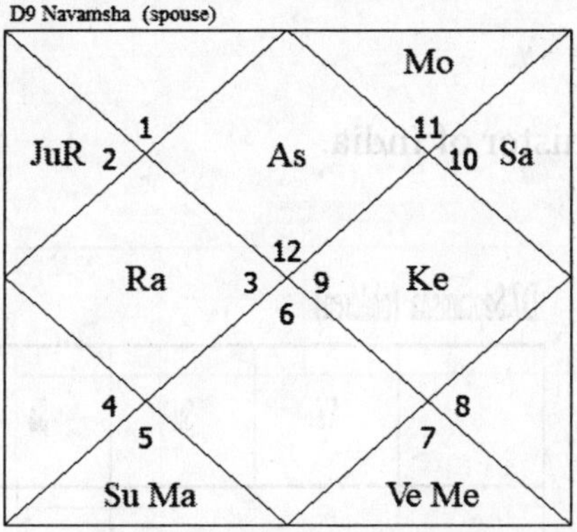

D9 Navamsha (spouse)

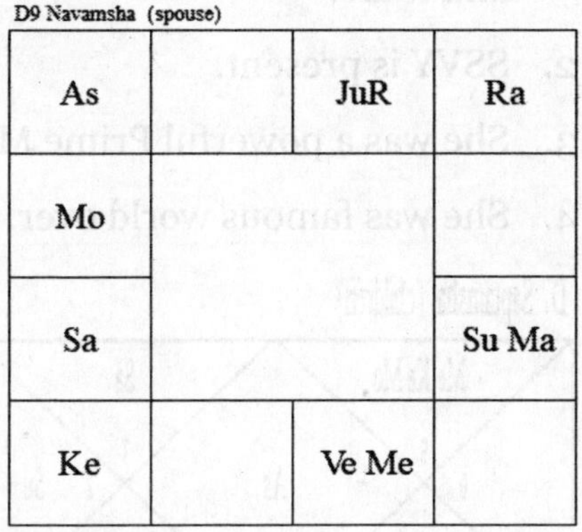

1. Third lord Venus is in eighth house.
2. Venus is with Mercury and is aspected by Saturn.
3. SSVY is present. The Jeeva effect of Navamsha is spoiled.
4. She was very religious and followed her religion.

D10 Dashamsha (great successes)

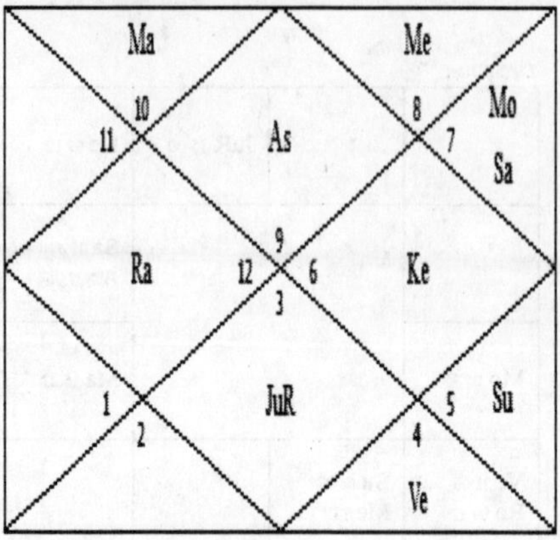

D10 Dashamsha (great successes)

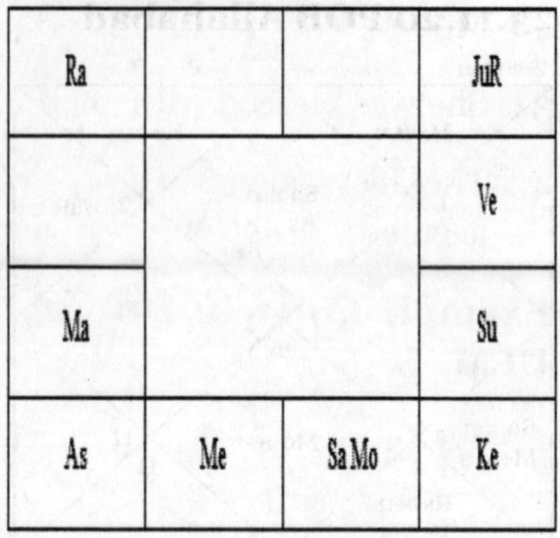

1. Sixth lord Venus is in eighth house and is aspected by Saturn and Mars.
2. SSVY is present.
3. She was a powerful Prime Minister of India.
4. She was famous world over.

D7 Saptamsha (children)

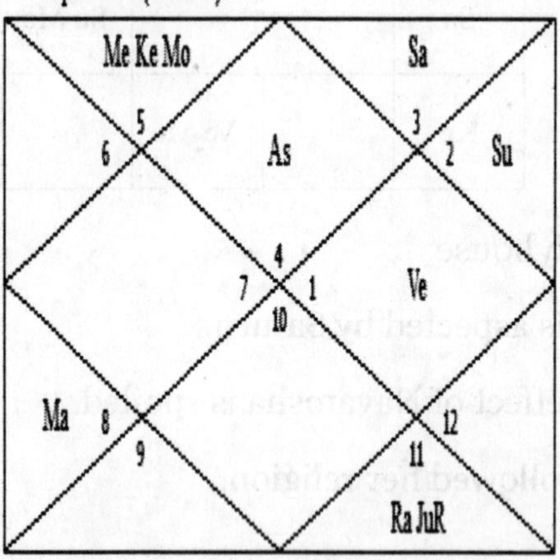

D7 Saptamsha (children)

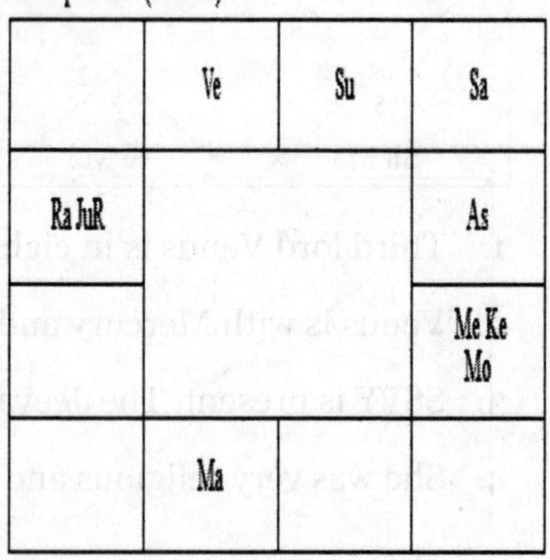

1. Sixth lord Jupiter is in eighth house.

2. Jupiter is with Rahu and is aspected by Mercury and waning Moon.

3. She was blessed with good intuition.

4. The Jeeva significations are spoiled. Her both sons died in accident.

Example Einstein DOB 14 March 1879 TOB 11.30 POB ULM

Birth Chart

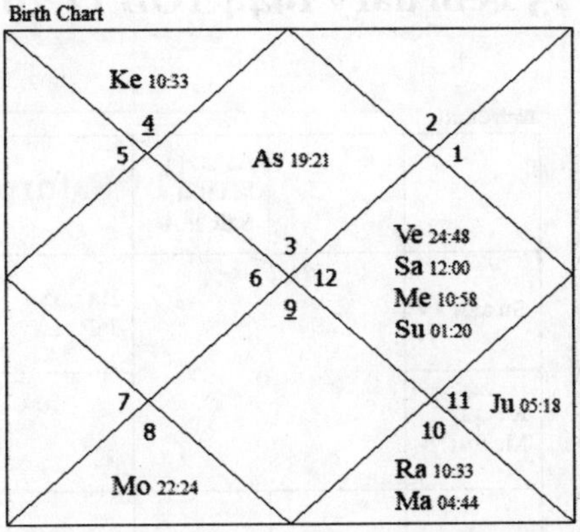

Birth Chart

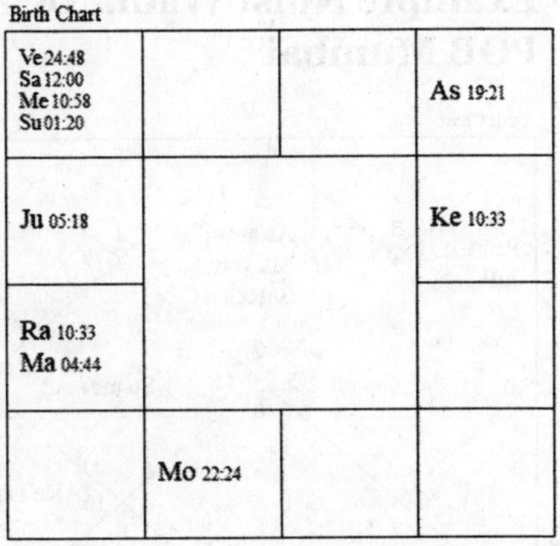

SSVY is present in birth horoscope and is discussed earlier.

D10 Dashamsha (great successes)

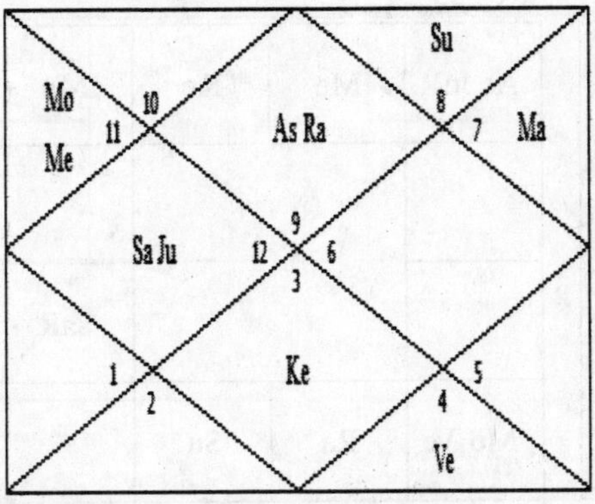

D10 Dashamsha (great successes)

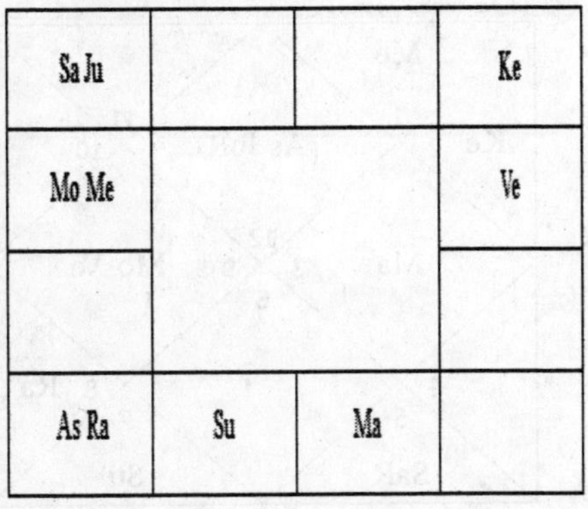

1. Sixth lord Venus is in eighth house and is aspected by Jupiter.
2. Eighth lord Moon is in third house with Mercury.
3. There is no malefic association with Venus or Moon.
4. The complete SSVY is not formed.
5. He was good in his work and got Noble Prize for his work.

Example Nulsi Wadia DOB 15 February 1944 TOB 13.30 POB Mumbai

Birth Chart

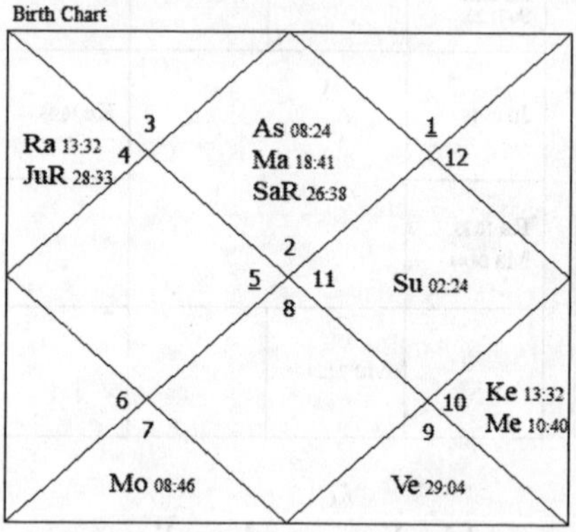

Birth Chart

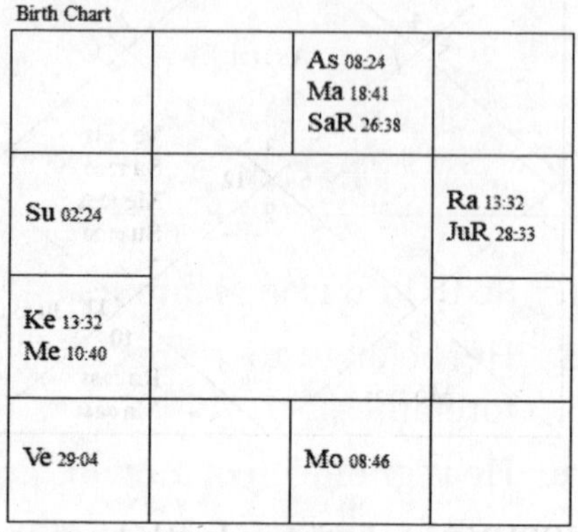

1. SSVY is present in birth horoscope and has been discussed.

D9 Navamsha (spouse)

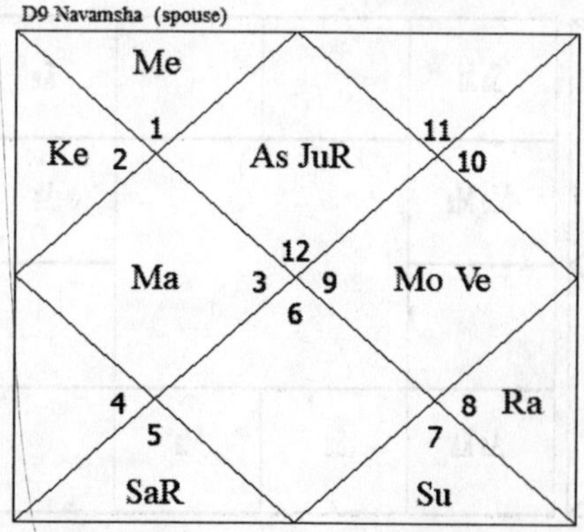

D9 Navamsha (spouse)

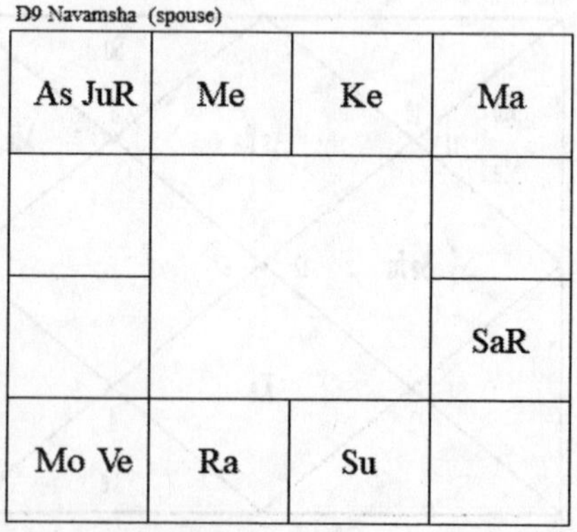

1. Sixth lord Sun is debilitated in eighth house.

2. Sun is aspected by malefic Mercury and Saturn.
3. He followed his religion faithfully.
4. This is not helpful for marriage bliss.

D12 Dwadashamsha (parents)

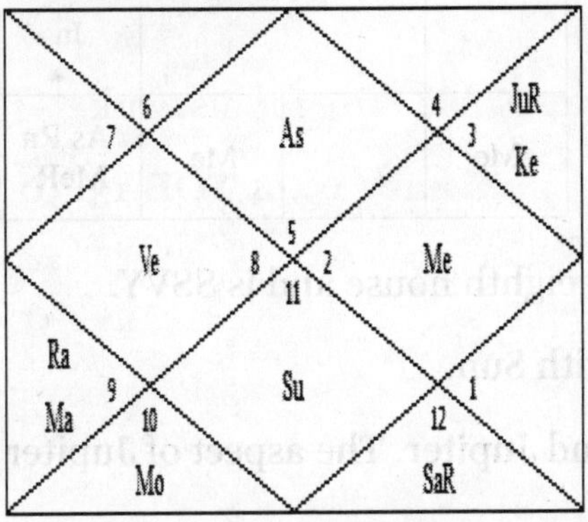

D12 Dwadashamsha (parents)

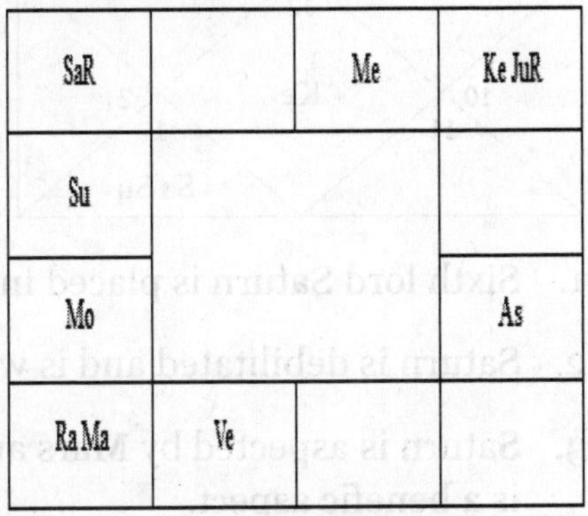

1. Sixth lord is in eighth house. Saturn is aspected by Mars.
2. He belongs to respectable lineage. This grant blessing of forefathers.
3. He is grandson of Jinnah, Father of Nation of Pakistan.

Example Lata DOB 28 September 1929 TOB 22.39.59 POB Indore

Birth Chart

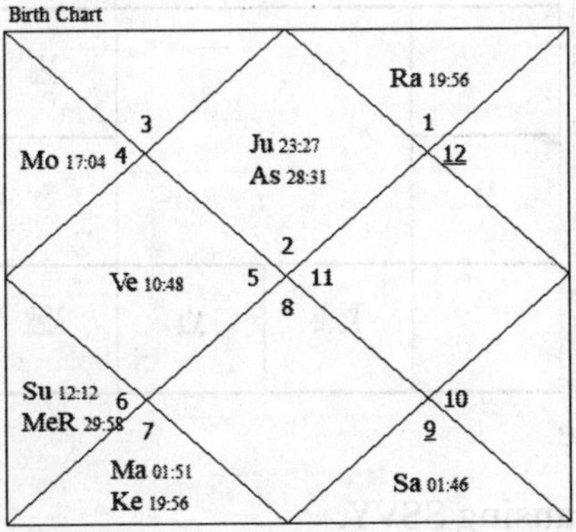

Birth Chart

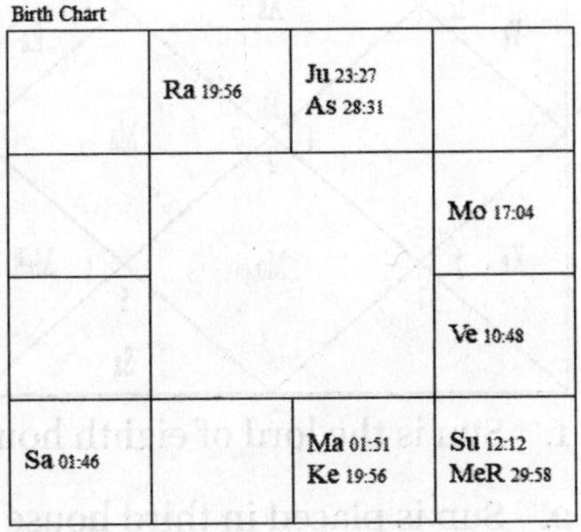

SSVY is not present in birth horoscope.

D9 Navamsha (spouse)

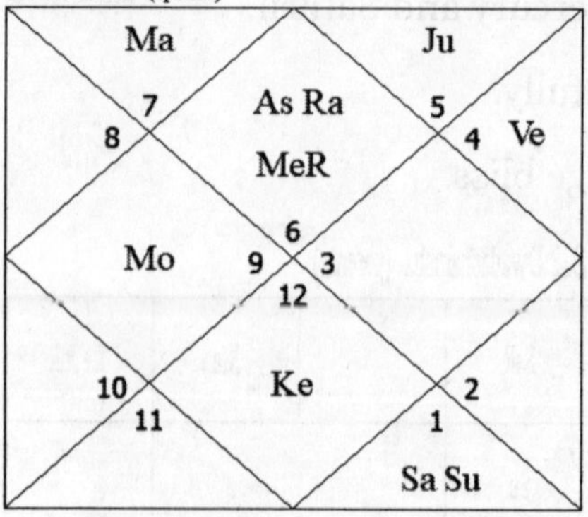

D9 Navamsha (spouse)

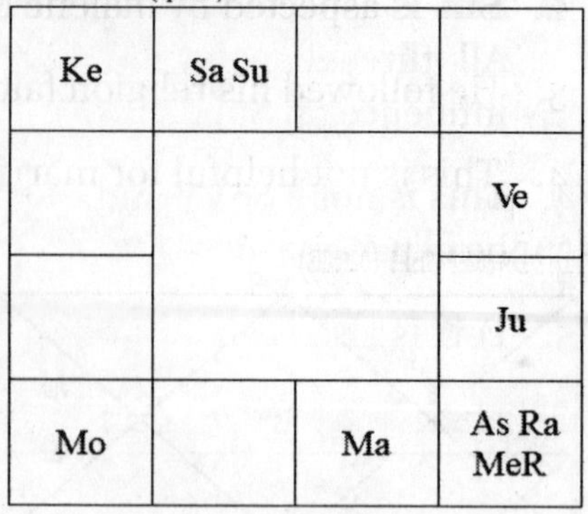

1. Sixth lord Saturn is placed in eighth house and is SSVY.
2. Saturn is debilitated and is with Sun.
3. Saturn is aspected by Mars and Jupiter. The aspect of Jupiter is a benefic aspect.
4. This gives strong religious attachment to her religion.
5. She is not married.

D11 Ekadashamsha 1/11 Cure

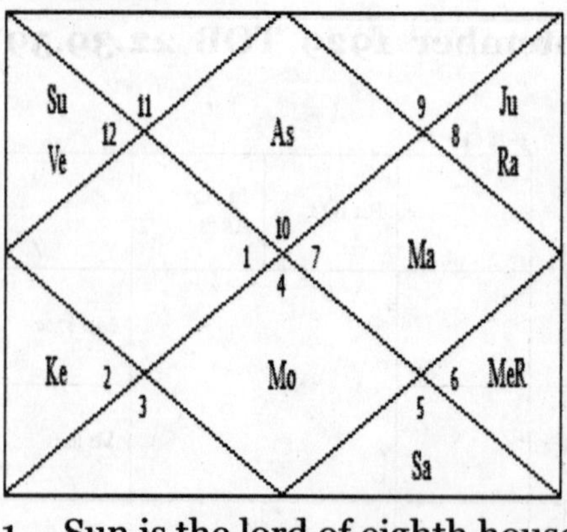

D11 Ekadashamsha 1/11 Cure

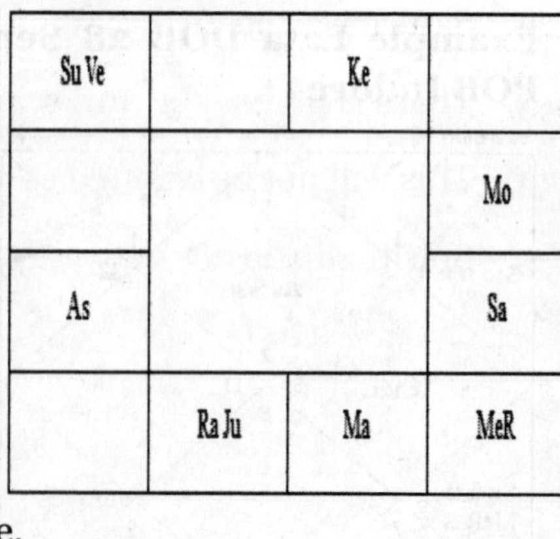

1. Sun is the lord of eighth house.
2. Sun is placed in third house causing SSVY.

3. Sun is aspected by Mercury and Jupiter. Venus is with Sun. All three benefic are related to Sun. there is no malefic influence on Sun.

4. This is not a SSVY and the problems of eighth house will also be experienced.

5. D 11 is also seen for honors. She was awarded Bharat Ratan.

D20 Vimshamsha (spiritual progress)

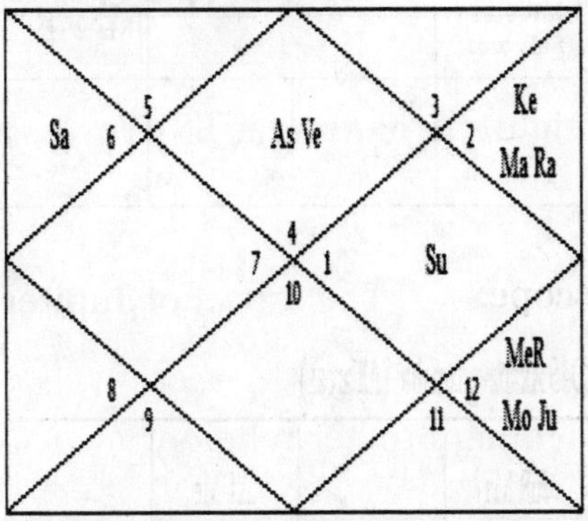

D20 Vimshamsha (spiritual progress)

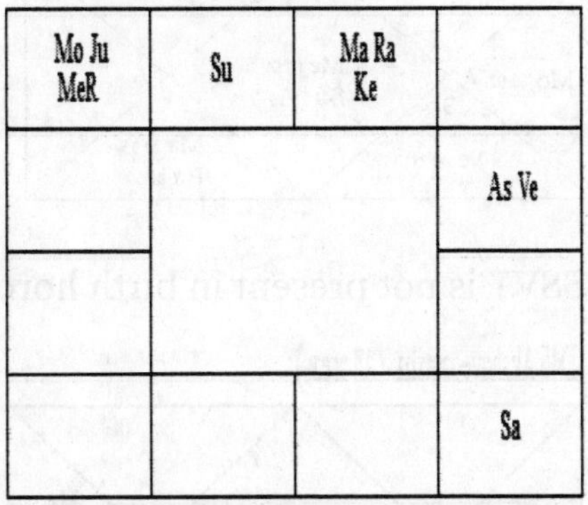

1. Saturn is eighth lord and is placed in third house.

2. Saturn is aspected by Moon, Jupiter and Mercury.

3. There is no malefic influence on Mercury.

4. This will not be counted as SSVY.

5. Spirituality is not stronger than religious attachment.

Example Barack Obama DOB 4 August 1961 TOB 19.24 POB Honolulu

Birth Chart

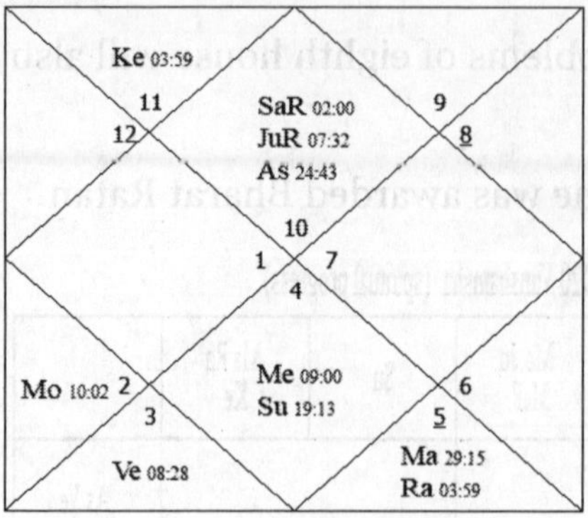

Birth Chart

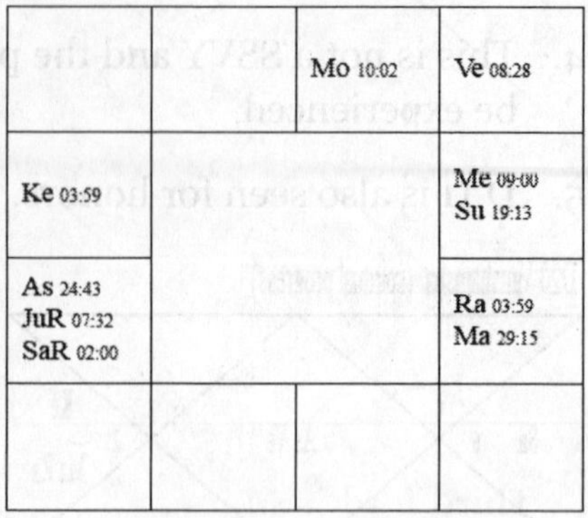

SSVY is not present in birth horoscope.

D45 Akshavedamsha (All areas)

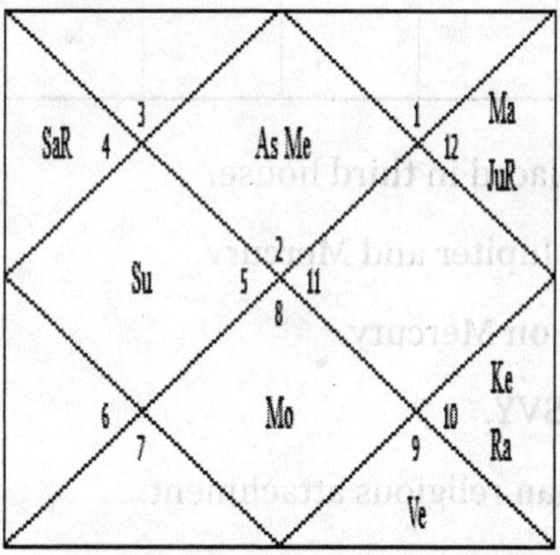

D45 Akshavedamsha (All areas)

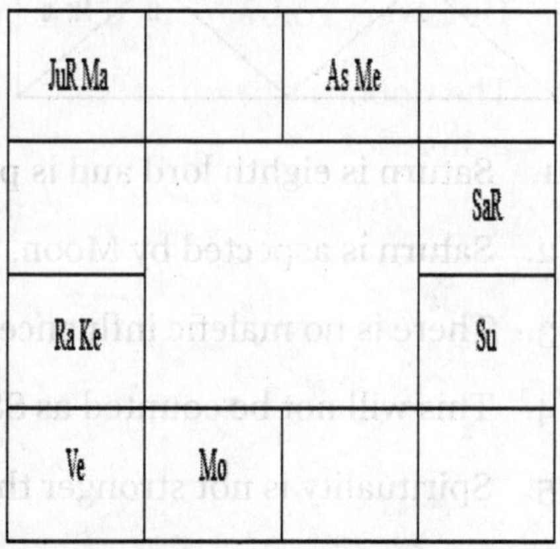

1. Sixth lord Venus is placed in eighth house.
2. Venus is having no relation with any other planet.
3. SSVY is present.
4. He was President of USA for two terms lasting 8 years.
5. D 45 gives results of all areas of life.

D3 Dreshkana (happiness siblings)

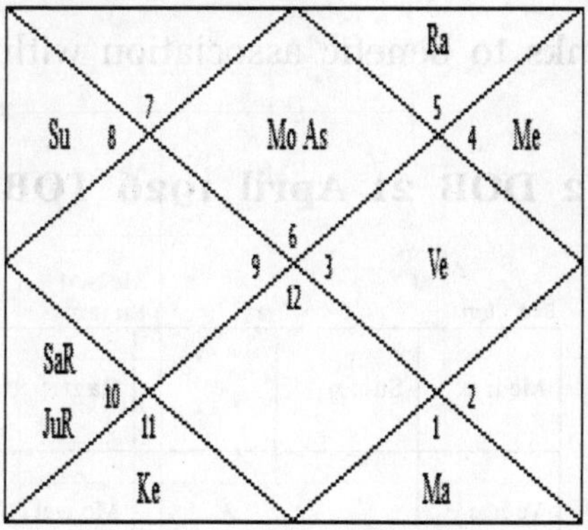

D3 Dreshkana (happiness siblings)

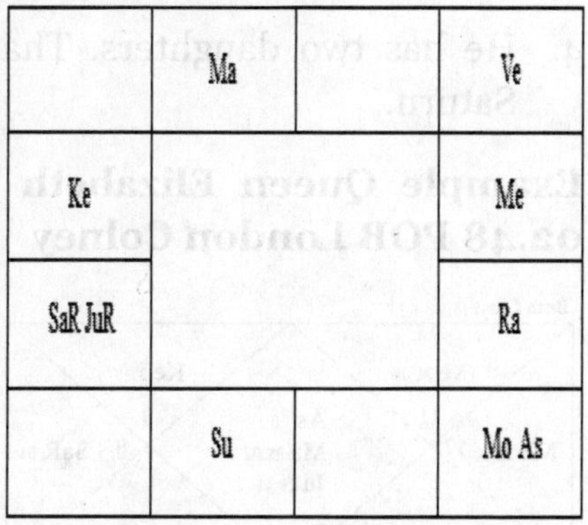

1. Third lord is Mars and is placed in eighth house in its own sign.

2. Mars is not aspected by any planet.

3. He is very courageous in taking hard decisions.

4. The Coborn can suffer. Mars is not related to any malefic and is in Aries.

D7 Saptamsha (children)

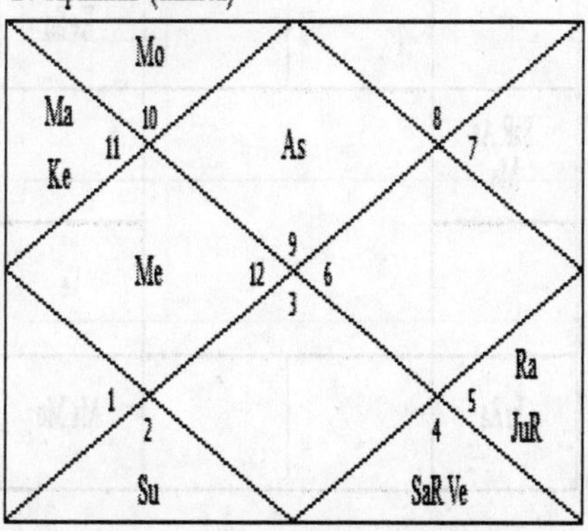

D7 Saptamsha (children)

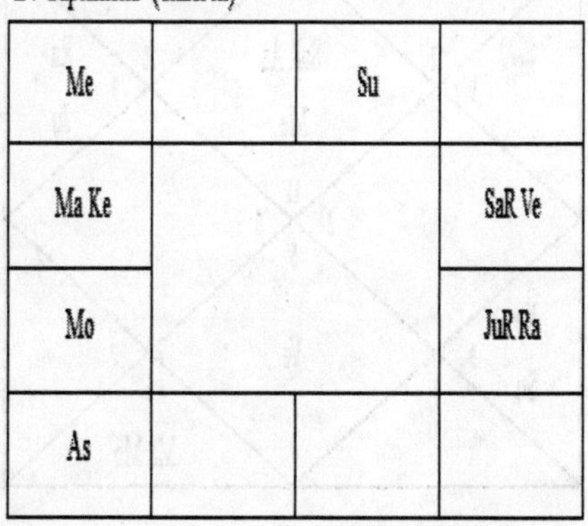

1. Third lord Saturn is in eighth house.

2. Saturn is with Venus and is aspected by Moon.

3. He has intuitive power.

4. He has two daughters. Thanks to benefic association with Saturn.

Example Queen Elizabeth 2 DOB 21 April 1926 TOB 02.48 POB London Colney

Birth Chart

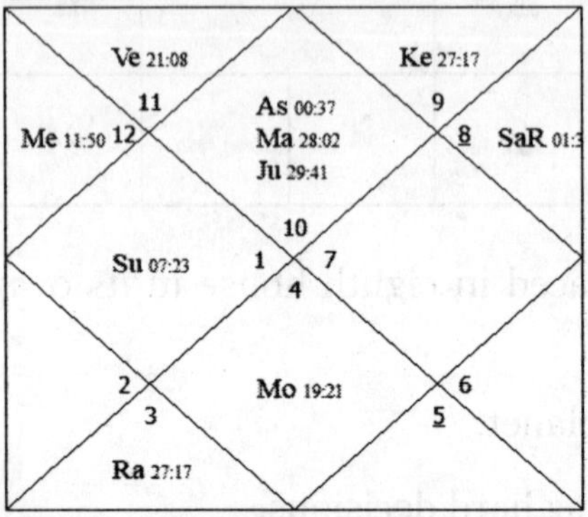

Birth Chart

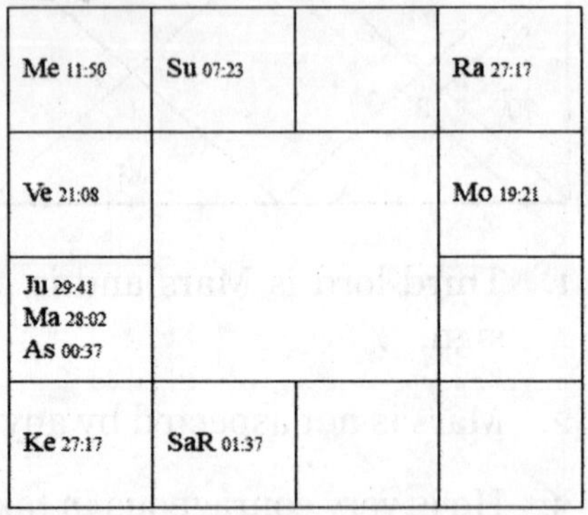

SSVY is not present in birth horoscope.

D60 Shashtiamsha (All areas)

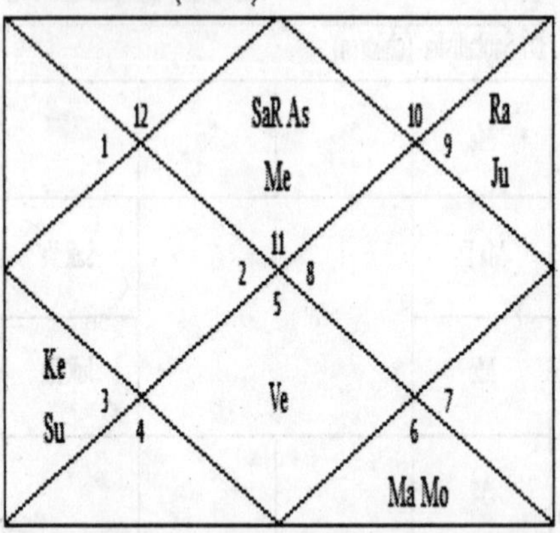

D60 Shashtiamsha (All areas)

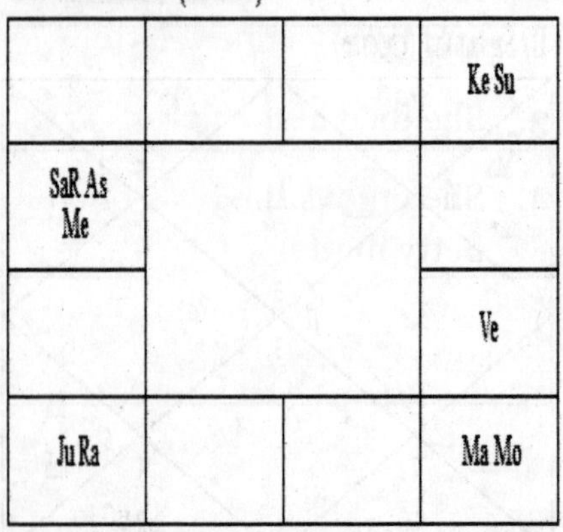

1. D 60 is given maximum importance by Parashar.

2. Third lord is Mars.

3. Sixth lord is Moon.

4. Mars and Moon are in eighth house causing double SSVY.

5. Moon is waning. There is no other relation with Mars and Moon.

6. She was the longest serving Queen of UK.

D8 Ashtamsha 1/8 Accidents

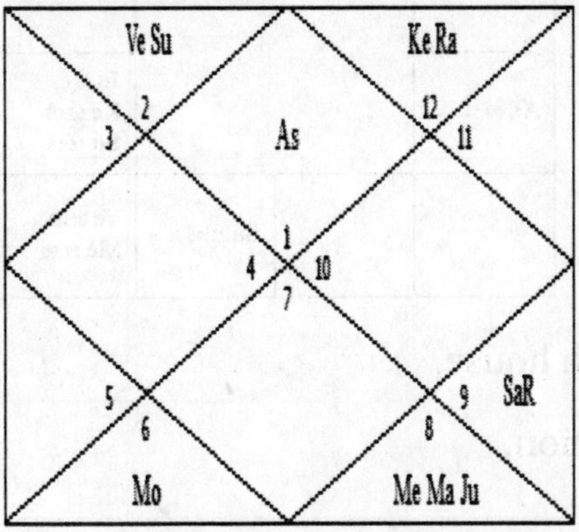

D8 Ashtamsha 1/8 Accidents

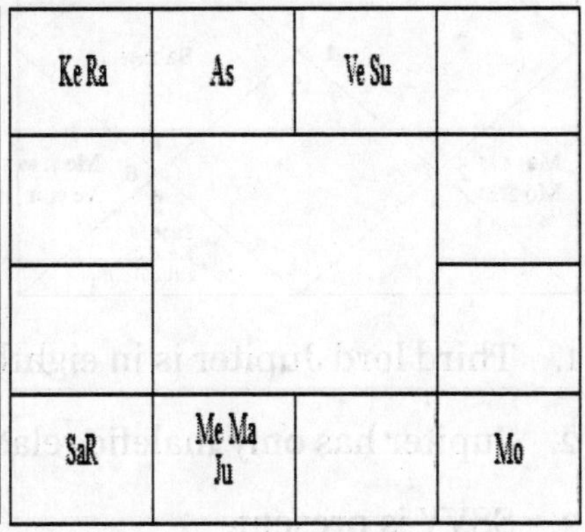

1. Mercury is third and sixth lord.

2. Mercury is placed in eighth house. Mercury has two malefic and two benefic relations.

3. She died at the age of 96.

4. She enjoys the bliss of concentration and is not disturbed by petty matters.

Example Prabhupad DOB 1 September 1896 TOB 15.45 POB Calcutta

Birth Chart

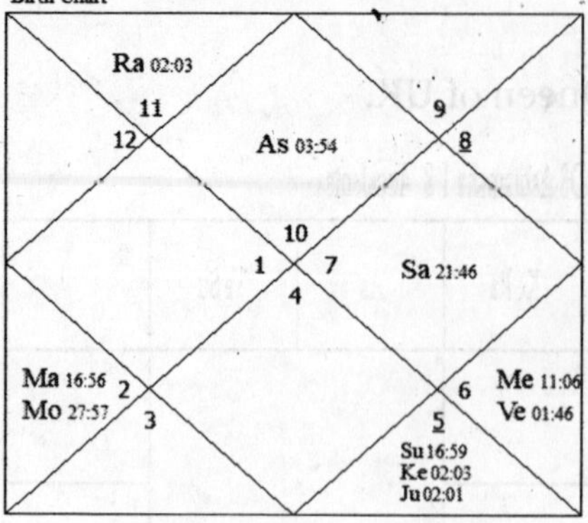

Birth Chart

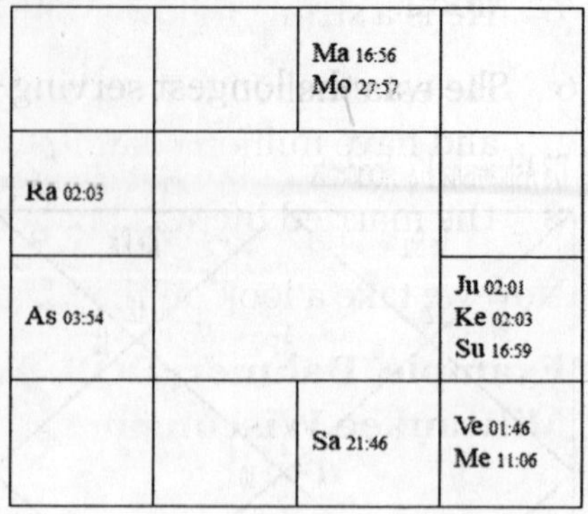

1. Third lord Jupiter is in eighth house.
2. Jupiter has only malefic relation.
3. SSVY is present.
4. He is a famous person and had all luxuries but after big sufferings. This is Vipreet Yoga.

D9 Navamsha (spouse)

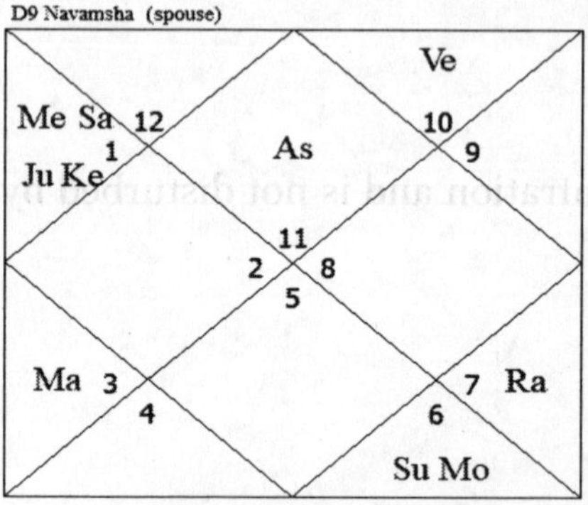

D9 Navamsha (spouse)

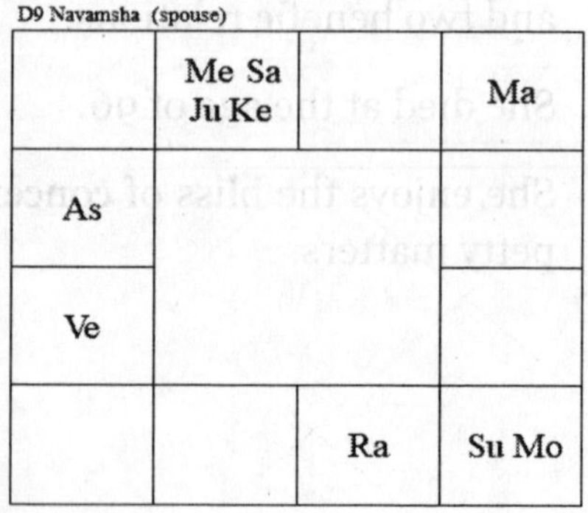

1. Eighth lord Mercury is in third house.
2. Sixth lord Moon is in eighth house.
3. Moon is with Sun and aspected by Mars.

4. Mercury is with Ketu and Saturn.
5. Two SSVY are present.
6. He is a strong follower of his religion.
7. He established ISKON which has branches all over the world and have millions of followers.
8. His married life was not good.

Now we take a look on the horoscope of a hardened criminal.

Example Dahmer DOB 21 May 1960 TOB 16.34 POB Milwaukee Wisconsin

Birth Chart

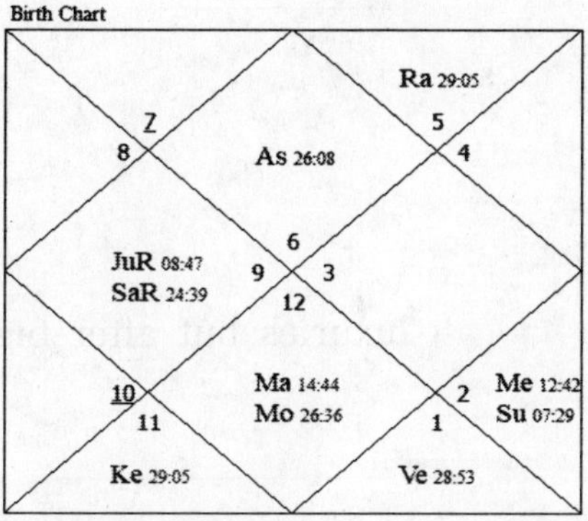

Birth Chart

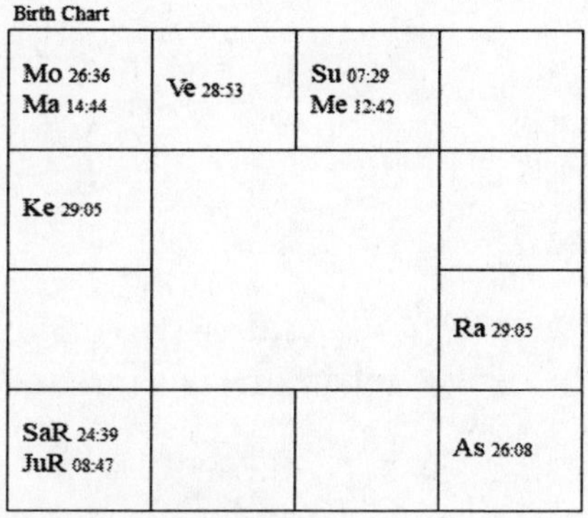

D30 Trimshamsha (misfortunes)

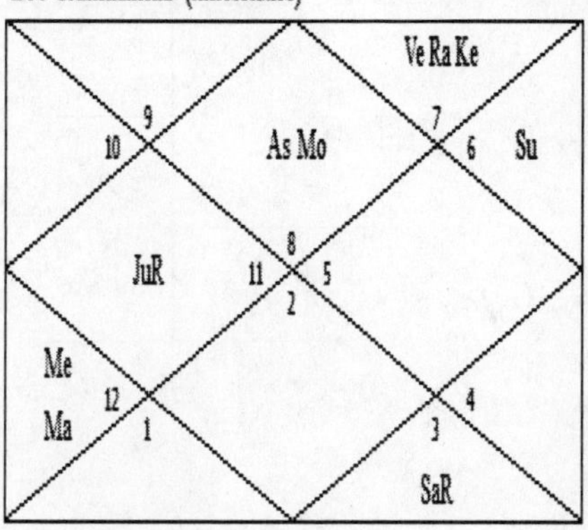

D30 Trimshamsha (misfortunes)

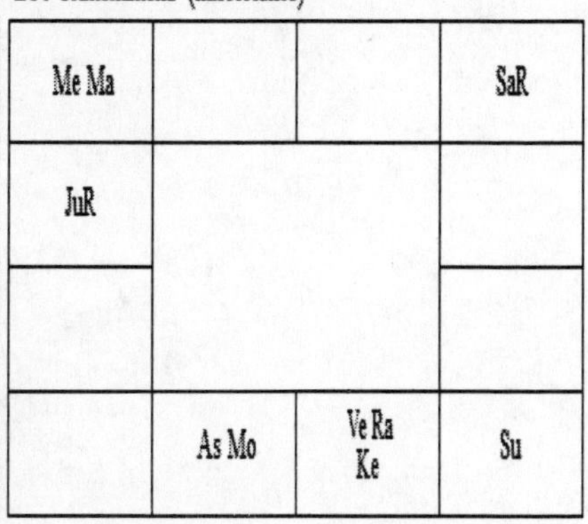

1. No SSVY is present in birth horoscope.

2. In D 30, Saturn is the lord of third house and is placed in eighth house.
3. Saturn is aspected by Jupiter and Mars.
4. This chart is of misfortunes.
5. His misfortunes are increased manifold.
6. He was awarded 16 life terms in jail.
7. After two years in jail, he was killed by a fellow prison mate.